Principles
of
Workers
Compensation
Claims

Principles
of
Workers
Compensation
Claims

Edited by

JAMES J. MARKHAM, J.D., CPCU, AIC, AIAF

Director of Curriculum
General Counsel and Ethics Counsel
Insurance Institute of America

First Edition • 1992

INSURANCE INSTITUTE OF AMERICA
720 Providence Road, Malvern, Pennsylvania 19355-0770

First Edition • 1992

Library of Congress Catalogue Number 90-86333
International Standard Book Number 0-89462-059-2

Printed in the United States of America

Foreword

The American Institute for Chartered Property Casualty Underwriters and the Insurance Institute of America are independent, nonprofit, educational organizations serving the needs of the property and liability insurance business. The Institutes develop a wide range of programs—curricula, study materials, and examinations—in response to the educational requirements of various elements of the business.

The American Institute confers the Chartered Property Casualty Underwriter (CPCU®) professional designation on those who meet the Institute's experience, ethics, and examination requirements.

The Insurance Institute of America offers associate designations and certificate programs in the following technical and managerial disciplines:

Accredited Adviser in Insurance (AAI®)
Associate in Claims (AIC)
Associate in Underwriting (AU)
Associate in Risk Management (ARM)
Associate in Loss Control Management (ALCM®)
Associate in Premium Auditing (APA®)
Associate in Management (AIM)
Associate in Research and Planning (ARP®)
Associate in Insurance Accounting and Finance (AIAF)
Associate in Automation Management (AAM®)
Associate in Marine Insurance Management (AMIM®)
Associate in Reinsurance (ARe)
Associate in Fidelity and Surety Bonding (AFSB)
Certificate in General Insurance
Certificate in Supervisory Management
Certificate in Introduction to Claims
Certificate in Introduction to Property and Liability Insurance

The Institutes began publishing textbooks in 1976 to help students meet the national examination standards. Since that time, we have produced more than seventy-five individual textbook volumes. Despite the vast differences in the subjects and purposes of these volumes, they all have much in common. First, each book is specifically designed to increase knowledge and develop skills that can improve job performance and help students achieve the educational objectives of the course for which it is assigned. Second, all of the manuscripts of our texts are widely reviewed prior to publication, by both insurance business practitioners and members of the academic community. In addition, all of our texts and course guides reflect the work of Institute staff members. These writing or editing duties are seen as an integral part of their professional responsibilities, and no one earns a royalty based on the sale of our texts. We have proceeded in this way to avoid even the appearance of any conflict of interests. Finally, the revisions of our texts often incorporate improvements suggested by students and course leaders.

We welcome criticisms of and suggestions for improving our publications. It is only with such constructive comments that we can hope to improve the quality of our study materials. Please direct any comments you may have on this text to the Curriculum Department of the Institutes.

Norman A. Baglini, Ph.D., CPCU, CLU
President and Chief Executive Officer

Preface

Workers compensation laws are a crucial social welfare system for compensation of work-related injuries. Injuries, an inevitable part of industrial production, can be tragic for the worker, the worker's family, and the employer. A worker's physical and financial health can be ruined by an injury. The worker's family can be destroyed by the stresses of an injury. The employer has an enormous humanitarian and financial stake in the well-being of its employes.

If the payment of claims is an important purpose of most types of insurance, it is essential for workers compensation. Workers compensation is designed to be a "no-fault" system that ensures speedy compensation for work-related injuries.

Claim representatives play an essential role in this important system. Insurers, insureds, "self-insureds," and claimants in particular depend on the diligence, efficiency, and expertise of claim representatives. Traditionally, workers compensation claim representatives have learned on the job. There may be drawbacks to this approach. The quality of on-the-job training can vary from employer to employer or even from supervisor to supervisor. In general, the focus of on-the-job training may tend to be too narrow to be truly beneficial. For instance, workers compensation training often has been regarded as a state-by-state matter because of the differences in state laws.

This textbook reflects the belief that the similarities among state workers compensation laws and procedures are more significant than the differences. Indeed, the study of common features helps students understand the unique aspects of any given state's laws and procedures. This textbook is designed for use in the Insurance Institute of America's AIC 34 course, which as of 1991 addresses workers compensation and medical aspects of claims.

This text describes evolution of employers liability and workers compensation laws as well as the nature of the existing workers compensation system and the standard insurance policy coverage. It carefully explores compensability, the issue of what injuries and parties are covered by workers compensation, as well as the calculation of benefits and the administration of workers compensation claims. The text concludes with a discussion of factors contributing to the cost crisis in workers compensation.

The Institute is deeply indebted to the contributing authors of this book. They willingly accepted their assignments and generously shared their vast experience. In addition, they graciously accepted the editorial work on their manuscripts, and most of them served as constructive and compassionate reviewers of another author's manuscript. I designed the content of this course and edited the entire work, along with other members of the Institute staff.

The Institute deeply appreciates the work of the following individuals who reviewed manuscripts for this text and made valuable suggestions for improvement: Dennis D. Alves, Liberty Mutual Insurance Company; Gordon Berger, GAB Business Services, Inc.; Thomas E. Certain, Hanover Insurance Co.; Stephen Dansevich, Nationwide Insurance Co.; Richard E. Ehret, CPCU, The St. Paul Companies; William R. Gawne, CPCU, CIGNA; Larry D. Gaunt, Ph.D., CPCU, Georgia State University; Jonathan H. Gice, CPCU, EBI Indemnity Company; Don Gordon, County Line Claim Service; Mark J. Hartzer, Esq., Nationwide Insurance Co.; Samuel M. Meeks, CPCU, AIC, Associated Risk Services Corporation; Lewis P. Palca, CPCU, General Reinsurance Co.; E. Timothy Poindexter, Esq.; Everett D. Randall, CPCU, CLU, AU, APA, Insurance Institute of America; George W. Scherbak, CPCU, PMA Group; David H. Stonehill, Esq., American Insurance Association; John H. Sullivan, CPCU, Employers Reinsurance; Tony Vogel, Wausau Insurance Co.; and Ronald R. Wirsing, U.S.F.&G. Robert J. Gibbons, Ph.D., CPCU, CLU, of the Insurance Institute of America reviewed, and made valuable comments throughout the text.

While the above individuals made valuable contributions to the text, the responsibility for the final product rests with the Insurance Institute of America. We welcome corrections and suggestions for improvements—especially from AIC students and course leaders.

James J. Markham

Contributing Authors

The Insurance Institute of America acknowledges with deep appreciation the work of the following contributing authors:

David Appel, Ph.D.
Milliman and Robertson, Inc.

Kristin M. Bonner, CPCU
Moore Group Inc.

Michael Camilleri, Esq.
National Council on Compensation Insurance

P.E. Nony Capellan, CPCU
SAFECO Insurance Co.

Robert B. Dorsey
National Council on Compensation Insurance

Marletta England, CPCU
Farmers Insurance Group

James J. Markham, J.D., CPCU, AIC, AIAF
Insurance Institute of America

Marjorie L. Mowrey, CPCU, AIC
Crum and Forster

Kevin M. Quinley, CPCU, AIC, ARM
Medmarc - Hamilton Resources Corporation

Table of Contents

The Essential Statutory Formula ~ *Independence of the Tests; Liberality of Compensation*

Arising Out of Employment ~ *Acts of God; Street Risk and Positional Risk; Assaults; Heart Attacks and Idiopathic Injuries; Consequential Injuries*

Course of Employment ~ *Commuting To and From Work; Travel at the Employer's Direction; Dual Purpose Trips; Deviations; Personal Comfort Activities; Recreational and Social Activities; Horseplay; Other Situations*

Employee Misconduct ~ *Misconduct Apart From Statutory Defenses; Statutory Defenses; Intoxication; Suicide*

Summary

Indemnity Payments—Temporary Disability ~ *Temporary Total Disability Compensation; Temporary Partial Disability Compensation*

Indemnity Payments—Permanent Disability ~ *Permanent Total Disability Compensation; Permanent Partial Disability Compensation*

Other Benefits ~ *Medical Benefits; Rehabilitation Services; Death Benefits*

Summary

Requirements Under Compensation Law ~ *Notice Requirements; Adjudicative Procedure; Second Injury Funds*

Responsibilities of the Claim Representative ~ *Factual Investigation; Medical Determination; Subrogation; Workers Compensation Claim Reserving*

Outside Providers of Workers Compensation Claim Services ~ *Selecting and Managing an Independent Claim Service; Management of Litigation and Defense Attorneys*

Summary

CHAPTER 1

Role of the Workers Compensation System

Workers compensation is a comprehensive term used to refer to the statutes that provide for fixed awards and medical reimbursement to employees or their dependents in cases of employment-related injuries and diseases. These awards are granted without regard to negligence or fault on the employer's part, thus differentiating the compensation system from the more traditional common-law system. Workers compensation laws are intended to benefit the employee *and* the employer. These statutes created a "no-fault" system whereby the employee lost the right to sue for common-law damages in return for the employer's strict liability for work-related accidents.

Workers compensation and workers compensation insurance are so closely interrelated that many incorrectly treat these two terms synonymously. Actually, workers compensation insurance is but one method by which an employer can demonstrate the ability to satisfy obligations imposed by the workers compensation laws. Some state workers compensation statutes do not require insurance for those who can self-insure. However, most employers purchase workers compensation insurance to protect themselves from liabilities otherwise imposed, or as an integral part of a well designed risk management program.

Workers compensation premiums in 1988 totaled more than $26.1 billion, which represents a 53 percent increase over the total workers compensation premiums of only three years earlier, and approximately 23 percent of the total commercial insurance premium dollar spent in

1

1988. With the recession and high rate of unemployment in the early 1980s, premium growth was uncharacteristically slow before rising by 12.8 percent in 1985, and 19.8 percent in 1986. The workers compensation annual premium has grown from $11.3 billion in 1978 to over $26.1 billion in 1988. About nine out of ten people in the nation's work force have workers compensation insurance.[1] Workers compensation is compulsory for nearly all employments in all but three states—New Jersey, South Carolina, and Texas. Even in those states, however, most businesses provide the coverage in order to limit their risk of negligence suits.

This chapter describes the history and current status of the workers compensation system. The onset of industrialization and the inability of the traditional common-law liability system to efficiently and fairly resolve claims arising out of work-related injuries was the catalyst for the creation and proliferation of workers compensation statutes. The chapter begins with a lengthy discussion of the history and common law of employer liability prior to the enactment in the early twentieth century of modern compensation legislation. A review of this history is important for two reasons. First, workers compensation laws made an extraordinary departure from the common law that based responsibility for an injury on fault. This departure stems from the inadequacies in common law that prevented it from dealing with work-related injuries. Second, the common law is still important in regard to injuries not covered by workers compensation. The various workers compensation laws have exceptions for certain employments or circumstances. In addition, if an employer fails to provide security for its workers compensation liabilities, its employees may be entitled to elect their common-law rights.

Following the discussion of history, this chapter explains modern workers compensation laws, including federal legislation. Workers compensation is predominately a matter of state law. Compensation statutes have been enacted in all fifty states. Despite some differences in the law from one state to another, there is great similarity between the laws of the fifty states.

The chapter continues with a review of major features of the workers compensation system including the role of rating bureaus, loss control, and third-party handling of claims. It concludes with a review of the standard workers compensation and employers liability insurance policy.

THE HISTORY AND COMMON LAW
OF EMPLOYER LIABILITY

In order to comprehend the present role of the workers compensation system and some of the issues associated with workers compensation insurance, one should understand the history of, and common law that addresses, employer liability. This section reviews the common-law principles of employer liability and the defenses to liability that employers could assert. The unfortunate results of the common-law system as related to employer liability and the initial attempts at legal reform that followed are also described.

Prior to the eighteenth century, agriculture, the trades, and the sea were the principal sources of employment. The status of the agricultural laborer was little better than serfdom. Trade and industry were conducted under the guild system. Master craftsmen maintained and trained the apprentice; the guild controlled product prices, wages, hours of work, methods of work, and the obligations of master craftsmen to the apprentice and the journeyman. These obligations included the master's responsibility for the welfare of servants and employees.

From early times, seamen worked under a separate class of rights and duties based on maritime law and under the jurisdiction of the admiralty courts. An injured sailor was entitled to care, cure, maintenance, and wages to the end of the voyage. Like the master craftsman, the captain was responsible for the welfare of his crew.

The Industrial Revolution in England beginning in the eighteenth century, and in America in the nineteenth century, radically changed working conditions, and raised questions as to the relationship between the employer and employee. The Industrial Revolution gave birth to new industries and new manufacturing techniques. These brought together great numbers of employees—unskilled, undisciplined, and often selected without regard to character. These employees were exposed to new hazards. Work areas were poorly lighted and poorly ventilated; work hours were unendurably long. Child labor was employed. Labor was plentiful; wages were low. The reaction of the British and American courts was to protect the newly developing industry through the emergence of what became known as the employer's "common-law defenses."

The current compensation system arose out of the common law regarding compensation for work-related injuries. Following is an examination of the essential elements of negligence and how the common law relies on fault in the distribution of awards.

Negligence and the Common Law of Employer Liability[2]

Negligence is based on failure to exercise the care required by law to protect others from unreasonable risks of harm. Negligence can be the basis of a claim. Among the legally protected rights recognized by law is the *right of safety of person*. Everyone has the duty to exercise reasonable care to avoid invading this legally protected right of another. A breach of this duty may consist of (1) an *act of commission* (such as drunk driving) or (2) an *act of omission* (such as failing to maintain premises in a safe condition). However, a potential defendant is not a guarantor of the safety of all others with whom he or she comes in contact. The defendant's conduct is judged by the "reasonably prudent person standard" in a court of law. This means that if the defendant's conduct conforms to what the reasonably prudent person would or would not do under the same or similar circumstances, he or she is not negligent regardless of whether or not an injury is sustained by the plaintiff. On the other hand, if the defendant's conduct falls below the reasonably prudent person standard, he or she is deemed negligent.

Elements of Negligence. The following are the essential elements of a cause of action based on negligence. (The first two elements together are sometimes called "negligence.")

1. A legal duty owed
2. Failure to comply with the standard of care required by the duty
3. Proximate cause
4. Damages

The plaintiff must allege and prove all of these elements. If any one element is missing, there is no cause of action. This principle has been applied to the relationship of employer and employee. At common law, the employer had certain duties.

Common-Law Duties of Employers. The common law requires that the employer exercise reasonable care for the safety of employees. The following specific duties have been abstracted from this general duty of care.

Provide a Safe Place to Work. This duty requires the employer to provide not only a physically safe building or work area, but also to maintain the premises in reasonably safe condition, to provide proper housekeeping, and to make inspections at reasonable intervals. The length of a "reasonable" interval depends on the nature of the work and the frequency with which unsafe conditions occur. The reasonably prudent person standard is used to determine whether or not the employer has met this duty. The reasonably prudent person would not only make inspections to determine the presence of unsafe conditions, but would also take immediate steps to remedy such conditions. In addition, he or she would comply with all state, county, and city safety requirements, as well as any federal safety standards.

The employer's duty to provide a safe place to work is not limited to the physical condition of the premises. It also extends to other circumstances that might be unsafe for employees. For example, an employer would fail in its duty of exercising ordinary care for the safety of an employee if the employer's medical department allows an employee to be further exposed after finding that the employee suffers from a tubercular condition that makes it dangerous to continue working in the employer's plant.

Provide an Adequate Number of Competent Fellow Employees. The employer must exercise care in the selection and training of all employees and provide enough people for the work demanded. The extent of pre-employment screening and on-the-job training varies according to the work.

Provide Safe Tools and Equipment. The employer is required to provide safe tools, appliances, and machinery. This means that the machinery should be adequately guarded, properly maintained, and equipped with all normal safety features. It does not mean that the employer is bound to provide the newest and "safest" machinery possible. It is sufficient if the machinery provided can be used safely by a competent employee. Necessary equipment must be provided, such as goggles for employees engaged in grinding, respirators for those exposed to noxious fumes or dusts, and hard hats for construction environments.

Warn the Employee of Inherent Dangers. This duty obligates the employer to warn the employee of any work-related dangers of which the employee is unaware or would not discover by the exercise of reasonable care. For example, the employer should forewarn employees of the presence of any toxic chemicals, radioactive materials, or hazards created by the use of certain dyes and chemicals.

There is no duty to warn employees of readily apparent dangers since the employer has a right to assume that the employee, experienced or not, would be aware of the danger and would be able to protect against it. Accordingly, the employer would be under no common-law duty to warn the employee of the dangers of fire in a smelter, a caged lion in a veterinary clinic, the use of a grinding wheel or welding torch without goggles, the lifting of unusually heavy objects, and of putting a hand in operating machinery.

Make and Enforce Rules for the Safety of All Employees. The employer is required to use reasonable care in developing and enforcing rules for the safety of the employees. The rules thus devised must be adequate in light of the dangers to which the employees are exposed. The greater the danger, the more rigid the rules must be. The rules for the conduct of the employees must be enforced, and the employer must not tolerate repeated violations. Enforcement may require the discharge of employees who repeatedly violate the rules.

The employer is not obligated to make and enforce rules when the process is simple, and the dangers, if any, are open and apparent to all. Employees are expected to protect themselves against all such dangers without rules requiring them to do so.

Death Claims. The common law did not recognize the legal rights of a dead person. A dead person could not sue or be sued, and his or her legal existence ended with death. Therefore, if an employee suffered an accident that resulted in death, there was no action that could be taken against the employer even though the injury and death were caused by the negligence of the employer. No recognition was given to the damages suffered by those who depended on the deceased for support. Thus, such dependents had no legal remedy and in many cases were forced to join other destitute persons on the rolls of public charity. As a consequence, public pressure caused the British Parliament to enact legislation allowing a recovery against wrongdoers. This original wrongful death statute, the Fatal Accidents Act of 1846, is more commonly referred to as Lord Campbell's Act.

This act created a cause of action on behalf of the dependents of the deceased whenever the death was caused by a tortfeasor's wrongful act or omission. The purpose of the act was to enable the dependents to recover the pecuniary loss they sustained as a result of the death. There was no provision for recovery for mental anguish or bereavement. Recovery was limited to the monetary loss suffered by dependents.

All American states have passed wrongful death statutes, the majority of which are similar to Lord Campbell's Act. In most states, the meaning of "pecuniary" loss has been expanded to include loss of services, guidance, and in some states, even the loss of companionship. Other states base the amount of the recovery on the degree of culpability of the defendant's conduct, or on the loss sustained by the estate of the deceased.

Common-Law Defenses[3]

If the failure of the employer to meet one or more of its duties causes injury to an employee, the employee would have a cause of action for damages against the employer. However, the employer is protected by three common-law defenses: assumption of the risk, contributory negligence, and the negligence of a fellow employee. Under certain modern compensation laws, if an employer fails to provide security for its workers compensation obligations, its employees may elect their common-law rights, while the employer is barred from asserting the following defenses.

Assumption of the Risk. The assumption of the risk defense can be applied if two conditions are present:

1. The employee knows or is aware of the existence of the risk, and has a corresponding appreciation of the extent of the danger.
2. The employee voluntarily exposes himself or herself to the danger.

The employee is expected to have knowledge of a danger that is open and apparent. If the employee accepts employment under such circumstances, he or she will be deemed to have voluntarily exposed himself or herself to the danger and may not recover for any resulting injury. The same is true when an employer fails to meet a duty and an employee who is aware of this failure continues to work. The employee will be held to have assumed the risk of injury.

On the other hand, the employee cannot be held to have assumed a risk of which he or she is unaware. For example, if, unknown to the employee, radioactive materials are used in another section of the plant, and the employee suffers an injury from exposure to radiation, it cannot be said that the employee assumed this risk since he or she was not aware of it in the first place. The same is true when the employee's work involves contact with chemicals that are unfamiliar to the average person.

Contributory Negligence. At common law, everyone is required to exercise care for his or her own safety. If an employee fails to exercise such care, he or she will be deemed to be contributorily negligent even though the negligence of the employer was also a contributing cause of the injury. The common-law rule is that if the employee's contributory negligence is responsible *to any degree* in causing the accident, the employee is barred from recovery. Thus, at common law, a momentary lapse in behavior on the part of the employee could defeat recovery even though the negligence of the employer contributed to a much greater degree to the occurrence of, or the extent of, the injury.

The contributory negligence defense has been largely replaced by the comparative negligence defense. *Comparative negligence* is based on the principle that the contributory negligence of the employee is not a complete defense. Instead, the negligence of the employee is taken into account in reducing the amount of recovery. Comparative negligence laws enable employees to recover a portion of their damages even when they are substantially at fault.

There are two forms of comparative negligence statutes, *modified* and *pure*. Both require the jury to bring in a verdict indicating the percentages of negligence, if any, applied to the plaintiff and the defendant. Although there are two types of modified comparative negligence, each prevents any recovery for the plaintiff when the plaintiff's negligence exceeds the defendant's negligence. Under the pure form, the plaintiff may always recover something as long as the plaintiff is not 100 percent at fault. An injured plaintiff can be 90 percent at fault and still recover 10 percent of his or her damages under a pure comparative negligence law. Under pure comparative negligence, a claimant will be barred from recovery only when the defendant is totally blameless.

Assumption of risk is sometimes regarded as another form of contributory negligence. However, certain comparative negligence statutes do *not* eliminate the defense of assumption of risk. If the comparative negligence statute does not specifically include assumption of risk within its definition of contributory negligence, then the assumption of the risk defense is still available to the defendant.

Negligence of a Fellow Employee. The employer is not liable for an injury caused solely by the negligence of a fellow employee. This is an exception to the general rule of *respondeat superior* under which the negligence of an employee acting within the course and scope of his or her employment is imputed to the employer. This rule has been greatly criticized, but the courts still apply it in absence of legislation to the contrary.

A "fellow employee" is defined as an employee of the same rank as the injured employee. A supervisor of an injured worker is not, therefore, ordinarily held to be a fellow worker. The theory is that since the supervisor is an agent of management, his or her negligence should be imputed to the employer. Some courts have gone further, holding that the fellow employee defense does not apply to any management employee who would be deemed a vice-principal of the employer. *Vice-principal employees* are responsible for meeting the employer's duties to provide a safe place to work, to select competent fellow employees, and to warn employees of the inherent dangers of the work. In addition to these exceptions, some courts have held that an employee of another department is not a fellow employee.

In general, the courts have been reluctant to apply the fellow-employee defense. They have grudgingly applied it only when absolutely necessary and have found excuses not to use it.

WORKERS COMPENSATION LAWS

Prior to the enactment of workers compensation legislation, the harshness of the common law was only slightly modified. As noted above, courts adopted the vice-principal exception to the fellow servant rule. Certain courts rejected the assumption of the risk defense in regard to safety violations by the employer. A number of legislatures enacted employer liability statutes that restricted or eliminated the fellow servant rule, restricted the assumption of the risk defense, or applied comparative negligence in lieu of contributory negligence. All of these efforts were negligible compared to the changes in the law brought about by workers compensation legislation.

The Wisconsin workers compensation statute, effective in 1911, is the oldest comprehensive compensation law in the United States. By 1920, all but a few of the states had passed workers compensation laws. Today, all fifty states and the District of Columbia have such laws. Modern workers compensation law makes a significant break from the principles of the common law and employers liability statutes. This section explains the important principles embodied in modern compensation legislation and describes the features of compensation law typically found in state statutes. The section concludes with a review of federal compensation legislation.

Principles of Workers Compensation Law

Workers compensation involved an entirely new legal concept, employer liability without regard to fault. Under this concept, the cost of occupational injury and disease was to be assessed against the employer even though the employer was neither negligent nor otherwise responsible under common law or employers liability statutes. The various state investigatory commissions in the beginning of the century developed a consensus that under modern industrial conditions, the employment relationship alone was ample reason for assessing the employer for the cost of occupational injury. Industrial accidents were recognized as one of the inevitable hazards of industry, not necessarily the result of a lack of skill, but rather related to the nature of the industry, characterized by long hours, new and complex processes, untrained workers, mechanization, repetitive operations, speed, and the use of toxic materials. The cost of industrial accidents and diseases was regarded as a legitimate cost of production.

The workers compensation laws balanced the interests of both employer and employee. Workers gave up their existing legal remedy, the right of a tort action for negligent injury against the employer. In so doing, workers gave up the right to recover damages for pain and suffering or inconvenience. The employer gave up various defenses and became obligated to respond to the employee's injury in accordance with the terms of the compensation act. The law provided relative certainty as to the amount of benefits to be paid for specified injuries. The general purpose of the compensation legislation was to alleviate the plight of the worker. All of the following have been stated as specific objectives of the workers compensation system:

1. Prompt payment of adequate benefits, according to a fixed and predetermined schedule, to injured employees or their dependents

2. Elimination of the delays and costs of litigation to the employee and to society

3. Establishment of a guarantee of benefit payment; benefits to be secured by a form of "insurance"

4. Promotion of industrial safety and industrial hygiene; employers would observe the relationship between accident prevention and the reduced cost of workers compensation benefits

5. Payment for medical care services

Other benefits anticipated from workers compensation legislation included the reduction of friction between the worker and the employer, and the easing of public and private relief.

Workers compensation statutes were intended to cure the defects of the common law and employers liability statutes and to present simple and rational provisions devoid of legalisms. The relief provided was to be certain and immediate. Injury schedules attempted to make payments largely automatic, resulting in few occasions when adversary proceedings would be required. The remedial and beneficial purpose of compensation legislation is often cited as a justification for extending coverage in close or doubtful cases. This attitude has the support of legal scholars of workers compensation and is enacted in practice by compensation hearing officers and judges. Claim representatives should accept and understand this approach to compensation.

Common Features of Compensation Laws

The following features are particularly important in the American compensation system: (1) choice of law, (2) the description of persons and employments covered, (3) the description of injuries and diseases covered, (4) the benefits provided, (5) the method of financing benefits, (6) the procedure for obtaining benefits, and (7) administration. These features are introduced here and are explained more fully in Chapters 2 through 5.

Choice of Law. In any given case of an employment-related injury, the laws of numerous states may apply if the circumstances of employment occur in different states. The following are such circumstances: the place of injury, the place of hire, the place of employment, the location of the employer, the residence of the employee, and any state whose compensation laws are adopted by contract. In general, the laws of the states where the injury occurred, where the employment usually occurs, and where the employee was hired *all* apply to a loss. The employee cannot receive duplicate benefits but can select the state with the most generous benefits. Because the facts of cases involving multiple states can be complex, the claim representative faced with such a case should obtain legal counsel as to which states' laws apply.

Persons and Employments Covered. Since the original compensation laws were directed toward addressing a specific social problem, the only industries that were initially affected were those whose operations were considered to be "hazardous." Industries that did not expose employees to any great danger and that contributed little to the creation of the social problem were eliminated from the compensation laws. The definition of what is and what is not "hazardous" employment was contained in a given state's compensation statute—there was no real uniformity among states.

Today, workers compensation statutes cover most public and private employments whether or not they are "hazardous" in the traditional sense of the term. Some statutes include within the scope of their coverage civilian workers such as volunteer fire fighters, auxiliary police officers, and civilian defense workers. Some of the earlier statutes covered only employments carried on for pecuniary gain. Such a provision would eliminate all public employees such as police officers, fire fighters, and sanitation workers as well as those employed by a charity since they are not profit-making enterprises. A few laws still retain this provision. Most state compensation laws exclude domestic and farm workers, who therefore retain their entire common-law rights.

As a general rule, an employer's legal obligations for occupational injury or disease extend to employees only, not to independent contractors. The distinction between an employee and an independent contractor is an important one. It is best expressed in terms of the extent of the employer's right to direct and control the work-related activities of each. An employee is one for whom the employer typically fixes the hours of employment, provides the tools with which to do the work, and defines and supervises the results of the work as well as methods and means of doing the work. An independent contractor is one for whom the employer does not typically fix the hours of employment, may or may not provide the tools with which to do the work, defines the results of the work, but perhaps most important, does *not* define and supervise the methods and means of doing the work. The essential distinction between employees and independent contractors is that the employer has the right to control and direct the activities of an employee, not only as to the result to be accomplished, but also the methods and means by which the result is obtained.

Injuries and Diseases Covered. It has always been the purpose of workers compensation to provide benefits only for *occupational injury*, i.e., covered injuries should arise from the worker's employment. It would be difficult to rationalize coverage for nonoccupational injuries and diseases under a program financed exclusively by the employer.

A compensable injury or disease must be occupational in nature as defined by the law. The most obvious losses are caused by industrial accidents. Hence, early compensation laws often referred only to "accidents" occurring within the scope of employment; they contained no provision with regard to occupational disease. Even today, it is necessary to define by statute what is an occupational disease and the proof required to qualify both injuries and occupational diseases for coverage. Not all occupational diseases are covered and the requirements to prove compensability for injury and disease differ. With regard to injuries, it is necessary to show that (1) the employee suffered an injury caused by accident, (2) the accident arose out of employment, and (3) the accident occurred in the course of employment. To be compensable, (1) a disease must be covered by the statute as one that normally results from the nature of the employment, and (2) the exposure to the disease must arise from employment.

The laws of the great majority of the states define an occupational injury as one that "arises out of and in the course of employment." The framers of this definition wanted to be assured of a causal connection between employment and injury. To be compensable, the injury must not only occur while the employee is at work, but it must also be related to that work. Stated differently, the words "arising out of the employment" refer to the origin or the cause of the injury, i.e., that the accident, in order to be compensable, must arise out of some risk reasonably incidental to the employment. "In the course of employment" refers to the time, place, and circumstances under which the injury took place. The employee must have been doing something that he or she was employed to do, and the accident must have occurred while the employee was so occupied.

For compensation to be awarded, most jurisdictions require that there be an injury that is accidental. Generally, an *injury* may be defined as trauma to the body and such disease or infection as may naturally or unavoidably result therefrom. This definition of injury excludes internally produced systemic conditions and damage to property including clothing and prosthetic devices. The courts have defined *accident* as an event that takes place without foresight or expectation—an undesigned, sudden, and unexpected event. Hence, a person who willfully injures himself is not entitled to workers compensation because the injury is not "accidental" in the sense indicated. The compensation statute will often further define accidental injury by stipulating that injuries arising from certain causes are not covered, such as injuries caused by intoxication, willful failure to use a safety appliance or observe safety regulations, or failure to perform a duty required by statute.

Benefits Provided. There are four types of workers compensation benefits. The two most important are (1) indemnity payments for time lost from work and (2) payments for medical services. Rehabilitation services consist partly of medical services, but ideally they extend well beyond them, and are thus considered apart from medical services. Likewise, death benefits must be considered apart from medical and indemnity payments.

Indemnity Payments. Indemnity payments are designed to compensate for lost wages. In all jurisdictions, benefits are payable to disabled workers only after a "waiting period" that ranges from three to seven days after the injury. This feature is designed to reduce compensation costs and to discourage malingering. The majority of job-related disabilities are of very short duration and do not involve indemnity benefit payments, yet they can nevertheless account for substantial aggregate medical benefits.

Disability extending beyond the waiting period is classified for benefit purposes as *temporary* or *permanent*, and *partial* or *total*. *Temporary total disability* payments are made to a worker who cannot work at his or her usual occupation during the period of recovery. Permanent disabilities resulting from more serious injuries are classified for statistical purposes by the severity of the disabling condition as minor permanent partial, major permanent partial, and permanent total disability. *Permanent total disability* involves injuries that prohibit further employment.

The duration of the payments for a given permanent partial disability varies greatly from state to state. States also differ on the relative duration of payments for different disabilities. For example, two states may not only provide different benefits for the loss of a hand, but the relative value of those benefits compared to some other injury, such as loss of an arm, may also differ.

Payments for Medical Services. During the early development of workers compensation laws, only limited provisions were made for medical benefits. Today, however, all states cover 100 percent of necessary medical expenses. This liberalization in medical benefits has been the greatest single improvement in workers compensation. Medical benefits account for over 40 percent of the total payments under workers compensation.[4]

Rehabilitation Services. The most promising of recent benefit developments is the growth of provisions for physical and vocational rehabilitation. Under early workers compensation laws, after the medical care called for by law had been provided, there were no further services regardless of the extent of recovery from disability. When treatment ran out or no further benefit from it was apparent, permanent total disability became an acceptable condition. With advances in physical and rehabilitative medicine, paramedical services, and vocational training facilities, permanent total disability can no longer be accepted as the final result in every case of serious injury.

Rehabilitation programs are a means to reduce the seriousness and, thus, the cost of disabling injuries. They do so, in part, by providing vocational or physical assistance to the injured so that they can return to gainful employment. Although considered an integral part of complete medical treatment, rehabilitation may go much further and include such services as vocational training or training to drive a specially equipped car.

Although only some states include specific rehabilitation provisions in their workers compensation laws, rehabilitation is allowed and provided in all states even if unspecified in the law. Many insurers have been leaders in conducting rehabilitation programs for disabled workers, often providing rehabilitation benefits well beyond those required by the law. This often reduces the ultimate loss costs because the rehabilitated workers are able to seek gainful employment. Equally important is the social benefit of making disabled workers feel that they are a meaningful part of society.

Death Benefits. Like disability payments, death benefit payments vary from jurisdiction to jurisdiction. In over half the jurisdictions, these payments to dependents are limited in time. Both the amount and the duration of the weekly benefit typically depend on whether there are minor children. As is true for permanent total disability benefits, about one-fourth of the states adjust the benefits annually to match all or part of the increase in prices or wages. In addition to income replacement benefits, all states pay a burial allowance.

Methods of Financing Benefits. Because of wide year-to-year fluctuations in workers compensation obligations for most employers, and because of the long-term nature of some of the payments that must be made, state legislatures wanted to be certain that employers could meet their workers compensation obligations. All states require employers to insure these obligations or to demonstrate their ability to "self-insure." State laws differ, however, with respect to (1) whether both private and public employers must comply with these security requirements; (2) the penalties for noncompliance; (3) whether and under what conditions an employer can qualify as a self-insurer; (4) the types of insurers from whom employers can purchase workers compensation insurance; (5) whether insurers must provide coverage for all employer applicants; (6) how insurers must notify the state industrial commission or other public agency before canceling a workers compensation insurance contract; and (7) whether there must be some formal arrangement for the payment of claims of insolvent insurers and "self-insurers."

As of 1990, six states operated monopolistic state insurance funds, and thirteen operated funds in competition with private insurers. The remaining states and the District of Columbia require private employers to purchase protection from private insurers. In all of these states except Texas and those operating monopolistic funds employers may request permission to "self-insure" their obligation.[5] "Self-insurance" has become increasingly popular in recent years, especially among large employers.

Procedure for Obtaining Benefits. The compensation laws require the worker to notify the employer of an injury within a certain period of time (often thirty days) in order to obtain benefits. Notice must be given to the employer, or supervisor, or someone in a managerial position. A failure to give notice is generally excused when the employer witnessed or heard about the occurrence of the accident, or where the failure to give notice did not prejudice the employer's right to investigate and verify the details of the accident.

Compensation laws require the employee or his or her survivors to file a claim for compensation within a designated time, usually one year. Failure to file a claim within the statutory period renders the claim unenforceable even if it has merit. The statute of limitations, together with the notice requirement, recognize that the employer should not be required to respond to claims that cannot be investigated and defended, and that might result in an accrued liability for which the employer had not planned.

Administration. Broadly speaking, the traditional objective of compensation claim administration has been to ensure that the injured worker knows his or her rights and receives the benefits to which he or she is entitled. The principal administrative objective is to provide a simple, convenient, and inexpensive method of settling the claims of injured workers and their dependents. Full and prompt payment when due is the essential virtue of the compensation system. If payments are not made, the system must provide a speedy and effective method of settling controversies.

State compensation administration for the settlement of disputes is largely a quasi-judicial function. In general, two bodies administer benefits in the United States—the courts and special commissions. In all states, the courts serve as an appellate forum for workers compensation claims. However, in a few states the courts conduct the initial administration of workers compensation claims. These courts hear and determine compensation claims and issue judgments in exactly the same way as they would in any other type of case.

The administration of workers compensation by a commission or compensation board is far from perfect, but is usually better than court administration. The majority of jurisdictions have created quasi-judicial bodies for the administration of compensation claims, variously called a *workers compensation board* or *industrial accident commission*. These bodies supervise the administration of the compensation law and hear and determine disputes that arise under it. The decisions of the board are usually conclusive as to questions of fact, and an appeal to the courts may usually be made only on questions of law.

Federal Compensation Legislation[6]

All fifty states, the District of Columbia, Guam, Puerto Rico, and the Canadian provinces have workers compensation laws, and a large percentage of the work force is afforded compensation benefits. Nevertheless, state workers compensation laws do not apply to everyone. Persons who are employed by federal institutions or who work upon navigable waterways or federal lands, including federal projects abroad, or within the District of Columbia are covered by the federal laws discussed below.

Federal Employer's Liability Act. The Federal Employer's Liability Act (FELA) of 1908, which applied only to employees of interstate railroads, was a form of precompensation legislation. FELA provided that contributory negligence should only mitigate damages (thus applying comparative negligence), and that neither this defense nor assumption of risk should apply in cases involving safety-statute violations. It made the employer liable for the negligence of all its officers, agents, and employees, and for injuries due to negligent maintenance of equipment.

The Longshore and Harbor Workers' Compensation Act. Congress enacted the Longshore and Harbor Workers' Compensation Act in 1927 in response to a Supreme Court ruling that federal admiralty jurisdiction was supreme and state compensation laws inoperative in cases of accidents on the navigable waters of the United States. The immediate effect of this ruling was to leave longshoremen without compensation. Thus, Congress stepped in. The purpose of the United States Longshore and Harbor Workers' Compensation Act is to provide benefits to persons who are engaged in maritime and longshoring operations, stevedoring, harbor work, ship repairing and building, and who are outside the scope of state compensation laws. The act specifically excludes a master or member of the crew of any vessel or any person engaged by the master to load or unload a vessel under eighteen tons net. Also excluded are officers or employees of the United States or any federal agency, or of any state or foreign government, or any political subdivision of either.

Under a 1972 amendment to the act, compensation is payable for disability or death of an employee injured "upon navigable waters of the United States," including any adjoining pier, wharf, dry dock, terminal, building way, marine railway, or other adjoining area customarily used by an employer in loading, unloading, repairing, or building a vessel. Because the Longshore and Harbor Workers' Compensation Act applies to workers in on-shore facilities, there is a possibility of overlap with the coverage of state compensation laws. An injured employee who is covered by both can be expected to elect the compensation system with better benefits. Adjusters must recognize situations involving the possibility of overlapping coverage and must check the employer's policy for coverage under this act.

The Longshore and Harbor Workers' Compensation Act has been extended to cover civilian employees of the military, employees of contractors on overseas locations, and employees on offshore drilling platforms except masters and members of the crew of vessels. The rate of compensation payable under the act is two-thirds of the average weekly wage, subject to a weekly dollar maximum. For accidents occurring after September 30, 1975, the maximum average weekly wage is not to exceed 200 percent of the national average weekly wage as determined by the Secretary of Labor. Security for the payment of these benefits is compulsory and may be obtained by purchasing insurance from a private insurer authorized by state or federal law and approved by the United States Employees Compensation Commissioner. "Self-insurance" is permitted. Coverage required by this act is provided by using the standard workers compensation and employers liability insurance policy with the *Longshore and Harbor Workers' Compensation Act endorsement*.

Rights of Sailors. Sailors are among the best protected class of employees. Some of their rights and benefits came into existence thousands of years ago and are still enforceable today. Others came into existence as a result of judicial fiat and gained their standing from court actions that repeatedly upheld these rights and benefits, thus acknowledging their validity. Still others have come into existence as a result of modern statutes.

A sailor who is injured or taken ill in the service of the ship is entitled to exercise the following rights against the vessel or its owner: (1) to claim damages under the General Maritime Law including wages, transportation, maintenance, and cure, and (2) to claim damages under the Jones Act.

General Maritime Law. This law is generally referred to as the common law of the sea. Although not written as a statute, it derives its authority from court decisions. Under this law, the sailor is entitled to damages from the *vessel* for any injury or illness brought about by the unseaworthiness of the ship. In general, there is an implied warranty of seaworthiness arising out of the relationship between the vessel and the sailor. The warranty applies not only to the physical structure of the ship and its ability to withstand the ordinary perils of the sea, but it also ensures that the vessel is properly loaded, the cargo is properly stowed, that the vessel has been provided with a competent master, a sufficient number of competent officers and sailors, and that it has all the requisite appurtenances and equipment, such as ballast, cables, anchors, cordage, sails, and lights all in good condition, as well as food, water, fuel, and other necessary and proper stores and implements for the voyage. If the vessel lacks any of these items, it is unseaworthy. A sailor who is injured as a consequence of an unseaworthy condition may bring an action for damages against the *vessel*.

Wages, transportation, maintenance, and cure are the ancient rights given to sailors and are considered among the elements of the contract of hire whether or not the articles of employment mention them. Sailors who fall sick in the service of the ship are entitled to (1) wages to the end of the voyage, (2) transportation back to their home port, (3) maintenance, which means food and quarters to the end of the voyage and payments to cover expenses during medical treatment, and (4) cure, which means medical attention and other similar services that extend beyond the end of the voyage and that are required either to cure the condition or bring it to a point where it is pronounced permanent or incurable.

In admiralty law, the vessel is charged with the responsibility of responding to the rights of sailors. This liability is imposed on the vessel itself and not personally on the master or the owner. In order to recover, a sailor must initiate action by means of a *writ of attachment* (called a *libel*) against the vessel. This writ is served by a United States marshal and is physically attached to the vessel, at which time the marshal takes possession of the vessel. The plaintiff/seaman is referred to in admiralty as the *libellant*. The owner enters the litigation as the *ship's claimant* and usually offers a bond in order to release the attachment. The case then proceeds as any other lawsuit.

Under General Maritime Law, there is no recovery for wrongful death. The damages to be claimed are only those items that accrue to the seaman alone.

Additional Rights Under the Jones Act. The Merchant Marine Act of 1920 is commonly referred to as the Jones Act. It applies the same system and the type of remedy allowed to railroad employees to American sailors employed on American vessels. Pursuant to the Jones Act, a sailor may elect to bring an action directly against the owners of a vessel and, in the case of death, the sailor's representative may bring an action for wrongful death. The Jones Act thereby amends the General Maritime Law by permitting a direct action against the owners and by creating an action for wrongful death that never before existed.

Employers subject to the Jones Act can obtain protection in one of two ways. First, they can purchase protection and indemnity (P&I) insurance, an ocean marine coverage. Second, they can amend their standard workers compensation and employers liability insurance policy by endorsement. The insurer agrees to provide employers liability coverage in the event of bodily injury by accident or disease, including death that results from either, at any time, and sustained by any person employed as a master or member of the crew of any vessel of the insured.

Federal Employees' Compensation Act. This act provides workers compensation benefits for nonmilitary employees of the federal government. Since the federal government self-insures this exposure, coverage required by this act is not found in standard workers compensation insurance policies.

THE WORKERS COMPENSATION SYSTEM

The workers compensation system has been responsible for the development of several important features. They include (1) the role of the National Council on Compensation Insurance (NCCI) in the development of workers compensation insurance rates, (2) the need to engage in loss control and to abide by the Occupational Safety and Health Act (OSHA), and (3) the importance of third-party administration of claims.

National Council on Compensation Insurance and Compensation Rates

Early in the history of workers compensation insurance, it became evident that ratemaking and rate administration could not be ideally handled by each state alone or by the insurers acting alone. To be statistically reliable, loss data should be as numerous and as geographically widespread as possible. Thus, the development of an essentially nationwide rating bureau was important. Although independent private bureaus for the promulgation and administration of workers compensation rates exist today in eleven states, the principal privately operated bureau is the National Council on Compensation Insurance (NCCI). Formed in 1915, the National Council is a voluntary, nonprofit, unincorporated association of insurers. Its membership comprises stock and mutual insurers, reciprocals, and state funds.

The NCCI is a filing agency and rating organization in about thirty-five states, and serves as an advisory or service organization in many states where independent or state bureaus exist. It created the standard workers compensation and employers liability policy discussed at the end of this chapter. The National Council operates divisional offices throughout the country. It issues experience ratings and modifications, provides classification inspections, administers the residual market mechanism in many states, and assists agents, brokers, and underwriters with manual rules, classification, and rates. It also conducts test audits to ensure that the rules are being followed, and it reviews workers compensation policies and endorsements issued by member companies. In the vast majority of states, all insurers are required to use the same workers compensation insurance rates; however, some states now encourage price competition.

The NCCI's Rules for Rating the Workers Compensation Policy. The price that employers pay for their workers compensation insurance depends on their payroll size, loss experience, classification, and insurance arrangement. Businesses are classified according to their primary business activity into one of more than 600 class codes. Manual rates covering average losses plus overhead are based on the experience of all the firms in a given class and state. Manual rates are quoted in terms of each $100 of payroll, which provides an excellent indicator of the firm's size and the gross exposure the insurer is assuming. For example, a business with a payroll of $3,271,400 has 32,714 units of exposure ($3,271,400/$100). Payroll serves as an excellent premium base because it corresponds very closely with the workers compensation exposure. Most workers compensation benefits consist of indemnification for lost earnings. As payroll increases, so does potential lost earnings. Furthermore, inflation in payroll amounts helps keep the exposure base for compensation premiums commensurate with medical cost inflation.

Workers compensation is class rated first and may then be modified by experience, premium discount, or retrospective rating. Experience rating and premium discounts can eliminate some of the differences in premiums between competing employers with different wage levels.

As of 1990, the NCCI rates represent loss costs only. Individual insurers will have to add in a factor for their expenses, overhead, and profit. The NCCI shifted from fully developed rates to loss costs to avoid accusations of aiding price fixing. The NCCI's loss cost rates will provide actuarially reliable information about expected loss. Individual insurers will have to account for their own expenses.

Class or Manual Rating. All employers purchasing private workers compensation insurance are initially class rated. For the vast majority of these employers, this is the only rating method applicable. Under class rating, all employers engaged in similar business operations pay the same rate per $100 of payroll. The rating manual lists rates for over 600 classes of business operations.

If a business consists of a single operation or a number of separate operations that are normally associated with that type of business, the payroll, subject to certain exceptions, is normally assigned to the class that most accurately describes the entire business. Clerical office employees, however, who are not subject to the operative hazards, are separately classified, as are outside sales persons; collectors who do not handle any merchandise; drivers, chauffeurs, and their helpers; members of a flying crew; and a few other special kinds of workers. If a business includes an operation not normally associated with that business, that operation can, subject to certain exceptions, be separately classified. Unless a worker is assigned to aircraft operations, construction, sawmill operations, or stevedoring work, which always receive separate classification, the entire payroll is assigned to the most appropriate class applicable to any work or production operation associated with the business. Thus, the business itself is rated, rather than individual occupations within the business. Differences in rates account for differences in the extent of hazard from business to business. One business might have a rate of 4.84, while a much more hazardous business would have a rate of 15.06. With an identical payroll of $100,000, these two businesses would pay very different premiums. The first would pay $4,840 ($100,000/$100 x 4.84), while the second would pay $15,060 ($100,000/$100 x 15.06).

After the premium is determined by multiplying the number of $100 of payroll applicable to the business by the rate for that class, an expense constant is added to cover the cost of servicing the policy. In a few states, if the premium is under a certain dollar amount, such as $500, a loss constant may be added to this amount. No matter how small the insured's payroll may be, there is a minimum premium because the insurer expects to incur a minimum amount of expense in servicing any insured.

Because payrolls can only be estimated at the beginning of the policy year, the initial premium is an estimated premium, subject to adjustment following a payroll audit conducted after the close of the policy year.

Experience Rating. Although the vast majority of employers pay manual rates, "straight" manual premiums only account for a minority of the total premiums collected. The remainder of the premiums are also influenced by one or more modification rating plans. Large employers are relatively few in number, but account for most of the premiums collected.

The first of these modification rating plans is experience rating. The basic principle of experience rating is that employers should pay lower or higher premiums than their class premium depending on whether their experience is better or worse than the experience for the average employer in their rating class.

In most states, all employers whose payrolls during the last two years or more of the "experience period" would have produced an average annual premium at manual rates of at least a certain amount *must* be experience rated. As of 1990, the specific annual premium amount varies between $1,750 and $5,000 from state to state; $3,500 is the typical amount. The *experience period* is the period beginning not more than four years prior to the date the modification is to be applied and terminating one year prior to that date. The experience period is three years unless reliable experience is not available, in which case experience rating is not used.

Premium Discount Plan. The second type of plan that can modify the manual premium is a premium discount plan, which recognizes that as the premium increases, the proportion required to pay certain expenses decreases. Although some attempts were made to introduce premium discounts in the early thirties, and later retrospective rating plans incorporated this principle, it was not until 1943 that the National Council announced a premium discount plan available to all large premium insureds. In most states, any insured now paying over $5,000 in premium is entitled to a discount.

Retrospective Rating. The third and final rating modification plan used by the National Council is retrospective rating, which, like experience rating, relates the insured's premium to experience. Experience rating relates the premium paid to past experience. Retrospective rating, on the other hand, relates the premium to the employer's experience during the policy period. The insured pays a deposit premium at the beginning of the policy term that is adjusted at the close of the policy period when the insured's experience is known. Because the retrospective premium is so highly responsive to experience, employers must develop a standard premium of at least $25,000 to be eligible for retrospective rating. Unlike experience rating, retrospective rating is optional; both the employer and the insurer must elect to have the policy so rated prior to the beginning of the policy period.

Loss Control and Workplace Safety

The workers compensation system has provided tremendous incentives for employers and insurers to engage in loss control activities. Indeed, this was one of the chief purposes of compensation legislation. Nevertheless, the federal government created the Occupational Safety and Health Administration to further ensure safe workplaces.

The Importance of Loss Control. The workers compensation system does much more than provide injured workers with needed financial support. By imposing part of the costs of injuries on the employer, it creates financial incentives to prevent workplace injuries and diseases. It conveys these incentives directly to firms that self-insure. Experience and retrospective rating of insurance premiums create similar incentives for insured firms.

Loss control is also important because insurance does not eliminate loss exposures. If businesses are indifferent toward losses merely because insurance is available, they may soon find insurance too expensive to purchase or too difficult to obtain. In addition, the level of workplace safety will decrease. A business must, therefore, take whatever means are available to avoid, control, or reduce losses.

Even an insured business has incentives that automatically foster loss control. For every work-related incident, employers sustain two types of costs. First, there are settlement costs and the compensation benefits that are paid to workers on behalf of the employer by the insurer or by the employer who retains the exposure. Second, there are loss costs as a consequence of work injuries that are not recoverable under insurance. The uninsured loss costs may include any number of the following:

1. The cost of the injured employee's lost time
2. The cost of the time lost by other employees who stop work out of curiosity or sympathy, or to assist the injured worker
3. The cost of time lost by supervisors and others in similar positions who assist the injured employee, investigate the accident, prepare accident reports, attend hearings, arrange to have another employee continue the work of the injured person, or hire and train a new employee for the vacated position
4. The cost of time spent providing immediate medical assistance to the injured employee
5. Costs stemming from damage to machine, tools, or other property affected by the accident
6. Costs to the employer in continuing the wages of the partially recovered injured employee in full after his or her return even

though the productivity of an employee who is not fully recovered may be something less than before[7]

Beyond these financial incentives, most employers are genuinely interested in reducing employee injury, disease, and death for the sake of the workers. Insurance alone does not eliminate the financial and social costs of employee injury, disease, and death.

Most workers compensation and employers liability exposures cannot be avoided. Even if there were no workers compensation laws, workers and independent contractors would still be injured on the job. The existence of these potential liability exposures creates the need for employers to establish a safe working environment. Even the individual proprietorship or partnership with no employees has an interest in preventing, controlling, or reducing the direct and indirect costs that would be incurred if an owner were injured.

Loss control techniques are perhaps more important as a noninsurance means of dealing with workers compensation exposures than any other type of exposures. Probably more time and effort are spent in the area of employee safety than in any other area of loss control, yet not every employer has a safety program at work.

The Results of Loss Prevention. Loss prevention programs can be credited for much of the reduction over the years in occupational accidents. Formal programs, solidly backed by management, have produced favorable results.

The Bureau of Labor Statistics and the National Safety Council report that occupational accidents claimed 13,800 lives in 1970, and 12,500 in 1976. Fatalities per 100,000 workers in 1970 was 17.5 compared to 9.3 in 1988.[8] By 1988, occupational fatalities were reduced to 10,600 despite a 45 percent increase in the labor force. Compared to 1912, when workers compensation laws were first being enacted, the significance of the figures becomes more readily apparent. In 1912, an estimated 18,000 to 21,000 workers lost their lives. Yet in 1976, with more than double the work force and more than seven times as much production as in 1912, only 12,500 lives were lost.

The Occupational Safety and Health Act.[9] Despite the overall reduction in occupational deaths and disabilities, there was a period throughout the 1960s when the annual rate of approximately 14,000 deaths and 2.2 million disabilities was fairly consistent from year to year. Society could not accept this record. Although there were some industries, as well as particular firms within industries, that were doing remarkably well in reducing and controlling their occupational accidents, many others were not. There were conditions in many firms that had to be improved or eliminated to provide safe places to work. Many states provided erratic or no inspections of workplaces for occupational hazards. To address these conditions, the Occupational

Safety and Health Act (OSHA) of 1970 was passed by Congress.

The primary mission of OSHA is to ensure every worker in industry a safe place to work. OSHA attempts to free places of employment from hazards likely to cause occupational deaths, diseases, and serious injuries. The consequences of noncompliance with OSHA include not only stringent penalties, but also shutdowns for those who refuse to correct certain conditions following warnings by federal inspectors. Since the construction industry had one of the worst records of any major industry group, it became OSHA's initial target. The enforcement of OSHA requirements has now spread into other industries with poor safety records. The mere threat of OSHA inspections has brought about improvements in the physical environment of many firms.

OSHA administrators have been criticized for being overly zealous in their desire to warn workers of all possible occupational hazards. One widely publicized OSHA bulletin was written to inform farmers that wet manure is slippery. OSHA has also been criticized for going too far in encroaching on private enterprise. Despite the fact that many safety programs have been instituted as a result of OSHA, the value of OSHA is still questioned. OSHA standards concentrate on physical work hazards, whereas a majority of occupational accidents are caused by unsafe acts, not physical hazards.

Third-Party Administration of Claims

One of the important advantages of the workers compensation system is that claims are almost always handled by a third party. The employer bears the legal obligations toward its employees established by the compensation law but the employer rarely handles the employee's claims. Claims are handled by insurers or other third parties. This separation of duties protects the employer-employee relationship when the claim must be carefully scrutinized or resisted by the insurer. Insurers have performed this service for years through their claim departments. In recent years, more and more employers have chosen to self-insure their compensation exposures through retention plans. As a result, the services of third-party claim administrators have become more important.

Increased Popularity of Retention. Retention has increased in popularity over the past number of years. Several factors have contributed to this increase, especially the limited availability of coverage during the "hard market" of the mid-1980s and the increasing costs of insurance. From 1984 to 1987 aggregate compensation of employees throughout the economy increased 21 percent, yet written premiums for workers compensation increased 55 percent,[10] thus reflecting substantial rate increases.

Inflation has also had a powerful effect on workers compensation costs. The cost of workers compensation is directly affected by higher wages and higher administrative costs. Medical costs have in general risen faster than inflation.

Another reason for the long term increasing cost of workers compensation and the resulting popularity of retention is the liberalization in coverage and benefits that followed the 1972 recommendations of the National Commission on State Workers Compensation Laws. The commission endorsed the basic concept of separate state-run workers compensation programs, but reached the "inescapable conclusion...that state workers compensation laws in general are inadequate and inequitable." Among other recommendations, the commission recommended increases in benefits, which have subsequently been enacted by many states.

When a retention program for workers compensation losses is implemented, an employer usually secures other benefits. For example, an employer that pays all losses with company funds may take a more active interest in preventing losses than an insurer. (However, an experienced insurer may have more loss control techniques available to it than an employer and more knowledge of the complexities of claim handling and risk management.)

When a business is faced with a profit squeeze and a steadily increasing premium for, or unavailability of, its workers compensation and employers liability coverage, it may wish to establish a retention program. If the business has a high premium volume, a large payroll, a high concentration of employees at one or two locations within a given state or geographical area, and a fairly stable loss record, retention is a viable risk management alternative. The business will ordinarily engage a specialty firm to act as its agent in managing the retention program.

Managing Service Agents. If an employer does not have the expertise required for administering its claim handling, it can retain the services of a specialty firm or purchase the service from an insurer that specializes in workers compensation claim administration. If the employer can handle its claims but lacks the capabilities for handling loss control services, it can hire a firm to perform only that function.

An employer with a retention program often needs a full range of services. In other cases, an employer may be required to hire a managing service agent by an excess insurer as a condition to obtaining excess coverage. When a full range of services is required, the managing service agent must (1) fulfill all of the duties that are required of the employer by the workers compensation law; (2) establish and conduct loss prevention and engineering functions, and create the accompanying reports; (3) provide the insurance company with periodic claim records showing tabulations of claims, the amounts of payments made and reserves outstanding, plus the loss adjustment expenses involved in resolving those claims; (4) file all notices and reports required by the workers compensation board or industrial commission; (5) attend hearings and trials as may be required; and (6) handle whatever else may be required under the applicable workers compensation law. When this full range of services is provided, the only obligation of the employer is to provide ample funds so that the managing service agent may pay all claims as required.

There may be fewer benefits than are immediately apparent in the use of retention. The cost of providing for the workers compensation exposure is less predictable under a retention program than with insurance. Many of the costs supposedly saved by not paying insurance premiums are not really saved because of the expenses of running a self-administered program and the cost of excess insurance. Furthermore, the cost of handling a workers compensation exposure through insurance may be reduced by experience or retrospective rating.

THE WORKERS COMPENSATION AND EMPLOYERS LIABILITY POLICY[11]

The policy of insurance written to cover the workers compensation and employers liability exposure is among the most closely regulated. The state compensation laws usually require the incorporation of certain provisions and prohibit others. All jurisdictions require approval of the contract by either the insurance commissioner or the industrial commission. Although the provisions of every state compensation law differ, the standard workers compensation and employers liability insurance policy, with appropriate endorsements, is used in all jurisdictions permitting private insurance. It is not used by state funds because they are forbidden to cover the employers liability hazard. When permitted in states with monopolistic funds, the standard policy may be endorsed to provide protection for the employers liability exposure only.

The policy form in use since 1954 was developed through the collaboration of the insurers writing compensation coverage, committees of the National Council on Compensation Insurance, the New York Compensation Rating Board, and various other independent and state bureaus. The most recent NCCI revision of the policy into what is known today as "easy read" was introduced in 1984. This policy combines two separate coverages:

- The first of these coverages, *workers compensation*, is governed entirely by the applicable statutes. Its purpose is to pay whatever benefits are prescribed by statute.

- The second coverage, referred to as *employers liability*, protects employers from suits brought by injured employees to recover money damages separate and distinct from claims for workers compensation benefits. This protection is much like that provided under a commercial general liability policy in that it also provides employers with defense coverage. The standard policy is designed such that employers liability coverage does not overlap with general liability protection.

In jurisdictions where employees are permitted to purchase compensation insurance from private insurers, coverage for both workers compensation and employers liability exposures is provided under one policy. The policy contains uniform provisions even though workers compensation benefits vary by jurisdiction. The compensation statutes are simply incorporated by reference into the policy.

Part One—Workers Compensation Coverage

Under the workers compensation coverage, the insurer agrees to pay promptly, when due, the benefits required of the employer by the workers compensation law. The policy refers to the workers compensation law as the compensation and occupational disease law of each state or territory named in item 3A of the information page and defines "state" as any state in the United States of America and the District of Columbia. The basic policy refers only to state laws. No protection is provided against claims made under federal compensation laws, such as the Federal Employer's Liability Act and the U.S. Longshore and Harbor Workers' Compensation Act. Coverage for such claims can be added by endorsement.

No policy limits apply to the workers compensation section of the policy. The insurer is instead required to assume whatever liability is prescribed for its insured by the statute in question except for any punitive or exemplary damages that may be assessed against the employer. The absence of policy limits does not mean that benefits are unlimited. The kind and the extent of any benefits that may be payable depend on the nature of the disability and the provisions of the state law that apply.

Since the policy restricts protection to that required by the state law or laws listed or referred to in the policy, it is important that the information page (declarations) designate the state or states where all business locations or operations involving employee work exposures are or may be maintained.

Most state compensation laws are extraterritorial. An employee hired by an employer in state A may be injured on business in state B.

That employee, depending on the laws or circumstances, might file a claim under the compensation laws of either state A or state B. If the information page of the employer's policy lists only state A, there would be no insurance coverage for a claim filed under the laws of state B. The "other states" provision discussed later in this chapter provides coverage for situations where extraterritorial exposures exist.

The separate paragraphs of the workers compensation coverage part are best understood by examining each separately.

How This Insurance Applies. Workers compensation insurance applies to bodily injury by accident *during the policy period* or to bodily injury by disease caused or aggravated by conditions of employment if the last day of the last exposure that causes or aggravates the disease *occurs during the policy period*. Coverage also applies regardless of when death occurs so long as it results from an otherwise covered bodily injury or disease.

We Will Pay. The insurer agrees to pay promptly when due the statutory benefits as required.

We Will Defend. The insurer agrees to defend at its expense any claim, proceeding, or suit against the insured for benefits payable. While the insurer agrees to investigate and settle these claims, proceedings, or suits, it has no duty to defend an action that is not covered by this part of the policy.

We Will Also Pay. In addition to the statutory benefits, the insurer also agrees to pay the following costs in the event of any claim, suit, or proceeding:

- Reasonable expenses incurred by the insured employer at the insurer's request, other than loss of earnings
- Premiums for bonds to release attachments and for appeal bonds for an amount not to exceed the amount payable under this insurance
- Litigation costs taxed against the employer
- All interest that has accrued on a judgment as required by law until such time that the insurer offers the amount due under this insurance
- Any expenses that the insurer incurs

Other Insurance. If a claim, suit, or proceeding arises whereby other insurance or self-insurance also applies, the most the insurer will pay under this policy is its share. Thus, all shares are to be equal until the loss is paid. If any insurance or self-insurance is exhausted, the remaining insurance will contribute until the loss is paid.

Payments You Must Make. The provisions of workers compensation insurance specifically disclaim any payments *in excess of* those benefits regularly provided by law, including any payments that may be required because of the following attitudes or actions by an employer:

1. Serious or willful misconduct
2. Employment of an employee in violation of law
3. Failure to comply with any health or safety law or regulation
4. Discharge or discrimination of any employee in violation of the workers compensation law

If the insurer is required to make any payments *in excess of* what is normally required by statute, the employer is required to reimburse the insurer promptly.

Recovery from Others. In the event of any payment under the policy, the insurer is subrogated to the insured's rights of recovery, as well as to the rights of other persons who receive the benefits of workers compensation, against other persons or organizations. Furthermore, the insured must do everything to protect those rights and to assist the insurer in exercising them.

Statutory Provisions. This paragraph comprises statements that apply where required by law. Thus, it is agreed that the employer's notice of injury is deemed to be notice by the insurer as well. Furthermore, neither bankruptcy nor insolvency of the employer or its estate will relieve the insurer of its duties under workers compensation insurance after an injury occurs. If any person is entitled to the benefits as prescribed by statute, the insurer is contractually liable. This part of the policy conforms to the workers compensation law that applies to benefits payable by this insurance, as well as special taxes, funds, and assessments that are payable by the insured under law. Finally, any terms of the insurance that conflict with the workers compensation law are amended to conform to such law.

Part Two—Employers Liability Coverage

Statutory workers compensation benefits are *said* to be the exclusive remedy that covered employees have against covered employers for injuries and diseases. Employees normally cannot reject the statutory benefits after an injury and decide to sue their employers with the idea of obtaining higher awards at common law. Nor can employees accept the benefits and later decide to sue their employers for additional money damages.

Yet, there are ways for employees or their families to circumvent the exclusive remedy of workers compensation laws and bring tort suits for money damages. These different ways, as discussed further in Chapter 6, include suits for loss of consortium by family members, dual capacity actions, and suits by employees of subsidiaries against parent companies. Employers liability coverage is also needed to protect employers against tort suits brought by injured employees who have rejected the compensation benefits under elective statutes, as well as suits brought by employees who are excluded from the acts by numerical or types-of-employment exemptions. There are times, too, when the injury, disease, or death of a victim does not meet the criteria for coverage, or in some cases, the workers compensation act specifically permits (or is interpreted as permitting) suits against employers by third parties, such as dependents of an employee.

We Will Pay. According to this paragraph, the insurer agrees to pay sums that the employer must legally pay as damages because of bodily injury sustained by employees and otherwise covered by employers liability insurance. Specifically included hereunder are damages, otherwise permitted by law, involving third-party-over actions, care and loss of services, consequential injuries, and dual capacity actions.

- A *third-party-over action* arises when an injured employee sues and recovers from a negligent third party. The third party, in turn, sues the employer for at least partial recovery based on contributory or comparative negligence of the employer. For example, suppose an employee is injured while operating a vehicle that the employer, with knowledge of a safety defect, allows to be operated. The employee sues the manufacturer of that vehicle rather than accepting the compensation benefits of the employer in order to obtain a higher recovery. The manufacturer then sues the employer on the basis that the employer was partially negligent in permitting the vehicle to be operated in an unsafe condition.

- *Care and loss of services* includes loss of affection and consortium.

- A *consequential injury* can occur when a spouse or family member contracts some occupational disease that is transmitted by the employee, or, for example, when silica or another hazardous substance is carried home on the employee's work clothes.

- *Dual capacity* claims, explained further in Chapter 6, deal with actions against the insured both in the capacity of an employer and in some other capacity.

The fact that each of the four preceding exposures is specifically excluded under all commercial general liability coverages and auto policies makes employers liability insurance the only recourse of protection in the event of claim or suit. Where workers compensation coverage is provided by a monopolistic state fund, employers would require *stop gap coverage*, which is the equivalent of employers liability coverage.

Exclusions. Part Two of the policy is subject to seven exclusions.

Contractual Liability. Under employers liability coverage, liability assumed by the insured (employer) under any contract or agreement is not covered. Tort liability assumed under any contract or agreement, including the assumption of any liability to compensate or to pay a third party for a work-related injury (other than one that the insured or its insurers is obligated to cover under workers compensation insurance) can be covered under contractual liability insurance.

Agreements dealing with the assumption of the tort liability of another to third parties are common. General contractors are often required to enter into such agreements with owners of work projects. Subcontractors also enter into assumption-of-liability agreements with general contractors, often as a condition to obtaining the jobs. An owner of a work project is open to suit by an injured employee of a contractor (or subcontractor), particularly when an owner contributes to the injurious exposure in some way. To avoid adverse judgments and the inconvenience of being confronted with suits, owners frequently require contractors to agree, under contract, to handle and settle the entire matter without involving owners, whether or not owners are negligent. Since agreements such as these may also be covered under contractual liability insurance, it is unnecessary to duplicate coverage under employers liability coverage.

However, employers liability coverage, as an exception to the exclusion, does extend to liability under any warranty that work performed by or on behalf of the insured will be done in a workmanlike manner. Such liability coverage does not come within the scope of contractual liability under the commercial general liability policy. To avoid any gap in protection, employers liability covers the exposure.

Punitive or Exemplary Damages. Workers compensation laws require employers to retain any punitive or exemplary damages assessed against them for violations of law. Under employers liability coverage, employers are denied coverage for any punitive or exemplary damages because of bodily injury to an employee in violation of the law.

Employment in Violation of Law. Even in the absence of any punitive or exemplary damages, employers are still denied protection under the policy if bodily injury to an employee is sustained while he or she is employed in violation of the law with the actual knowledge of the employer or its executive officers.

Workers Compensation. Employers liability coverage does not apply to any statutory benefit obligations imposed by workers compensation, occupational disease, unemployment compensation, disability benefits law, or similar law.

Intentional Injury. Bodily injury intentionally caused or aggravated by the employer is generally not covered by workers compensation insurance. Such offenses are likewise excluded under employers liability coverage.

Foreign Nationals. With the exception of a citizen or resident of the United States of America or Canada who is *temporarily* outside these countries, no coverage is provided because of any claim or suit brought by others, such as foreign nationals.

Wrongful Discharge or Discrimination. The policy precludes coverage for any damages arising out of the discharge of, coercion of, or discrimination against any employee in violation of law. Since it is the damages that are not covered, the employer at least is given the benefit of any defense coverage until the matter is resolved.

Common Conditions. Three provisions of employers liability coverage are identical to those of workers compensation coverage. These provisions are We Will Also Pay, Other Insurance, and Recovery from Others. The provision entitled We Will Defend is similar to the one under workers compensation coverage. The only difference is that with employers liability coverage, the insurer has no duty to defend or continue defending after the insurer has paid its applicable limit.

Limit of Liability. The policy is subject to specific limitations as to the amount payable by the insurer. Two such limits of liability are designated in item 3B of the information page. The first is a *bodily injury by accident limit.* The limit shown for "bodily injury by accident— each accident" is the maximum the insurer will pay for damages covered by this policy because of bodily injury (or death) to one or more employees in any one accident. The second limit deals with the *bodily injury by disease limit.* The limit shown for "bodily injury by disease- policy limit" is the most the insurer will pay for all covered damages arising out of bodily injury by disease, regardless of the number of employees involved, whereas the limit shown for "bodily injury by disease—each employee" is the maximum amount payable to any one employee. It is stipulated that a disease is not bodily injury by accident unless it results directly from bodily injury by accident; also, bodily injury by disease does not include disease that results directly from a bodily injury by accident. The rationale is to avoid any argument that an injury is attributable to both an accident and a disease. The two terms are mutually exclusive. It is also clear that the insurer has no contractual obligation to pay any claims for damages after it has paid the applicable limit of its liability under this section.

Action Against the Insurer. This provision, like the suit provision of commercial general liability forms, states that no right of action is permitted against the insurer under the insurance policy unless the employer (insured) has complied with all terms of the policy and the amount that the employer owes has been determined with the insurer's consent or by actual trial and final judgment. Finally, this insurance does not give anyone the right to sue the insurer as a defendant in any action against the employer in order to determine the employer's liability.

Part Three—Other States Insurance

The purpose of "other states insurance" is to provide coverage against those exposures that develop during the policy period in any state designated on the information page. The states where operations are known to exist are designated in item 3A. If exposures could arise in other states, they should be listed in item 3C. However, monopolistic fund states where workers compensation insurance is available through the state government cannot be listed, and insurance companies that are not licensed to operate in all the states, such as regional insurers, cannot list states where they are not permitted to operate. National insurers sometimes use standard wording that includes all nonmonopolistic fund states. There is no premium charge for listing a state in item 3C.

Part Four—Your Duties If Injury Occurs

Part Four explains the duties of the employer in the event of injury. *The first and most important requirement is to inform the insurer at once if injury occurs that may be covered by the policy.* The following are other duties of the employer under the policy:

- Provide immediate medical and other services that may be required by the compensation law
- Give the insurer or its agent the names and addresses of the injured persons, as well as the names and addresses of any witnesses
- Provide the insurer promptly with all notices, demands, and legal papers related to such incident
- Cooperate and assist the insurer, as may be requested, in the investigation, defense, or settlement of any claim, proceeding, or suit

- Do nothing after any injury that may interfere with or impair the insurer's right to recover from others
- Refrain from making any voluntary payments or assuming any obligations or incurring any expenses except at the insured's own cost

Part Five—Premium

This part of the policy explains how the premium is developed. It is also subject to an agreement whereby the insurer is permitted to examine and audit all of the insured's records that relate to the policy. Such audits may be conducted within three years after the policy ends.

Part Six—Conditions

The workers compensation and employers liability policy is subject to certain conditions that concern the duties and obligations of both parties, the most significant of which concerns inspections.

Inspection. The insured agrees to permit the insurer to inspect the premises and operations covered by the policy. Insurance company inspections are highly important in workers compensation insurance not only for providing insurers with underwriting information, but also in connection with insurer loss control activities. This condition contains the statement that the inspections are not safety inspections, but that they relate only to the insurability of the workplaces and the premiums to be charged. The insurer also states that it *may* give the insured the reports on the conditions it finds as well as any recommended changes. While these inspections may be helpful to the insured, the insurer attempts to clarify that it (1) does not have the duty to provide for the health and safety of the insured's employees or the public and (2) does not warrant the workplaces as being safe or in compliance with the laws. These qualifying statements are considered necessary as a defense against possible allegations that the insurer is responsible for unsafe working conditions that might result from the failure to perform an inspection, or from an inadequate inspection.

SUMMARY

Workers compensation laws evolved out of a common-law system that did not satisfactorily address work-related injuries. Workers compensation laws provide workers with specified benefits and protect the employer from tort suits.

Workers compensation responsibilities are usually handled through workers compensation insurance. The National Council on Compensation Insurance has developed standard rates and policy forms for such insurance. The standard workers compensation policy also protects employers from employer liability claims. Despite the broad protection of workers compensation laws, employers still face the possibility of liability claims from their employees.

Chapter Notes

1. Insurance Information Institute, *1990 Property/Casualty Insurance Facts*, pp. 15-16, 28, based on statistics from A.M. Best Company, Inc., *Best's Aggregates and Averages*.

2. This section was adapted from Donald S. Malecki, James H. Donaldson, and Ronald C. Horn, *Commercial Liability Risk Management and Insurance*, 1st ed. (Malvern, PA: American Institute for Property and Liability Underwriters, 1978), pp. 368-371, 376.

3. This section was adapted from Malecki, Donaldson, and Horn, 1st ed., pp. 371-375.

4. National Council on Compensation Insurance, *Issues Report*, 1990, p. 10.

5. U. S. Chamber of Commerce, *1990 Analysis of Workers Compensation Laws*, pp. 1-4.

6. This section was adapted from Donald S. Malecki, Ronald C. Horn, Eric A. Wiening, and James H. Donaldson, *Commercial Liability Risk Management and Insurance*, vol. II, 2nd ed. (Malvern, PA: American Institute for Property and Liability Underwriters), pp. 152-157.

7. Adapted from "Accident Cost Control," Bureau of Labor Standards Bulletin, 1965, as cited in Malecki, Donaldson, and Horn, p. 451.

8. *1990 Property/Casualty Insurance Facts* (New York: Insurance Information Institute), p. 87.

9. This section was adapted from Malecki, Donaldson, and Horn, 1st ed., pp. 458-460.

10. U.S. Department of Commerce, *Statistical Abstract of the United States 1989*, Table 691, p. 425, and Insurance Information Institute, *1990 Property/Casualty Insurance Facts*, p. 28.

11. This section was adapted from Malecki, Horn, Wiening, and Donaldson, 2nd ed., pp. 173-186.

CHAPTER 2

Compensability: Employments and Injuries Covered

Broadly speaking, workers compensation protects against injuries to employees. However, neither all employees nor all injuries are covered by workers compensation. This chapter explores covered employments and injuries.

It begins with an explanation of the essential elements of the employment relationship. Not everyone who performs work is an employee. Independent contractors are the most important category of nonemployee workers. The distinction between employees and independent contractors is explained in detail, yet in many cases the distinction is a fine one and remains hard to make. In addition to independent contractors, certain workers are excluded from coverage under various workers compensation laws even though such workers are clearly employees.

Almost any injury to an employee is covered, yet a few may not be. Generally, workers compensation statutes require injuries to be "accidental," or to occur "by accident," to be compensable. The evolution of the meaning of this requirement is explained. Some particular injuries whose "accidental" quality is often doubtful are given special consideration under the law and at the end of this chapter. These injuries include occupational disease, cumulative trauma, hernias, and psychological injuries.

THE EMPLOYMENT RELATIONSHIP AND COVERED EMPLOYMENTS

The modern term "workers compensation" might be refined by referring to it as "employees compensation" because not all workers are employees. Workers compensation laws are designed to protect all employees except those specifically excluded.

A worker's status as an employee depends on the existence of an employer-employee relationship. The employer may be an individual, a partnership, a corporation, or any other entity. The employee is the individual who has agreed to perform personal services for the employer in exchange for consideration. This underlying consent implies that the employee agrees to be under the authoritative direction and control of the employer.

Elements of the Employment Relationship

Workers compensation is a "no-fault," strict liability system. The obligations are determined not by who is at fault, but simply by whether the worker is an employee subject to the workers compensation law and whether the injury or disease is connected to the employment. Determining whether or not an employer-employee relationship exists requires an analysis of three elements that define the relationship:

1. Control
2. Consent
3. Consideration

Control. State workers compensation laws generally define the term "employee" broadly or not at all, allowing the courts and administrative judges considerable latitude in deciding who are subject workers. Workers compensation laws replaced employers liability laws, which imposed legal obligations on the master (employer) for injuries to its servants (employees). The element of control is an overriding factor in determining the existence of an employment relationship. Control establishes who the employer (master) is and who the employee (servant) is. As discussed further below, control is the key factor in distinguishing employer-employee relationships from independent contractor relationships.

Control includes the employer's rights to do the following:

1. Give orders
2. Control the manner in which the work is to be done
3. Hire and discharge

Any worker who is under the control of an employer as defined above is generally deemed to be an employee subject to the workers compensation laws unless he or she is specifically excluded by statute or fails to meet the tests of consent and consideration.

A distinction must be made between the common-law tests of the master-servant relationship and the tests of the employer-employee relationship used in workers compensation. The common-law concept of master-servant is important to the workers compensation scheme only in that it establishes the element of control as *one* of the tests in establishing that a worker is an employee subject to workers compensation laws. The relevance stops there. The purpose of the master-servant concept in common law is to determine the extent of the master's vicarious liability for injuries to third parties caused by its servants. This liability was determined by the extent of control the master had over the details of the servant's work. Since liability to others was the key issue, control was the key test. In workers compensation, the issue is responsibility to the servant (employee) who is injured, not to a third party. Thus, the extent of control is not the only factor determining the existence of an employment relationship for purposes of workers compensation, but it is an important one. The many factors that should be considered in distinguishing employees from independent contractors are set forth in a subsequent section. These factors are based on the common law and, to the extent that they are cited as evidence of control, should be given somewhat less weight in the workers compensation setting.

Consent. The employment relationship assumes that there is an underlying contract of hire whereby the employee voluntarily accepts the terms of the employment and is competent to enter into such an agreement, and the agreement has a lawful purpose.

Based on the failure to meet the consent requirement, there are states that expressly exclude from workers compensation coverage employments of a spouse by a spouse, children working for their parents, inmates working to serve their sentence, volunteers working for nonprofit organizations, and workers employed in illegal trades.

Intrafamily employments generally lack genuine assent. In a genuine employment contract, the employer must freely make an employment offer and the worker must freely accept the terms. Children, particularly those not yet emancipated, are not competent to enter into a contract of hire. Furthermore, because of the nature of the family relationship, the bargain may not be mutually beneficial to all the parties involved. There is also a problem of moral hazard when it comes to claims by family members against the family business. For example, it may be difficult to find an objective witness to corroborate a claim made by a wife against her husband or the family business.

Consideration.   In an employment relationship, a thing of value is exchanged between the employer and the employee. In the law, this thing is called "consideration." It need not be monetary or tangible. However, it does mean that the services cannot be gratuitously given.

A typical employment involves an employee providing personal services in exchange for wages. However, working for meals or room and board can also be consideration, thus creating a valid employment relationship. Other types of exchanges can be consideration, such as working in exchange for the privilege of using the facilities at a health club or golf club. There are cases in which the exchange of labor has been judged sufficient to find a valid employment relationship.

One significant difference between an "employee" as defined in the context of workers compensation and "servant" as defined by common law is that an employee must be paid (or receive consideration) under an express or implied contract of hire. A servant does not necessarily have to be remunerated. Workers who offer services gratuitously are uniformly excluded from coverage under workers compensation laws because they fail to meet the test of consideration.

Distinctions Between Employees and Independent Contractors

Discussions of the elements required in an employment relationship naturally lead to what distinguishes an employee from an independent contractor. The distinction between the two is based on the twenty criteria described below. Simply entering into an agreement and calling it an independent contractor relationship does not necessarily create that relationship or relieve an employer from workers compensation obligations. If the facts show that the elements of an employer-employee relationship exist, then absent specific statutory exclusion, courts will find coverage.

When examining the relationship between an employer and a worker hired to perform personal services, courts tend to presume that the relationship is that of employer-employee under workers compensation law unless the facts establish that the worker is indeed an independent contractor. This presumption is consistent with the remedial purposes of compensation legislation—to provide indemnification to injured workers regardless of fault and without excessive legal action. The following criteria are not necessarily listed in order of importance, but all may be relevant in determining whether a worker is an employee or an independent contractor:

1. Control over details of work
2. Distinct business or occupation

3. Special skills
4. Tools, materials, and equipment
5. Place of work
6. Method of remuneration
7. Integration of services into the business operation
8. Compliance with instructions
9. Training requirements
10. Duration of relationship
11. Time constraints
12. Availability of services to the public
13. Status of employer
14. Right to discharge
15. Right to quit
16. Right to hire subordinates
17. Personal service requirement
18. Reporting requirements
19. License requirements
20. Understanding of both parties

Control Over Details of Work. An employer has the right to control not only the result of an employee's work, but also the manner in which that result is accomplished. An independent contractor is simply given specifications for the final product or result. The means of accomplishing the result, or the pattern and sequence of completing the final product, is left to the judgment of the independent contractor. The distinction between employee and independent contractor is therefore made on the basis of whether or not the employer has the right to control the details of the work. *Control is the decisive test of the employment relationship.* The actual exercise of such right is not as important. The right of control may sometimes not be exercised because the worker is experienced and highly competent, but this fact will not change an employer-employee relationship. Although possibly of less weight in a workers compensation claim than in a liability claim, the right of control is still regarded as the most crucial distinction between employees and independent contractors.

Distinct Business or Occupation. An independent contractor is more likely than an employee to have a significant investment in its business, such as maintaining an office or other facilities. The contractor's investment exists apart from any customer for whom services are provided. Because of overhead and other costs, an independent contractor may realize a loss on any given job. An employee receives remuneration regardless of the result.

It becomes more difficult to distinguish between an employee and an independent contractor on the basis of distinct business or occupation when the worker provides, through an allegedly distinct business or occupation, a service that is an integral part of the employer's business operation. It is not wholly clear that the worker is an independent contractor if the service provided, although able to be performed as a distinct business or occupation, is a necessary component in the employer's business operation. Examples of services performed by workers who may be difficult to classify include window cleaning, security, and maintenance operations. The argument that workers offering such services are employees rests on the notion that their services are an integral part of the employer's business. On the other hand, despite what they provide for the employer, if they are in fact in business for themselves, the law should not cover all such workers. In these cases when the distinction is difficult to make, the degree of dependence upon the employer becomes the critical factor. A window washer hired from the yellow pages to do a one-time two-hour job is an independent contractor; a window washer on a permanent retainer, most of whose time is spent regularly performing a service for the building owner, is likely to be considered an employee.[1]

Special Skills. The need to hire an independent contractor is usually based on the need for a specialized skill or service that cannot be performed or provided by employees either because they do not have the skill or training for the job or because it is not economically feasible to make the additional investment in human resources to develop the necessary expertise. Having specialized skills usually denotes "independence" and suggests that a worker with such skills may be an independent contractor. In contrast, employees are dependent on their employers because their skills are such that they cannot simply go out and offer personal services to the general public.

Workers such as doctors, nurses, lawyers, architects, and other skilled professionals may be either employees or independent contractors. To determine the status of such a professional, the test is not whether the employer can control the worker's professional discretion. Instead, the test is how much control the employer can exercise over the time the professional works for the employer's benefit versus working only for his or her own benefit. For example, a hospital cannot tell a doctor how to perform surgery, but a doctor is an employee if he or she is employed full time by the hospital and is paid a salary.[2]

The status of a professional worker as an employee is further strengthened if that professional performs duties that are more administrative than professional. For example, a doctor employed as a hospital administrator is more easily classified as an employee, not as an independent contractor.

Tools, Materials, and Equipment. Tools, materials, and equipment also help to make the distinction between an employee and an independent contractor. An employee is usually hired to provide only labor, but an independent contractor is likely to provide tools, materials, and equipment in addition to labor. Furnishing tools, materials, and equipment by the employer almost invariably establishes an employer-employee relationship. However, workers who provide their own tools, materials, and equipment are not necessarily independent contractors. A worker who satisfies other employee tests may be deemed an employee.[3]

The furnishing of tools, materials, and equipment carries with it the right to control their use, whether or not that right is exercised. For example, if a trucking firm owns the truck the operator drives, the firm has an interest in how the truck is driven, and control can and will be exercised. This test assumes that the tools, materials, and equipment are substantial investments, and thus implies that the employer will want to control how they are used. If the tools, materials, and equipment are of small value and size, the implication is no longer compelling, and other tests of the employee-employer relationship may be more important.

The worker who provides his or her own tools, materials, and equipment is not necessarily presumed to be an independent contractor. Control over the operator or user is not necessarily relinquished because the operator or user owns his tools. However, if the tools, materials, and equipment are of significant size or value, it is likely that the worker has made a substantial financial investment in these items and is, by implication, in a distinct business or occupation. The ultimate question remains: Is control actually relinquished by the employer?

Place of Work. Workers who are required by their employer to work on the employer's premises are likely to be deemed employees. Workers who are free to work wherever they please are more likely to be deemed independent contractors, but many may be considered employees if other indications of employment are present. Obviously, this test is inapplicable to work that can *only* be performed on the employer's premises, such as construction and maintenance, the performance of which may be done by bona fide independent contractors.

Method of Compensation. Workers paid by the hour, week, or month are likely to be considered employees, unless the method of payment is for convenience only and is actually part of a lump sum payment for the completion of the job. The practical rationale for this test is that if the method of compensation is based on a unit of time spent on the job, the employer will be interested in controlling the efficient use of the time spent on the job.[4] By contrast, if the pay is a set amount for an end result, the employer will not be concerned about how the time is spent, as long as the end result is as specified.

It is more difficult to use payment by commission or on a piece-work basis to test a worker's status because the above rationale is not easily applicable. Such forms of compensation may be present in either employment or contractor relationships. On one hand, when the worker is paid by commission or "by the piece" it can be argued that the employer is only interested in the end result, not the means of accomplishment. On the other hand, such an arrangement may represent a continuous employment, a characteristic of an employer-employee relationship. Furthermore, employers who pay by commission or "by the piece," may also invest time, materials, and training in the worker.

Integration of Services Into the Business Operation. If the service performed is an integral part of the business of the employer for whom the service is provided, the worker is likely to be an employee. The employer's dependence on such service is especially strong evidence of an employment relationship. Dependence suggests that the employer is likely to retain the right to exercise direction and control.

This consideration is known as the "relative nature of the work test." Legal experts in the field of workers compensation point to this criterion as an appropriate and decisive test.[5] It simplifies the analysis of the employment relationship. Rather than focusing on the mechanics of the work being performed to determine the extent of control (or the *right* to control), it simply raises the question of whether or not the services provided are an integral part of the business of the employer. For example, a seamstress who assembles clothes for a clothing manufacturer would be regarded as an employee even if she performed her work at home, set her own hours, and was paid by the piece. Assembling clothing is the essential activity of a clothing manufacturer, and the workers who perform such work should be treated as employees. In contrast, a landscaper who tends the grounds of the clothing manufacturer would be less likely to be regarded as an employee even if a substantial portion of the worker's time is devoted to that employer.

An example from an actual case is a dairy hiring a cheesemaker. In view of the specialized skill of a cheesemaker, a contract may be written designating the cheesemaker as an "independent contractor," who would be paid piecemeal and would work without supervision or set hours; the contract would also state that the dairy is only interested in the final product. Nevertheless, in the final analysis, if a cheesemaker's job is considered an integral part of the dairy business, the relationship may be that of employer-employee, not employer-independent contractor.[6]

Compliance With Instructions. An independent contractor is not given instructions as to when, where, how, and by whom the work should be done. An employee, on the other hand, may receive and is expected to comply with set instructions.

Training Requirements. If a worker is required to attend meetings or to receive training on how a given task is to be performed, it would appear that the employer is not only interested in the final result, but also in the means by which the result is accomplished. Workers subject to such training are likely to be employees.

Duration of the Relationship. If the services provided by a worker are recurrent, even if performed at irregular intervals, the relationship is more characteristic of employer-employee than employer-independent contractor. However, a worker who is otherwise a bona fide independent contractor does not lose that status by providing regular and continual services.

Particular Time Constraints. An independent contractor may be given a schedule to complete the job. However, imposing specific time constraints, such as set hours of work and full-time devotion to the job, creates the appearance of an employer-employee relationship.

Availability of Services to the Public. If a worker advertises his or her services, offers them to anyone in need of such specialized skills, and provides them to more than one employer at a time on a regular and consistent basis, he or she will likely be considered an independent contractor. Conversely, a person working solely or substantially for one employer is likely to be considered an employee.

However, the relative-nature-of-the-work test should also be applied when considering a worker's availability to the public as a test for the employment relationship. A worker performing a service that is an integral part of the employer's business may be regarded as an employee even if the worker also works for others. One of the fundamental purposes of workers compensation law is to compensate workers and their dependents regardless of fault. To deny coverage simply because the worker also considers himself or herself as an independent business will defeat this purpose.

Status of Employer. If the employer is not engaged in a business enterprise and a worker is hired (e.g., a church hiring a maintenance worker) because there are no employees to do a particular job to begin with, then the worker is likely to be considered an independent contractor. Workers compensation is a form of commercial insurance designed to protect employees of commercial enterprises. In some states there are statutory exclusions for nonbusiness employments.

Right To Discharge. If a worker can be summarily dismissed by an employer, the worker is an employee, not an independent contractor. This is a fairly decisive test because the right to discharge indicates the right to control. However, this test is neither absolute nor always conclusive. Although the right to discharge is a key test, courts are reluctant to rule out exceptions.

Just as there are valid reasons to break a contract, there are also valid reasons to terminate agreement with an independent contractor. If the right to discharge were completely determinative of independent contractor status, the fundamental purpose of the compensation system might not be served.

Right To Quit. In a similar context, if the worker can terminate the employment at will without incurring any legal liability for a contract breach, the relationship is likely that of employer-employee, not employer-independent contractor.

Right To Have Subordinates. If a worker can at any time hire, supervise, and pay assistants to fulfill the agreement and complete the job, then control does not rest with the employer, but with the worker, who would likely be considered an independent contractor. If the employer has the right to hire subordinates, then the worker would probably be considered an employee because he or she is under the employer's direction and control.

Personal Service Requirement. If the services must be performed by the person specifically designated by the employer, then the employer is probably interested not only in the result, but also in the methods used to accomplish the desired result. The person designated to perform the personal service has the characteristics of an employee rather than an independent contractor. Hiring an independent contractor does not normally allow the employer to dictate who will do the job, although such right may exist in the case of bona fide independent contractors who perform professional services.

Reporting Requirements. If the worker is required to submit oral or written reports at regular intervals while performing the job, this indicates that the employer has a degree of control over the worker. In this case, the worker is likely to be deemed an employee, not an independent contractor.

License Requirements. If a worker is hired because the job must be performed by someone with a special license and the worker makes himself or herself available to anyone in need of someone with such a license, then the worker is likely to be an independent contractor. However, this test alone is not decisive or compelling because many kinds of employees may have licenses, such as employees at an insurance agency.

Understanding of Both Parties. Courts do not generally recognize a signed contract indicating that a worker is an independent contractor if the facts show that the elements of employer-employee relationship exist. However, if it can be established that (1) there is clear understanding by both parties that they entered into an employer-independent contractor agreement and (2) the agreement is written, then courts will consider these conditions along with the other factors that have been discussed.

Noninsurance Transfer of the Workers Compensation Loss Exposure

The cost of workers compensation insurance is a very significant item in any budget. Consequently, risk managers and other corporate officers continually explore alternative risk management techniques for transferring the financial impact of this particular loss exposure.

Independent Contractor Agreements. One risk management technique for treating the workers compensation loss exposure is to hire independent contractors, instead of employees, thereby transferring the workers compensation statutory obligations to the independent contractor. However, courts frown upon attempts to circumvent workers compensation obligations through contracts if the workers are in fact employees. Courts will not enforce a written contract under these circumstances, particularly if the "independent contractor" does not have workers compensation insurance coverage. In addition, as discussed further below, contractors may become liable under certain conditions for the workers compensation obligations of uninsured subcontractors.

Independent contractor agreements may be created, but in order to be enforceable they must meet two criteria:[7]

1. An employer-independent contractor relationship must exist in fact, not simply in name and form.
2. The nature of the work subject to the agreement is not normally performed by an employee.

Hiring the Equipment and the Owner. Another noninsurance transfer technique that has been attempted in the trucking industry is for the employer to own the trailers and to hire owner-operators of the tractor as independent contractors. A close examination of this arrangement shows that the employer typically has a significant investment and may insist on certain rights of control such as giving instructions and requiring the trailers to display the employer's name. Under such circumstances, if the tractor-owner is injured and has no insurance, the employer will likely be responsible.

Worker-Lessor Arrangements. Another approach to transferring the workers compensation exposure is to try to establish that the worker is in a distinct business or occupation. In arrangements of this kind, the employer owns equipment and leases it to the worker at an agreed price. The worker is not paid with wages, but earns "profits" based on the income generated from use of the equipment less the costs of leasing it. A close examination of this arrangement may reveal evidence of control, including the employer's signs on the equipment and detailed instructions as to where, when, and how the worker must perform the services.

Employer-Landlord Arrangements. There have been cases involving oil companies that have attempted to circumvent workers compensation obligations to gas station operators by styling the relationship as that of landlord and tenant. The companies charged the operators rent and made the operator responsible for all operating expenses. This technique has been somewhat successful, but it has generally failed when the arrangement allowed the oil company to terminate the relationship at will. Courts generally equate the right to discharge to the right to control.

Judicial Response to Noninsurance Transfers. There is a common thread that runs through the court analysis of the preceding noninsurance transfer techniques. Whenever the worker is not able to bear the costs of the workers compensation premium, the courts, serving the basic purpose of the system, will go out of their way to find coverage. The actual test used by the courts appears to be the answer to the question: Is the worker able to independently bear the risk of an industrial injury? If the answer is negative, the courts are likely to reject attempts to circumvent workers compensation loss exposures by hiring "independent contractors."

Special Employment Relationships

Certain employees and relationships raise important questions about the nature or existence of an employment relationship or coverage under workers compensation laws. They include statutory employees, loaned employees, joint and dual employments, and employments covered by federal law.

Statutory Employees. The preceding discussion has focused on the different tests for establishing an employer-employee or an employer-independent contractor relationship. Some workers are covered by workers compensation laws even though they are independent contractors. These workers are called *statutory employees*.

In the usual scenario, a general contractor hires a subcontractor (independent contractor) who is uninsured for workers compensation, and the subcontractor's employee is injured. Since the purpose of the workers compensation law is to provide a remedy to all employees exposed to the hazards of employment, most state statutes impose workers compensation obligations on the general contractor. The injured worker in this scenario is considered a "statutory employee," and the general contractor is the "statutory employer." Although it may appear that the general contractor is unjustly burdened, this scenario must be understood in the context of the primary purpose of the workers compensation system—to compensate employees and their dependents regardless of fault. Furthermore, there is justification for imposing vicarious liability on the general contractor because it presumably has control over which subcontractor to hire and the responsibility to insist that the subcontractor be insured.

When there is a hierarchy of contractors and some at various levels are uninsured, the law will generally move up the hierarchy until it finds the first insured contractor. Workers compensation obligations will be imposed solely on that contractor. The assumption is that control flows downward, so liability should flow upward.

A risk management technique for general contractors under these circumstances is to require proof of workers compensation insurance from a subcontractor before it can bid on a job. In addition, the law does not absolve the irresponsible subcontractor. Most states allow the insured contractor legal remedies against the uninsured subcontractor.

Loaned Employees. When a regular employee is temporarily assigned to another employer (hereinafter designated as the "special employer"), the question arises as to whether the special employer is responsible for workers compensation benefits. The lending employer is hereinafter designated as the "general employer."

The tests, or criteria, already described can be applied to determine if the special employer is considered the employer for the specific purposes of workers compensation. If the relationship between the worker and the special employer includes the elements of control, consent, consideration, and the other employment criteria, and injury is sustained while the work is being done for the special employer, then the special employer is liable for workers compensation benefits. If the employment criteria are not met, the general employer will remain liable. The element of control is critical. The special employer becomes liable only if there is an actual transfer of control.

Another issue related to loaned employees is which employer, if not both, is immune from common-law suits by virtue of the workers compensation exclusive remedy principle. States have differed on the question of immunity. Some states make workers compensation the exclusive remedy against both the general and special employers, but other states allow common-law suits against either the general or special employer who did not provide the statutory benefits.

By entering into an express or implied contract of hire with the special employer, the employee effectively accepts the benefits of the workers compensation laws and the exclusive remedy principle that comes with it. As far as the general employer is concerned, it is presumed that the general employer remains the employer[8], and is therefore likewise immune. However, where there has been a complete transfer of all elements of employer-employee relationship from the general employer to the special employer, the general employer has the status of a third party and is subject to suit.

Joint and Dual Employments. The key element of a joint employment is that an employee performs the same personal services for two or more employers at the same time. If the employee has an employer-employee relationship with all employers, the employers are jointly and severally liable for workers compensation benefits. If any of the critical criteria of an employer-employee relationship are missing for a particular employer, that employer will not be included among those jointly liable. That employer will be excused from paying workers compensation benefits, but will also lose immunity from common-law suits. Some states impose joint and several liability on joint employments, and other states apportion liability. No state allows double recovery to the employee.

Dual employments are different from joint employments. In dual employments, an employee performs separate and distinct services for two employers at different times. Under dual employment situations, the only employer responsible for workers compensation benefits and immune from common-law suits is the employer whose interests were being advanced at the time of the injury.

Federal Compensation Statutes. In 1982 the District of Columbia Workers' Compensation Act replaced the Longshore and Harbor Workers' Compensation Act as the compensation statute for nongovernmental employees working in the District of Columbia. The Longshore and Harbor Workers' Compensation Act now covers "any person engaged in maritime employment, including any longshoreman or other person engaged in longshoring operations, and any harbor-worker including a ship repairman, shipbuilder, and shipbreaker...." This act is the exclusive compensation remedy for covered workers while they are working on the navigable waters of the United States, such as on board a ship. While working on land, covered maritime employees may also be covered by a state compensation act.

The most significant exception to the coverage of the Longshore and Harbor Workers' Compensation Act is for any "master or member of a crew of any vessel...." Seamen are covered by the general maritime law and by the Jones Act, the provisions of which were discussed in Chapter 1. The term "seamen" is not defined under the Jones Act; its meaning is understood from the body of admiralty case law. The above quoted exception to the Longshore Act suggests who seamen are. In addition, anyone else regularly employed on a navigable vessel would be considered a "seaman." On a ship such as a cruise liner, the term seamen would include cooks, bartenders, and even entertainers.

Excluded Employments

Not all workers are employees, and not all employees are subject to the workers compensation laws. Certain employees are legislatively excluded in order to meet the needs of the citizens and business community; others are judicially excluded because they fail to meet one or more of the criteria of an employer-employee relationship.

Another factor that determines whether a worker is subject to the workers compensation laws is whether or not the relationship involves a commercial or "business" undertaking from the standpoint of both the employer and employee. The purpose of the workers compensation system is to promptly provide certain benefits to employees and to pass the costs along to consumers through the medium of insurance. Workers compensation laws were originally conceived to cover only business employments.

The employment relationships that are exempt from state workers compensation laws vary greatly from state to state. Various exclusions have evolved over the years in response to the needs of the citizens of each state and as a result of judicial interpretations. The following is a list of excluded employees and employments that, in one form or another, are found in various state statutes:

1. Domestic employees
2. Casual workers
3. Newspaper carriers
4. Minimum number of employees exclusion
5. Agricultural employments
6. Sole proprietors, partners, and corporate officers
7. Intrafamily employments
8. Real estate salespeople and brokers
9. Religious, charitable, and nonprofit employments
10. Public and federal employments
11. Miscellaneous exclusions
    a. Illegal workers

      b. Nonhazardous employments
      c. Athletes
      d. Ministers
      e. Jockeys
      f. Taxicab drivers

Domestic Employees. Domestic workers are hired to work in a home or for the maintenance of a household. They typically meet the criteria for being employees; that is, the elements of control, consent, consideration, and the other employment criteria will likely be found in their relationship with their employer. However, their employment usually has no business purpose. Some state workers compensation statutes refer to "business," "trade," "industry," and other similar terms. Courts have concluded that the system does not apply to every odd job performed for a homeowner.

As of 1991, approximately twenty-six states had statutory exclusions in one form or another for domestic servants. Some states exclude them only under certain conditions or only in conjunction with other factors. For example, states that generally cover domestic employees may still exclude them if the employment is part-time or the employment fails to meet the required minimum number of employees.

Casual Workers. When the relationship between the worker and the employer is not continuous or recurrent, then the worker may not be considered an employee for compensation purposes. Some states have set temporal or monetary thresholds in defining "casual" employments. For example, California excludes domestics who worked less than fifty-two hours during the preceding ninety days or earned less than $100 during the same period.

Some states have abandoned the casual employment exclusion altogether. Most apply the casual employment exclusion only if the employment is also outside the usual business of the employer. Typical statutory language defining the casual employment exclusion reads "casual and not in the employer's trade or business."

States that exclude casual employment only when the work is also outside the usual business of the employer reflect the rationale that the casual employment test should apply to the nature of the work, not the relationship between the worker and the employer. So, for example, if a building owner hires a worker for one job, painting the building, the employment may not be continuous or recurrent, but if it can be shown that maintenance of the building is an integral part of the employer's business, the employment will not meet the definition of "casual" employment and the worker will be a covered employee.

The primary reason for excluding casual employments is administrative. Workers compensation benefits are calculated based on past earnings and are provided on the assumption that such earnings are regular and continuous. It would be difficult and impractical to determine what the benefit rates would be for employments in which earnings are irregular and nonrecurrent.

There may also be moral and morale hazards in compensating workers more than what they would normally earn from irregular, unpredictable employments. If a transient worker who only takes odd jobs were injured and paid regular weekly benefits, the payments would significantly exceed the worker's usual income, and there would be no incentive to get off disability. This would also increase the temptation to file frivolous and noncompensable claims.

Newspaper Carriers. Newspaper carriers are generally minors who work part time and are paid on a piecework basis. They also create their own work pattern—they are not strictly subject to established routines or schedules set by the newspaper company. The newspaper company is typically interested only in the result and not in the methods used to accomplish the work. Thus, newspaper carriers are typically considered independent contractors. However, newspaper carriers following set routes may be considered employees under appropriate circumstances. New York and Wisconsin have legislatively brought minor newspaper carriers under their compensation acts.

Minimum Number of Employees. Recognizing the many informal and casual employment relationships, particularly in agricultural and domestic settings where the general tests of employment cannot be conclusively applied, some states have excluded employments where the number of employees is less than the statutory minimum required for coverage. Employers with fewer than three, four, or five employees are exempt on the basis of various state statutes. The primary reason for this statutory exclusion is administrative. It is not practical to require small businesses to keep and maintain the records necessary to administer and comply with the workers compensation requirements.

This numerical criterion is quite arbitrary. Employers might move in and out of the technical scope of the law as the number of their workers fluctuates. To overcome this problem, state statutes are usually written to include the term "regularly employed." This means that an employer who regularly maintains a certain number of employees in excess of the minimum number must provide coverage even when the number of employees happens to drop below the minimum.[9]

There is also a question as to which workers are to be counted for purposes of the statutory exclusion. States vary greatly on this issue. Some states only count covered employees, which means that casual workers, domestic servants, corporate officers, and the like are not to be counted. Other states include all workers, particularly those states with broad statutory language using such terms as "persons" and "workmen," which have been judicially interpreted to include gratuitous workers and other persons who are not employees under compensation laws.[10] The distinction between employees who are counted and those who are not is important for small businesses because of the severe penalties imposed on nonexempt employers that fail to comply with the workers compensation obligations.

Agricultural Employment. The workers compensation system came about partly because of an increase in injuries caused by employment hazards associated with industrialization. Traditional agricultural employments do not pose the same hazards and do not always have the elements of an employer-employee relationship. Many labor exchanges and gratuitous services are performed for farmers by the family members and friends they traditionally hire.

Another reason for the agricultural exclusion is the difficulty of compliance with administrative requirements. Small farms have little or no payroll record keeping and employ a small number of seasonal workers.

Agricultural employment has historically been excluded. By 1991, only about ten states retained an exemption for agricultural labor. The distinction between agricultural employments and nonagricultural employments has become blurred in modern times, particularly when the farm operation is an integral first stage in the industrial production of consumer goods. If an agricultural process is actually a stage in a manufacturing process, it may lose its agricultural standing and its statutory exclusion.[11]

Instead of analyzing the nature of the employer's operation as farm or nonfarm, the courts interpret agricultural exclusion statutes according to the character of the employee's work and if and at what stage it is part of an industrial process. The test being applied is whether the work involves the handling of an agricultural raw material or a finished agricultural product. The latter would give the work a commercial character that takes the worker's job out of the realm of the agricultural exclusion.

Many states only apply the agricultural exclusion in conjunction with other factors. For example, it is applied only if the farm workers are also volunteers or part of employments having less than a minimum number of employees.

Because of the changing character of agriculture, states that still have a statutory farm exclusion generally allow farmers to elect to have their employees covered and given the benefits of the workers compensation laws.

Sole Proprietors, Partners, and Corporate Officers. A moral hazard exists when the employer is also the employee. Most states exclude sole proprietors, partners, and corporate owners from workers compensation coverage. However, in recognition of the fact that there are working partners and officers, these states allow the option to elect coverage, or such parties may be automatically covered unless they opt not to be. Corporate officers in particular are often given the same coverage as any employee because many perform nonexecutive, supervisory, and even manual work. Unless a corporate officer is also the owner of the business, the officer is an employee subject to the control of the corporation and its stockholders. Generally, corporate officers are covered unless they elect not to be, an option in about half the states.

Exclusions of sole proprietors and partners are common because the employer-employee distinction is very difficult to establish. Coverage for such individuals is possible only a few states in which coverage must be specifically elected. The owners' proprietary interests in the business and their separate legal standing as business entities prevent them from losing their status as employers and becoming employees. However, the exclusion becomes problematic when it involves working partners or joint venturers. The exclusion of working partners is especially problematic when they are placed on the payroll, the basis from which compensation premium rates are determined. However, the calculation of proper premiums is a problem for premium auditors.

Intrafamily Employments. Only a few states still exclude family members working for the family business. This exclusion is becoming obsolete. Idaho still maintains a statutory exclusion by excluding from the definition of employee members of the employer's family dwelling in his or her household. Michigan is the only other state with a statutory exclusion for family members and then only to the extent of allowing family members to elect to be excluded from coverage.

Real Estate Salespeople and Brokers. Real estate salespeople and brokers often simultaneously represent more than one firm and do not follow a pattern of work or work hours established by their employer. They are compensated substantially from commissions, and many operate under a contract specifying that they are independent contractors. Although courts do not generally honor such independent contractor designations in what is an otherwise employer-employee relationship, many states have recognized the special relationship between realty companies and their sales force and have expressly excluded real estate sales occupations. Thus, real estate sales personnel are excluded even if a court concludes that they are employees.

Religious, Charitable, and Nonprofit Employments. The workers compensation system was created with the industrial sector of the economy in mind, where it is presumed that the services provided by the workers are not gratuitous. Accordingly, many state statutes and court decisions provide that volunteers, particularly those working for religious, charitable, and nonprofit organizations, are not subject to workers compensation laws.

Today, only a few states exempt paid religious, charitable, and nonprofit employers from workers compensation obligations because of the nonbusiness character of the employment. In recognition of the fact that such organizations employ paid, nonvolunteer workers, the majority of states does not exclude them. In the absence of an explicit statutory exclusion, the courts will find coverage for such employees since their work generally meets the criteria of an employment relationship.

Public and Federal Employments. In recognition of the distinction between private and public employment, particularly in regard to public officials who have some sovereign power, state workers compensation laws do not always make coverage for public employees compulsory. There are vast differences between states in this area. Some cover all public employees. Some exempt some and cover others. Some exempt only elected officials. In addition to the rationale that public employees exercise sovereign power, another argument that has been used to justify the exclusion is that public officials act independently of any master (employer), and they are answerable only to the laws they are sworn to serve and uphold. The status of a public official as an employer or an employee is difficult to discern.

Miscellaneous Exclusions. Most states exclude workers in illegal employments as a matter of public policy even absent a statutory exclusion. Some states have specific statutory language excluding such employments. However, the distinction must be made between a worker employed in an illegal trade and a worker employed illegally. If the trade is illegal, such as operating an illicit drug lab, it is not a covered employment. If the illegality is a function of the employment relationship, such as employing a minor in an otherwise lawful enterprise, a valid employment relationship for the purposes of workers compensation laws will be found to exist. The purpose of the law is to compensate injured workers.

Workers compensation laws were enacted in response to the increase in injuries associated with hazardous occupations in the industrial sector. Consequently, when the original laws were drafted, they were limited to "hazardous" work only. Statutory exclusions of nonhazardous employments are virtually obsolete; only the state of Wyoming still has such a provision.

Some states have recognized the professional calling and the nonprofit nature of paid ministers. In order to avoid confusion and unnecessary litigation, many states have made specific statutory exclusions for this occupation.

Some states have expressly excluded professional and amateur athletes and officials, jockeys, and taxicab drivers from coverage, mostly in response to an outcry from the citizenry and the business community alarmed by judicial decisions finding coverage for such "employees." It is easy to see, using the usual tests of coverage, how college athletes can argue that they are employees. They are under the control of the school, they generate revenue from their work, and they are given consideration in the form of scholarships and the like. Because the states did not intend to expand workers compensation to amateur athletes, states had to exclude them by statute. Jockeys are in the same category, although they could arguably also be properly classified as independent contractors. The employment status of taxicab drivers can be ambiguous. Recognizing that the facts usually suggest they are independent contractors, some state legislatures have removed the uncertainty by a statutory exclusion.

COVERED INJURIES

Not every type of employment is covered by workers compensation laws. Similarly, those laws do not cover every type of on-the-job injury. Rather than list all of the conceivable covered injuries, the following section discusses coverage in terms of (1) the requirement that injuries be accidental, (2) occupational diseases and cumulative trauma, (3) hernias, and (4) nonphysical injuries.

Accidental Injuries

In the majority of states, an injury must be accidental to be compensable. The wording "accidental" or "by accident" appears in the statutory workers compensation language of most states. It is important to understand how each state defines and interprets the term "accidental injury" and whether the term "by accident" is included in the statutory definition of compensable injury. The "by accident" requirement is a remnant of employers liability law, which required the event or occurrence causing injuries to be fortuitous and traumatic; the injury could neither be expected nor designed by the injured employee. The significance of this definition is that it indicates two essential conditions that must exist before injuries are covered by the workers compensation law: (1) unexpectedness and (2) being traceable to a definite time, place, and cause.

Unexpectedness Requirement. This requirement raises the question of whether or not an injury must be unexpected as to both cause and result, or whether an unexpected result alone, from the standpoint of the injured worker, is enough to meet the requirement for coverage. Does the unexpectedness requirement allow for compensation for an injury caused by normal and usual strains on the job, under a strict and narrow statutory definition of "injury by accident?"

In the past, some courts interpreted the statutory definition of "injury by accident" literally and stringently. Injuries involving usual, normal, and routine work strain were not covered because they failed to meet the narrow statutory definition. A back injury caused by repetitive lifting of heavy boxes, for example, was not deemed to have been caused "by accident." Over time, however, the courts made gradual concessions, and most states began to award coverage for injuries caused by normal strain at work.

The majority of states now recognize that such a cause-oriented approach to workers compensation is obsolete. The liability laws were designed to establish who was at fault, and injured workers were denied benefits accordingly. Workers compensation statutes were designed to provide coverage irrespective of fault. Covered injuries are simply those that "arise out of employment," regardless of the expectedness of the cause.

The "accidental" or "by accident" requirement is thus satisfied merely by an unexpected result. Most states now agree that any injury that is not self-inflicted is accidental, even if the cause is not unexpected, unusual, or abnormal.

Limited in Time, Place, or Cause. Some states have interpreted their compensation statute such that causes of injuries and injuries themselves must be traceable to a definite time and place. This second condition raises questions about compensation for nonspecific injuries resulting from nonspecific causes. States that strictly construed the terms "injury" and "accident" as used in their compensation statutes had difficulty awarding compensation for nonspecific injuries resulting from nonspecific causes.

These states gradually moved away from the strict interpretation of the "by accident" language. Recognizing the no-fault, strict liability concept built into the workers compensation scheme, the majority of states now only require the injury or disease to be unexpected from the standpoint of the employee. To be sure, the injury or disease must also arise out of and in the course of employment. This test for compensability will be discussed in Chapter 3.

Occupational Disease and Cumulative Trauma

An injury that is unexpected and definite in time and place is clearly compensable (provided, of course, that it also arises out of and in the course of employment). Traumatic injuries such as cuts and broken bones are obviously compensable because they meet both criteria. However, assessing the compensability of diseases and cumulative trauma can be problematic because injury in such cases is not traceable to a definite time, place, or even cause.

Coverage for Diseases. Unlike traumatic injuries, the causes for diseases are not always clear. Determining that a disease is occupational is difficult. Proof of a condition is not proof of causation. Although courts have largely abandoned the distinction between an industrial injury and an occupational disease, many states still have separate occupational disease laws that enumerate covered occupational diseases or define a covered occupational disease. Occupational disease statutes serve mainly to distinguish between diseases that are caused by and are peculiar to the industrial setting and the ordinary diseases of life. Occupational diseases are covered; ordinary diseases are not.

Occupational disease statutes and court rulings have provided guidelines for determining when an injury is presumed to have occurred so that a loss date can be assigned for purposes of insurance coverage. The loss date triggers the applicable insurance policy. The date of injury can be one of the following:

1. The date of last injurious exposure to the harmful stimuli on the job. This is often the last day of employment.

2. The date the disease or generalized condition becomes disabling.

3. The date the disease first manifests itself.

or

4. The date the employee is notified by a doctor that he or she is suffering from a work-related disease.

In specific cases, the applicable ruling in that state must be determined.

Hearing Loss as an Occupational Disease. Loss of hearing as a result of explosion or a traumatic head injury clearly meets all of the requirements of a covered injury. However, early workers compensation laws did not recognize hearing loss caused by protracted exposure to a noisy environment because of the fear that there would be a swell of claims by workers in noisy work environments, such as boiler rooms, shipyards, and machine shops, making such employers commercially uninsurable. Also, it was recognized that many workers lose their hearing to some degree because of age, heredity, infectious disease, military service, noisy hobbies, and noise not related to employment. In states where hearing loss is classified in the statutes as a *scheduled disability* (that is, disability benefits are paid regardless of its relationship to loss of earnings), there was a fear that many workers would collect hearing loss disability benefits while drawing their regular wages.

Gradually, states began recognizing hearing loss caused by protracted exposure to industrial noise as a covered injury or disease. States handled the problem of preexisting, nonoccupational causes by making allowances for the nonoccupational causes in the calculation of disability benefits by allowing apportionments and by establishing second-injury funds so employers would be given relief if they are found liable.

Allergy as an Occupational Disease. Allergic reaction to hazards in employment presents a special problem because of the personal nature of allergies. Not all workers react the same way, if at all, to stimuli in the employment environment. As a result, some state courts have denied allergic conditions as a covered injury or disease. However, most states now recognize allergies as a covered occupational disease if (1) the employment caused the allergic reaction; (2) the hazard causing the allergic reaction is peculiar to an employment; and (3) the employment exposes the employee to the hazard to a greater degree than other employments in general.

Accidental Infectious Disease. A variation of the same problem presented by allergies is accidental infectious disease. Infectious diseases are common to the general population and are not easily traceable to employment hazards. However, if the cause of an infectious disease is traceable to a specific incident or incidents at or related to work, then contracting the disease meets the definition of accident and qualifies as a covered injury. For example, if contracting typhoid fever could be traced to polluted water in a factory, then the illness is a covered injury. However, some state courts may be forced to deny coverage if the state occupational disease law limits coverage for occupational injuries to those specifically named.

Cumulative and Progressive Injuries. Sometimes a condition is traceable to a certain time period and to separate incidents, but not to identifiable points in time and place. These conditions are known as "microtraumas" and "cumulative traumas." For example, an employee suffering from a generalized condition may be able to identify a special project at work where he had to perform specific tasks or was exposed to specific stimuli. The project may have lasted for a given period of time, but he cannot pinpoint the exact task or the specific exposure that caused the condition. The test for coverage in this scenario will be similar to that of an occupational disease.

Progressive diseases present the most difficulty in determining compensability because not only are they not specific to time, place, or cause, but they can also involve diseases that are not directly associated with employment hazards. Pulmonary diseases are common examples. An employee may have been exposed to foreign particles at the job site, but pulmonary diseases are also associated with personal habits such as smoking and alcohol, genetic predisposition, environmental pollution common to all, and other personal risks and hazards. Progressive diseases are a source of a great deal of litigation in workers compensation and will continue to be so for years to come. The true cause of a progressive disease is always very complex.

Hernia Statutes

Hernias present special coverage problems and require separate treatment. It is known that hernias are generally congenital and that their onset usually occurs in everyday life. It is also recognized that the onset of a hernia can be caused by trauma or strenuous effort at work. For this reason, a significant number of states have specific statutory provisions that govern coverage for hernias. States differ in their specific requirements, but they generally fall within the following:

1. The hernia must result from a sudden effort, severe strain, or trauma.
2. The hernia must appear suddenly and the employer must be notified promptly.
3. The onset must be accompanied by severe pain.
4. There must be no preexisting rupture or protrusion.
5. The employee must promptly seek medical care.

Hernias are one injury to which most states still apply the requirements of unexpectedness and being traceable in time and place to both the cause and result. A special provision generally found in hernia statutes is a limitation on the length of time benefits are payable. Twenty-six weeks is a common limitation.

Nonphysical Injuries

Workers compensation statutes were originally drafted to cover only bodily injuries and diseases. Many states initially required, and some still do, the injury to involve damage or harm to the body before an injury or disease is covered.

Statutory definitions of an "injury" may or may not include the term "bodily" and may or may not include the term "personal" when describing covered injuries. Some states only cover nonphysical injuries if they are accompanied by, or result from, a physical trauma. In these states, emotional problems are only covered if they arise from the

64—Principles of Workers Compensation Claims

pain and trauma of a covered physical injury. Otherwise, they do meet the definition of an "injury."

Liberal interpretation of the workers compensation law and the advances in medical science that clinically establish the cause of psychiatric problems have allowed the courts to expand coverage to emotional problems not accompanied by bodily injury or disease. A common example is coverage for an emotional breakdown because of an unusual emotional trauma at work.

There is little or no coverage dispute when the nonphysical "injury" is caused by physical violence, and there is only a little more dispute when an emotional trauma causes a physical injury. However, nonphysical injuries that result from nonphysical causes are controversial compensation cases. A convenient conceptual framework for determining coverage can be constructed by dividing cases into three categories:

1. Mental-Physical
2. Physical-Mental
3. Mental-Mental

Mental-Physical Category. This category includes physical symptoms caused by mental phenomena. As long as the mental cause can definitely be attributed to work origins, these injuries are covered. Examples include unusual job-related tension and stress causing ulcers or heart attack. The character of the mental stimulus and the suddenness and definiteness of the physical injury are relevant factors in finding coverage. Because the "accidental" requirement in the statutory definition of an "injury" may again be a consideration, it makes a difference whether the mental stimulus is unusual, traumatic, gradual, or sustained, and whether the physical injury is immediate or protracted.

Physical-Mental Category. This category includes mental suffering or consequences caused by physical injuries. Without exceptions, these are covered injuries. A typical example is an employee who develops traumatic neurosis after a physical injury. The unexpectedness and definite time, place, and cause requirements are clearly satisfied.

Mental-Mental Category. This category includes mental injuries caused by mental phenomena. States are sharply divided about how to treat this category, and it has prompted much litigation. The rulings cover a wide spectrum: some states never cover injuries in this category and other states find coverage even when the mental stimulus is not unusual or traumatic and the mental injury is not sudden or definite. Between these extremes are states that provide coverage only if the mental stimulus is unexpected and traumatic and the mental injury is sudden and definite.[12]

Because of the liberal interpretation of the workers compensation laws, state courts are moving toward finding coverage for injuries in the mental-mental category. Most states have already recognized that emotional injuries meet the definition of "bodily injury." Some states have extended workers compensation coverage to emotional injuries resulting from harassment and criticisms on the job. More and more states are finding coverage for "injuries" with no physical component whatsoever. This expansion of coverage is one of the important issues facing the workers compensation insurance industry today as discussed further in Chapter 6.

Exhibit 2-1 illustrates the typical ruling as to compensability including various mental conditions and mental causes of injury. The exhibit further expands the conceptual framework for determining compensability by introducing the elements of unusualness and specificity. This chart is by no means controlling as to all situations and all states because there is great variation in both. The chart serves only as a general guide. It illustrates that disputes in coverage increase as the cause or injury moves from physical to nonphysical and from unusual, traumatic, and specific to gradual, usual, and generalized.

The "maybe" and "probably" outcomes are results of the requirement that the injury must meet the legal causation test ("arising out of" and in the course of employment) and both the injuries and diseases must meet a medical causation test. The "injury" must be, within reasonable medical probability, connected to the employment. The medical causation test includes an evaluation of personal risks such as preexisting conditions, personal habits, medical and family history, and other factors.

Some courts have examined claims for physical and mental injuries and have determined that such injuries are compensable depending on whether or not their cause was a usual or an unusual stress. Injuries caused by unusual stresses are covered; those caused by usual stresses are not. The *usual-unusual exertion* criterion has been criticized as a legal test of coverage because "usual" does not necessarily mean it is not stressful or physically strenuous. [13] Digging ditches may be usual work, but it is definitely strenuous and may easily meet the legal and medical causation test for a heart attack. The lifting of a heavy box by someone in a sedentary occupation, on the other hand, may be "unusual." Should the sedentary worker be compensated and the ditch digger not? Many states nonetheless still use the usual and unusual causation test when analyzing coverage of mental injuries. It is unfortunate that the use of such rules causes analytical confusion. The real issue in these cases is the question of whether the injury arises out of and in the course of employment,[14] a question examined at

Exhibit 2-1
Compensability of Mental Conditions and Mental Causes of Injury

Cause \\ Result	PHYSICAL		MENTAL	
	Specific	Generalized	Specific	Generalized
PHYSICAL				
Traumatic	Yes	Yes	Yes	Yes
Protracted	Yes	Maybe	Maybe (if accompanied by bodily injury)	Maybe
Unusual	Yes	Yes	Yes	Yes
Usual	Yes	Maybe	Maybe (if accompanied by bodily injury)	Maybe
MENTAL				
Traumatic	Yes	Yes	Probably	Maybe
Protracted	Probably	Probably	Probably not	No
Unusual	Yes	Yes	Probably	Maybe
Usual	Maybe	Maybe	Probably not	No

length in Chapter 3. This issue can be quite difficult to resolve in certain cases but should not require a modification of the *legal* standard of compensability.

SUMMARY

Applying to real situations the simple idea that workers compensation is limited to injuries to employees requires careful understanding of exactly what covered "employees" and "injuries" are. This understanding is based in part on the existence and the nature of the employment relationship. The existence of an employment relationship depends on the existence of three factors: control, consent, and consideration. If these factors characterize the employment relationship, various workers such as independent contractors, involuntary labor, and volunteers are excluded from employee status. The employee-independent contractor distinction is extremely important but is sometimes very close and therefore difficult to make. Many factors are relevant to this distinction, but the common law regards the extent of control as most significant. Nevertheless, many scholars of workers compensation law have advocated the relative-nature-of-the-work test, which treats all workers whose work is integral to the employer's purposes as employees. This test would generally result in wider coverage for compensation, a result that the test's advocates assert is consistent with the beneficial purposes of compensation legislation.

This chapter reviewed the special coverage rules applicable to statutory employees, loaned employees, joint and dual employments, and employments covered by federal law. Various types of employments are excluded from some compensation laws, including domestic workers, casual workers, newspaper carriers, employers having fewer than a statutory minimum number of workers, agricultural workers, proprietors of businesses, family members, real estate sales people, employees of religious, charitable, or other nonprofit entities, public employees, and various others.

After some evolution in case law, the requirement that injuries be accidental has come to mean that the result of the injury must be unexpected or unintended from the employee's point of view. Self-inflicted injuries are still excluded from coverage as being nonaccidental in nature. Occupational diseases and cumulative traumas are treated specially under occupational disease statutes, the purpose of which is to distinguish occupational diseases from ordinary diseases of life. Likewise, hernias are frequently addressed by special statutes since they can also occur outside employment. Many courts have created special standards of compensability for mental injuries. Other courts have recognized that mental injuries should be subject to the same standards of compensability as physical injuries even though they may present difficult issues of causation.

Chapter Notes

1. Arthur Larson, *Workmen's Compensation*, Desk Edition (Albany, NY: Matthew Bender), §45.31.
2. Larson, §45.32(a).
3. Larson, §44.34.
4. Larson, §44.33(a).
5. Larson, §43.50 - §43.54.
6. Green Valley Cooperative Dairy v. Industrial Commission, 27 N.W. 2d 454 (Wisc. 1949).
7. Larson, §46.10.
8. Larson, §48.14.
9. Larson, §52.20.
10. Larson, §52.30.
11. Larson, §53.00.
12. Larson, §42.25(b).
13. Larson, §38.81.
14. Larson, §38.83.

CHAPTER 3

Compensability: Arising Out of and in the Course of Employment

Not every accidental injury to an employed person is covered by workers compensation. The compensation system was created to make employers responsible for the cost of injuries related to employment. Thus, one would not expect workers compensation to cover injuries not related to employment. The fact that an accident victim is employed would not involve the workers compensation system unless the accident was work-related.

The simple idea that workers compensation should be limited to work-related injuries is easy to apply in the vast majority of cases. However, because the line between work-related and nonwork-related has been a fine one since the inception of the compensation system, this idea has been among the most heavily litigated in legal history. Litigation also occurs frequently because the applicable legal rules are very general, and the resolution of each case depends heavily on the facts of that particular case.

To be compensable, most jurisdictions require that an injury arise out of and in the course of employment. Courts have offered many explanations of this principle, not all of them consistent with one another. Nevertheless, because courts in the various jurisdictions have been interpreting the exact same phrase, a working consensus as to its meaning and application has evolved.

This chapter explains how courts have interpreted the phrase "arising out of and in the course of employment," and how different courts have interpreted each element of the phrase. Much of the apparent inconsistency between various courts is explained by the different facts of each case and by the differences in each court's standards for compensability. It appears that most courts judge the compensability of an injury by its degree of work-relatedness. Although the official legal standard is "arising out of and in the course of employment," courts do not apply the standard literally when there is an otherwise strong relationship between an injury and employment.

There are particular situations that account for the questionability of compensation in the vast majority of cases. In response, courts have developed working rules for some of these situations. Nevertheless, other situations have defied general rules. Most of this chapter is devoted to describing and illustrating both kinds of situations.

THE STATUTORY STANDARD

The statutory standard for compensability is the same in most jurisdictions. Courts have interpreted this standard and its components similarly throughout the country. Nevertheless, claim representatives must be familiar with case law in the jurisdictions in which they work, since there can be some important variation. Some of the apparent inconsistency in court interpretations of the standard can be explained by the work-relationship test of compensability, suggested and described below. When otherwise compensable, the fact that injuries are due to an employee's misconduct is generally irrelevant.

The Usual Statutory Formula and Its Exceptions

The usual formula for compensability has two parts that must be considered separately. In some jurisdictions, the formula for compensability is different from, and usually more liberal than, the standard formula.

Arising Out of and in the Course of Employment. Over forty states have adopted the identical test of compensability: injuries must be "arising out of and in the course of" employment. This formula includes two separate tests, the "arising out of" requirement and the "in the course of" requirement. In states that adopt the standard language, both tests must be met for compensation to be awarded.

Independence of the Tests. The "arising out of" and the "in the course of" tests are separate tests that must be independently fulfilled. In most cases, both requirements are either satisfied or not satisfied. However, some cases meet either one or the other requirement, that is, an injury will arise out of employment but will not occur in the course of employment. There are also cases for which the reverse is true; injuries that occur in the course of employment may not arise out of the employment.

Because of this variability, courts consistently hold that both tests must be separately satisfied. Nevertheless, the actual outcome of many cases suggests that courts will overlook the failure of a case to meet one test when the other test is strongly satisfied. This issue is explained below in the section on the work-relationship test of compensability.

Other Formulations. The "arising out of and in the course of" standard is not universal. West Virginia requires compensation for injuries that occur "in the course of and resulting from" employment, a standard that is essentially the same as the usual formula. Wyoming requires that injuries "result" from employment, a standard similar to the "arising out of" rule alone. North Dakota, Pennsylvania, Texas, and Washington only require an injury to occur "in the course of" employment. This is a more liberal standard of compensation than the usual formula, since in these states it does not matter *how* the injury arises, as long as it occurs "in the course of" employment. Utah applies the even more liberal standard, "arising out of *or* in the course of employment" (emphasis added). In Utah, anyone injured in the course of employment would be compensated (as in North Dakota, Pennsylvania, Texas, and Washington), but so would anyone whose injury arises out of the employment.

The "Arising Out of" Test

The "arising out of" test concerns the cause of an injury. An injury is considered to have arisen out of the employment if it was caused by some circumstance of the employment. Determining the exact meaning of this idea has been a difficult task for courts over the years.

In the compensation context, cause does not mean proximate cause. Proximate cause is the tort standard for determining liability. Tort law is more concerned than compensation law with moral culpability. Therefore, the concept of proximate cause is narrower than it should be in order for it to be applicable to compensation law. Thus, unlike the way in which liability is determined under tort law, the determination of compensability under workers compensation does not depend on the fact that the injury was foreseeable.

The liberalization of court interpretations of the "arising out of" test is demonstrated in the following sections. Although courts now universally reject the historic interpretation of this principle that placed unwarranted limits on compensation, they have not yet agreed on a new interpretation.

Historic Interpretations. In the early years of compensation law, certain courts did not deem an injury to "arise out of" employment unless it was the result of a risk specific to that employment. Injuries caused by hazards common to other employments or society at large were not compensable. Thus, for example, a worker at a saw mill could be compensated for injuries caused by the sawing equipment or by falling lumber, since these are special risks of saw mills, but that worker could not recover for an injury caused in a fall on a defective floor, since defective floors are found in all kinds of workplaces and homes.

Nothing in the statutory language of the compensation laws supported or required such a strict interpretation of "arising out of." As it became evident that such a strict interpretation would defeat the purpose of compensation laws, courts became more liberal. Today, no jurisdiction adheres to the strict historic interpretation.

Increased Risk Due to Employment. Today, most courts would deem an injury to "arise out of" employment if it results from a risk to which the employee is more subject than is the public at large. For example, although the public at large is exposed to the danger of being struck by an automobile, an employee whose job requires him or her to be on the street more often than the general public is in greater danger of being struck. Any injuries to such an employee caused by an automobile accident would be deemed to have arisen out of the employment. Similarly, a laborer required to work outdoors may experience the same weather as everyone else, but he or she experiences it to a greater extent. Any injuries to this laborer caused by exposure to heat or cold would be considered to have arisen out of employment and therefore would be compensable. The principle of increased risk is illustrated by the following actual cases.

- A claimant, a driver of a garbage truck, was struck by an apple thrown from a passing school bus. Because the court ruled that the claimant was at greater risk for this injury because of his employment, the injury was considered to have arisen out of the employment.[1]

- A claimant regularly made large deposits of money to the bank for her employer, a precious metals dealer. During one such visit to the bank, the claimant was assaulted and robbed by armed robbers. The court ruled that the injury arose out of the employment because the employment exposed the claimant to an increased risk of robbery.[2]

- A cocktail waitress at a hotel in an area of the city with a high crime rate was sexually assaulted in a public restroom. The court ruled that the assault arose out of the employment because the employment exposed the employee to a higher risk of crime.[3]

- A claimant's job involved sales and collections. While waiting in his car outside a customer's office, the claimant was shot by two assailants who admitted that they had seen the claimant earlier with a large sum of money and that they had intended to rob him. The court held that collecting and holding large sums of money was a condition of the claimant's employment and was therefore the cause of the assault. Compensation was awarded.[4]

- An off-duty policeman was shot by a gunman after the policeman had identified himself. The court ruled that when the gunman shot him, the claimant was acting as a policeman and was required by law to do so. Compensation was awarded.[5]

"But For" Causation. Certain jurisdictions, including such populous states as California, Massachusetts, New Jersey, and New York, have further liberalized the interpretation of "arising out of." These jurisdictions and a significant minority of others would allow compensation whenever an injury results from a risk to which the employee is exposed because of the employment. Regardless of whether the risk was the same in type and degree as that faced by the public, courts in these jurisdictions ask whether the employee would have been exposed to the risk "but for" the employment. If not, the resulting injuries are compensable. Thus, whenever an employee is exposed to a risk because of the employment, any resulting injuries are compensable.

This approach is also known as the *positional risk doctrine.*[6] According to the doctrine, whenever the employment places the employee in the time and place where an injury occurs that would not have otherwise occurred, the injury is compensable. For example, an employee who is struck by a stray bullet while running an errand for his employer would be compensated. Although the stray bullet is unrelated to the employment, the employment placed the employee in the position to be injured. The injury is therefore said to "arise out of" the employment.

The "but for," or positional risk, test would allow compensation in all cases except when the injury is caused by strictly personal factors that would have operated regardless of the employment. For example, someone who dies of a sudden cerebral hemorrhage would not be compensated just because it happens at work. The fact that the event occurs at work is sheer coincidence. Likewise, when someone is assaulted at work by a personal enemy or by a jealous spouse, the connection with work is purely coincidental and any resulting injuries would not be compensable. The "but for" principle is illustrated by the following actual cases.

- A claimant's work as a road-grader operator required him to be outdoors in the cold. Because of his diabetic condition, the claimant wore electric socks to keep his feet warm. The socks injured his feet. The court ruled that the claimant was injured because his employment required him to be out in the cold.[7]
- While entering his car after lunch, a salesman was shot and killed by a stranger who acted without provocation. The court found that the salesman would not have been at the place of attack at that time "but for" his employment and therefore awarded compensation.[8]
- A worker contracted tuberculosis from a co-worker. The two worked in extremely close proximity and, because of the noise in their workplace, had to shout six inches from each other's faces. Compensation was awarded because this case of tuberculosis was found to have been caused by the workplace conditions.[9]
- A bookkeeper was struck by a car after posting letters for his employer. The court ruled that the injuries arose from the employment because the employment exposed the claimant to the danger that caused the injury.[10]

The "in the Course of" Test

The "in the course of" employment test refers not necessarily to the cause of an injury, but to the circumstances of its occurrence, including the time and place where it occurs and the activities in which the employee is engaged when it occurs. The "course of" employment is essentially the same as the common law "scope of" employment. An employee is within the course of employment whenever engaged in work-related or incidental activities at the time and place required by the employment.

Work-Related Activities. An employee is within the course of employment whenever performing work-related activities. They include the actual performance of job functions and any incidental tasks that someone in that position would be expected to perform, such as setting up work, cleaning up, moving from one work station to another, and helping co-workers.

Ordinarily, but not necessarily, an injury suffered by an employee in the course of employment will also arise out of the employment. For example, the employee who dies of a cerebral hemorrhage at work may well be within the course of employment. Yet, the *cause* of injury is not employment related, so it does not arise out of the employment. Similarly, a strike-breaking worker who is assaulted and injured at home by strikers whose job he took may sustain injuries that arise out of the employment, but not in the course of it.

In most cases, however, the activities in which the employee is engaged are also the cause of injuries. For example, a worker who is injured while lifting boxes at work is injured in the course of his employment since moving boxes is a work-related task. The injury also arises out of the employment because the risks of lifting boxes are a part of that job.

Although both tests of compensability are often simultaneously satisfied, claim representatives must be able to distinguish between what caused an injury and what an employee was doing when injured. In difficult cases of compensability, the distinction is not easy to make. However, the inability to make the distinction will cause confusion between the "arising out of" and "in the course of" tests.

Time and Place of Employment.   "In the course of employment" also refers to the time and place of employment, which are fixed for most employees. In these cases, it is easy to determine whether employees are within the course of employment by where and when they are injured. In general, injuries that occur at work during work hours to employees with a fixed schedule are compensable.

However, not all employments have a set location and hours. Employees who travel to various locations and work irregular hours can also be injured in the course of employment. Such employees are within the course of their employment whenever they are engaged in work duties at a particular place and particular time required by the employment. However, because the time and place of employment are not fixed, it is typically more difficult to determine whether employees are injured "in the course of" employment as a basis for awarding compensation. For instance, it might be more difficult to determine whether or not to award compensation to a traveling salesman who is injured in a hotel at 9:00 P.M. after he has completed the day's business.

An employee who performs work at a certain time and place for personal convenience is not necessarily within the course of employment. For example, an employee who takes work home and is injured while working at home is generally not deemed to be within the course of employment. Usually, such cases also raise issues as to whether the injury "arises out of" the employment.

Work-Relatedness of Injuries—The Real Test?

As stated, courts generally maintain that the "arising out of" and the "in the course of" tests must be fulfilled separately. Yet, the results of a number of close and difficult cases suggest that this is not strictly so. Compensation has been awarded when the circumstances of a claimant's injury have fulfilled one of the tests only very weakly, if at all. For example, there have been a number of cases in which the cause of injury is completely unknown. Nevertheless, such cases usually result in compensation if the employee is diligently engaged in the course of employment when injured. Likewise, compensation is regularly awarded to claimants clearly not engaged in work activities when injured.

Professor Arthur Larson, the leading scholar of workers compensation law, asserts that courts are actually looking for a sufficient connection, or relationship, between the injury and the employment regardless of whether the "arising out of" and "in the course of" tests are each separately fulfilled. A strong showing on one test may make up for a deficiency in the other.[11]

Larson's analysis is consistent with the liberal standard of compensation intended by the law. Accordingly, claim representatives who analyze compensation claims must consider the overall relationship of the injury to the employment.

Liberality of Interpretation. Workers compensation is intended to be a no-fault system in which injuries due to employment are promptly compensated. As a practical matter, the employer or its insurer bears the burden of proof to show that an injury is not compensable. Unless the employer or its insurer can prove that an employee's injury is not work-related, most industrial commissions will award compensation. This approach is consistent with the law's remedial purpose. New York's law explicitly includes a presumption that injuries are work-related.[12] In light of the system's orientation, claim representatives should expect compensation to be awarded whenever some relationship between an injury and the employment can be shown.

The Elements of an Injury's Work Relationship. Claim representatives should look for the following circumstances, or the absence of such circumstances, when determining whether an injury is related to employment.

- Cause of injury. This element of the work relationship is the essence of the "arising out of" test. An injury is deemed to be related to employment whenever it *is caused by* some hazard of the employment.

- Employee's activities. What was the employee doing when injured? An injury is deemed to be related to the employment whenever the employee is directly engaged in job duties or is performing any task incidental to the job duties.

- Place of injury. Was the employee injured on the employer's premises or at some place he was required to be because of the employment?
- Time of injury. Was the employee injured during regular work hours or at some time when the employee's services were required by the employment?

The greater the number of these circumstances that indicate a work relationship, the greater the likelihood that compensation will be awarded. Obviously, compensation will be awarded when all four circumstances indicate a work relationship.

When three of the four circumstances indicate a work relationship, an award of compensation is extremely likely. The only cases that may be denied compensation in this situation are those in which the cause of the injury (the "arising out of" test) is obviously unrelated to the employment, such as the previous example of the person who died suddenly on the job of a massive cerebral hemorrhage.

Cases in which only two circumstances indicate a work relationship are the most difficult to decide. Compensation is probably awarded in most of these cases, but one should not generalize. The facts of such cases should be investigated carefully. The lunch break cases discussed below illustrate this problem.

Suppose a worker is injured while on a lunch break as a result of a defect on the employer's premises. Three of the circumstances (cause, time, and place) indicate a work relationship, and compensation would most likely be awarded. Alternatively, suppose the worker left the employer's premises during a scheduled lunch break and was injured in a car accident. Since it is possible that only one circumstance would indicate a work relationship (the time of accident), compensation would likely be denied. The most difficult case is somewhere in between. Suppose, during a lunch break on the employer's premises, the worker chokes on a sandwich brought from home. At best, only the time and place of the accident have any relationship to the employment. Most courts would probably grant compensation in this case, but some would not.

Compensation is very doubtful in cases in which only one circumstance indicates a relationship between the injury and the employment. For example, an employee who suffers a heart attack while doing work at home for his own convenience would probably not receive compensation. Assuming that the heart attack cannot be related to the employment, only one circumstance (the employee's activity) indicates a work relationship. The cause, time, and place of injury are unrelated to the employment. However, given the liberal standard of compensation required by the law and practiced by industrial commissions, claim representatives should not deny compensation in such cases without the advice of counsel.

Cases in which none of the circumstances indicate a relationship between the injury and employment are so obviously not covered that they are not even submitted by claimants for compensation, and claim representatives are unlikely to ever see them.

Employee Misconduct

One of the clearest rules in compensation law is that the employee's fault in causing an injury is generally irrelevant in determining the compensability of that injury. Injuries are compensable if they "arise out of and in the course of" employment regardless of the employee's fault. The few exceptions to this rule are discussed in this section. The employee may receive compensation despite negligence, gross negligence, or even certain intentional wrongdoing.

Willful Misconduct and Violation of Safety Rules. Slightly less than half the states have a specific statutory exception to compensation in cases of willful misconduct or violation of safety rules. In the remaining jurisdictions, it is argued that such behavior removes the employee from the course of employment, and compensation should therefore be denied.

Courts have construed these exceptions to compensation very narrowly. Compensation is denied only in cases in which the employee deliberately and knowingly violates a safety rule.[13] The employee must both know of the rule and intend to violate it before compensation is denied. In some jurisdictions, the willful misconduct must be the sole cause of an injury before compensation can be denied. Certain courts have allowed compensation, despite violations of rules, in cases where the employer was aware of repeated violations of a rule and failed to enforce it.

Courts have also allowed compensation when the employee was injured while attempting to perform job duties by *prohibited means*.[14] These courts would only deny compensation if the employee were engaged in *prohibited activities*. According to these courts, employees injured while attempting to perform job duties should be compensated no matter how reckless and prohibited are the means by which they do so.

Intoxication. A number of jurisdictions have statutory exceptions to compensation for injuries to an intoxicated employee. The specific application of this exception varies widely. In some states, an intoxicated employee cannot be compensated even if the intoxication had nothing to do with the injury. In other states, intoxication must be the sole cause of injury for compensation to be denied, a condition that rarely occurs. Most states that recognize this exception require the injury be "due to" intoxication.[15]

Claim representatives who discover that an employee was intoxicated when injured should carefully investigate all other circumstances of the injury and should obtain the advice of counsel before denying compensation.

Self-Inflicted Injury. A number of jurisdictions have a statutory exception to compensation in cases of self-inflicted injury. In jurisdictions without such a specific exception, it is argued that self-inflicted injury is outside the course of employment.

Courts also interpret this exception carefully. This exception does not apply to anything other than intentional and deliberate behavior. No matter how grossly reckless an employee may be, he or she can recover for injuries that are not *intentionally* and *deliberately* self-inflicted.

Courts have also allowed recovery in suicide cases when a compensable injury caused the suicide. Identifying such circumstances is a complex medical and legal issue. They are most likely to occur in cases in which the original injury caused such terrible suffering that the victim commits suicide as an escape.[16] Other cases of suicide are unlikely to be compensable since it is obvious that the employee has in the act of suicide departed from the course of employment, and it is very doubtful that the suicide arose from the employment.

APPLICATION OF THE STATUTORY STANDARD

The remainder of this chapter addresses typical circumstances in which compensability is doubtful. Over the years, the facts of the many court cases that turn on the issue of "arising out of and in the course of" have shown similar patterns. This section presents these cases according to their characteristic facts.

Although many cases share a variety of facts, claim representatives must be careful not to categorize a case improperly as compensable or not based solely on certain facts. For example, the lunch break cases previously described result in compensation or denial of compensation according to the complete facts of each case. It would therefore be incorrect for a claim representative to memorize a rule of compensability for lunch breaks. The central issue in every case is the relationship of the injury to the employment, not that the case appears to fall into a certain category.

The first group of cases presented below includes those in which the cause of the injury may not be related to the employment. These are the cases in which it is doubtful the injury "arises out of" the employment. The next group of cases includes injuries occurring while it is possible that the employee was doing something other than employment duties. The final group of cases includes injuries occurring outside of the usual place and time of employment.

Relationship of Cause of Injury to Employment

The cases in which the cause of the injury is not related to, or has a dubious relationship to, the employment include claims based on street risk and positional risk, acts of God, exposure to the elements, health risks peculiar to the claimant, and assaults.

Street Risk and Positional Risk. Street risk includes all dangers characteristic of public streets, including traffic accidents; defective street and sidewalk surfaces; criminal assaults; and random encounters with people, animals, or objects that share the street.

The analytical difficulty of awarding compensation for injuries resulting from street risk is that such risks are experienced by everyone who uses the streets, employed or not. Thus, it is difficult to say that injuries related to such risks arise out of the employment.

Nevertheless, all courts will award compensation for an injury caused by street risk to an employee whose job requires him or her to be on the streets more often than the general public. Such employees include traveling salespeople, police, delivery personnel, road repair crews, trash collectors, and any other person who frequently uses streets and sidewalks as a function of his or her job.

It is probable that a majority of courts also allow compensation to any employee injured on the street in the course of employment. This is true regardless of whether the employee must regularly travel the streets or even if injury occurs during the only visit to the streets ever made by an employee. This approach is a clear application of "but for" principles of causation to street risk injuries: "But for" the employment, the employee would not have been out on the street and would not have been injured. The application of this rule of compensability requires the employee be in the course of employment when injured. A typical case is when an employee runs an errand for the employer. An employee on the street for personal reasons during the working day cannot expect compensation.

The positional risk doctrine is a generalization of the "but for" principle to any cause of injury, not just street risk. That is, compensation should always be awarded when the injury would not have occurred but for the employment (assuming the employee is in the course of employment). For example, a bee flies into an open window at a workplace and stings an employee who suffers a severe allergic reaction. But for the employment the employee would not have been present to be stung. Compensation should be awarded even though the employment itself may not present an increased risk of bee stings, and therefore did not directly cause the sting. A significant minority of jurisdictions apparently adopt the positional risk doctrine though it may not be identified as such. The principles that underlie street risk and positional risk are illustrated by the following actual cases.

- A miner who was required to return a lamp to his employer's office slipped on ice on the road. The court ruled that the employment required the claimant to be on the road and that this occurrence was therefore a hazard of the employment and, as a result, compensable.[17]

- After leaving the workplace where she worked as a bookkeeper, a claimant was attacked while depositing mail for her employer. The court applied the street risk doctrine and ruled that the claimant's injuries arose out of her employment.[18]

- The claimant, a schoolteacher, was walking to his home where he was required to grade examinations and was struck and killed by an auto. Compensation was awarded.[19]

- Compensation was awarded to a claimant who worked as a cook at the employer's residence and was injured while running an errand for the employer on the way to work.[20]

Acts of God. Acts of God include such natural phenomena as lightning, floods, hail, tornadoes, hurricanes, and earthquakes. The difficulty of awarding compensation for injuries caused by these phenomena is similar to that associated with awarding compensation for injuries caused by street risk. The risk does not really arise out of the employment. Most acts of God affect entire communities. Even those with a more localized impact, such as lightning and hail, are not directly associated with employment.

Courts have resolved this problem in the same way as they have resolved the street risk problem. All courts award compensation to someone whose job increases the exposure to acts of God,[21] such as agricultural workers, construction workers, and other outdoor employees. However, this rationale does not apply to all acts of God. Hurricanes devastate entire communities regardless of place of employment. Earthquakes likewise affect entire communities and are actually a greater danger to indoor workers than to outdoor workers.

As with injuries related to street risk, a significant minority of courts award compensation whenever the employment causes the encounter with nature regardless of whether the employment poses an increased risk. For example, if employment causes someone to be present in the path of a tornado, that person should be compensated for resulting injuries whether or not the overall risk of exposure was greater than that of the general public. The principles that form the basis for compensation for injuries resulting from acts of God are illustrated by the following actual cases.

- While in the course of employment, a claimant was struck by lightning in an open, level field. The claimant was a vice president of an agricultural company. The court ruled that the claimant's employment created a greater risk than other employments from acts of God and awarded compensation.[22]

- A claimant was killed at his place of employment by a tornado that affected 60 percent of the community and caused casualties at the claimant's workplace at about the same rate as it did in the community. Compensation was denied.[23]

Exposure to the Elements. Frostbite or heatstroke can strike anyone exposed to cold or heat for too long. Whenever the temperature is extreme, anyone might suffer such injuries. Yet, the general public is not required to stay outdoors in extreme weather. Certain employees are so required. Whenever such employees suffer injury as a result, courts deem the injury to arise out of the employment. Certain cases to the contrary are obsolete.

Idiopathic Injuries. Certain accidents and the resulting injuries are caused by medical conditions peculiar to the victim and unrelated to the employment. For example, an employee may lose balance and fall because of the side effects of a medication. Such medical conditions are called idiopathic conditions. "Idiopathic" means an obscure or unknown cause, or a cause that is peculiar to the individual. In the workers compensation context, an idiopathic injury is one that arises solely from within the employee and not from any circumstance of the employment.

By definition, idiopathic injuries should not be compensable. However, although all courts are prepared to accept this principle, claim representatives must nevertheless deal with two types of claims associated with idiopathic injuries.

The first type of claim occurs when an injury that appears to be idiopathic is not. In other words, the claim is that the employment somehow caused the injury. The incidences of heart attacks and psychological injuries have caused an increase in this kind of claim. Claim representatives who encounter an injury that appears to be idiopathic but is alleged to be work-related should immediately obtain expert assistance. Such claims involve highly complex medical issues as well as usually serious and expensive injuries.

The second type of claim associated with idiopathic injuries is a claim for *resulting injury*. The claimant may not claim compensation for an initial epileptic seizure, stroke, or heart attack, but will make a claim for resulting injuries. For example, a worker may faint because of an idiopathic condition and strike his head on an object in the work environment. The worker would claim compensation for the head injury, not for the event of fainting.

Courts allow compensation for resulting injuries whenever the work environment creates a special hazard for someone afflicted by the claimant's condition. Thus, if a worker who had to work at heights or around dangerous machinery fainted because of an idiopathic condition, he or she would be compensated for resulting injury. If the same worker simply fell to the floor and was injured, he or she probably would not receive compensation.[24]

A medical condition that simply makes a worker more vulnerable to workplace hazards is not an idiopathic condition. An idiopathic condition affects the worker on its own. A medical condition that makes a worker more vulnerable must interact with a workplace hazard to cause injury. The classic example of vulnerability is a weak back. Many workers have backs that are weak or in bad condition, and they suffer injury when they exert their backs in work-related activity. The principles underlying the issue of compensation for idiopathic injuries are illustrated by the following actual cases.

- A claimant died of a heart attack while driving in the course of his employment. The court found no evidence of an exertion or any other basis on which to attribute the heart attack to the employment and denied compensation.[25]
- A claimant suffered a fall that may have been caused by an idiopathic condition. She fell from a wooden platform, across a metal table, and onto a concrete floor. The court awarded compensation because of the increased danger caused by the work environment.[26]
- While a claimant was outside getting fresh air, he suffered a heart attack, fell into a large pool of water, and drowned. The court found that the claimant was in the course of his employment when the incident occurred and the fall and death resulting from a heart attack, an idiopathic condition, were compensable.[27]

Assaults. Injuries to employees caused by assaults may or may not be compensable, depending on the nature of the assault. Compensability is dubious in assault cases because being assaulted is not considered part of most jobs (except for certain professional athletes), and engaging in a fight may be deemed to be abandonment of the employment.

Although compensation may be in doubt, the fact that an injured employee was the aggressor in a fight is generally not relevant. The compensation system is not based on fault. An employee's role as aggressor is only relevant when it constitutes "willful misconduct." As noted above, misconduct is only found to be "willful" in compensation claims when it is intentional. Such willfulness in the case of an assault would constitute criminal behavior. The spontaneous or heat-of-the-moment fights that tend to erupt in the workplace would not be deemed "willful misconduct." Thus, aggressors can usually receive compensation if it is otherwise appropriate. This principle is illustrated by the following actual cases.

- After having his work corrected by a foreman, the claimant sprayed the foreman in the face with paint. The foreman struck and kicked the claimant, causing injury. The court rejected the aggressor defense and the willful misconduct defense and awarded compensation.[28]

- While unloading a truckload of insulation, a claimant was injured in a fight he provoked with a co-worker. The court rejected the aggressor defense because the dispute clearly arose out of the employment and awarded compensation.[29]

In addition to professional athletics, certain other employments actually involve an increased risk of assault. Because of the nature of their work, employees in these jobs are more likely than the general public to be assaulted. Such employees include police, armored car personnel, couriers of valuables, bill collectors, and people whose work requires them to be in high-crime areas. Injuries resulting from assaults against such employees are generally deemed to arise out of the employment and are therefore compensable.[30]

Most assaults on employees are committed by other employees. These assaults may arise out of work-related disputes, such as those between superior and subordinate or between disagreeable co-workers; they may also result from personal animosity. Assaults arising from work-related disputes are generally compensable even though fighting is outside the course of the employment. This principle is illustrated by the following actual cases.

- A dispute arose between two furniture salesmen as to which one would wait on a customer. One of the salesmen assaulted the other, and the second salesman sued the first for assault and battery. The court held that the assault arose out of the employment and remanded the case to the Bureau of Workers Compensation.[31]

- A claimant was attacked by the survivors of a deceased fellow employee. The assailants were displeased with how the claimant had handled the compensation claim of the deceased fellow employee. The court ruled that the claimant's death arose out of the employment and was therefore compensable.[32]

- An instructor working for an aircraft manufacturer was assaulted by a group of students in a dispute arising out of test grading. The instructor sued the employer for failure to provide adequate protection. The court dismissed the suit because the instructor's injury arose out of his employment, and workers compensation was his exclusive remedy.[33]

Compensation is much more difficult to assess in cases of assaults related to personal animosity between parties whose only connection is the employment. "But for" the employment, such parties would not assault other parties. Nevertheless, the employment duties and circumstances really play no role in causing the assault. It is probable that only those jurisdictions that follow the positional risk doctrine would award compensation in these cases.

A similar analytical problem exists in cases of mistaken or unexplained assaults, or assaults committed by an insane person. Again, the employment duties and circumstances really play no role in causing the assault. Only those jurisdictions that follow the positional risk doctrine are likely to award compensation in these cases. The principles that underlie compensation for injuries related to unexplained assaults are illustrated by the following actual cases.

- A claimant was assaulted by an unknown person in the laundry room of her employer, a nursing home. The claimant was engaged in work duties when attacked, was not robbed or sexually assaulted, and had no known enemies. Compensation was awarded.[34]

- A claimant suffered an unprovoked attack by an intoxicated co-worker with whom he had little prior dealing. The court awarded compensation.[35]

- The court ruled there was insufficient evidence to rebut the presumption that the claimant was in the course of his employment as a manager of nine department stores in New York City when he left a store in Queens at 11:30 A.M. and was found at 3:00 P.M. in Manhattan, cut, stripped naked, and mentally unaware. Compensation was awarded.[36]

- A claimant was shot by a paranoid schizophrenic co-worker who believed the claimant was a hit man out to get him. The two parties had no contact with each other except through work. The court ruled that the injury arose out of the employment and awarded compensation.[37]

Assaults at the workplace that arise from purely personal motives are not compensable. For example, if a cheating spouse who is clearly engaged in the course of employment is attacked and injured by a jealous spouse, the resulting injuries are not compensable. The cause of the injuries clearly arises from outside the employment, and the fact that injuries are sustained on the job is sheer coincidence. This principle is illustrated by the following actual cases.

- A claimant was shot and killed at her workplace by her boyfriend. The court ruled that the employment played no part in causing the occurrence even though a co-worker had revealed the claimant's exact whereabouts.[38]

- A claimant was attacked at work by his ex-wife's husband, who worked at the same auto assembly plant. The court found the animosity between the parties to be purely personal and unrelated to the employment. Compensation was denied.[39]

- During her lunch break, a claimant cashed her paycheck at a bank and returned to her employer's parking lot where she was assaulted and robbed. The court ruled that the robbery was strictly personal and did not arise out of the employment. Compensation was denied.[40]

Relationship of Employee's Activities to Employment

Cases in which the employee is clearly not performing work-related duties when injured present the best illustrations of the work-relatedness rule of compensation. The fact that an employee is not performing work duties when injured, by itself, is not usually enough of a basis on which to deny compensation. However, if the cause of the injury or the time and place of injury are also unrelated to the employment, it is very likely that compensation will be denied.

Employees have been injured on lunch breaks; coffee breaks; while taking breaks to rest, smoke, chat, or go to the toilet; at social affairs and sports events; while engaged in unauthorized activities, pranks, or practical jokes; and while deviating from business travel for personal reasons. The following discussion addresses the relationship of these activities to employment and how that relationship is interpreted under workers compensation law.

Personal Activities. The law recognizes that employees are not machines. Employees interrupt their work to rest, warm up, cool down, smoke, chat with fellow employees, attend to their personal appearance, use the toilet, eat lunch, and drink coffee. In general, these activities are deemed to be incidental to the employment even though they are clearly not work duties. This is true even if the break from work may be longer than a few minutes or if it is not compensated by the employer.

The law does not require the activity to be absolutely necessary in order to award compensation if injuries are sustained when that activity is performed. It is sufficient for the activity to be reasonable. Indeed, even if the extent and duration of these activities has become excessive, compensation will not necessarily be denied if the employer has known about and acquiesced to the activities.

Compensation may be denied when an injury is accompanied by

additional circumstances unrelated to the employment. Given the conditions discussed above, an employee who leaves the employer's premises and is injured during a lunch break is unlikely to receive compensation because the injury is likely to involve both a cause and place of accident unrelated to the employment. Similarly, an employee who uses a break to engage in horseplay or pranks, discussed further below, or who decides to try out tools, machinery, or equipment he or she has no business handling, or wanders onto parts of the employer's premises where he should not be is likely to be denied compensation. In addition, if the cause of injury is unrelated to the employment, if an employee is stabbed in the eye by a hairbrush bristle while brushing her hair, she is likely to be denied compensation.

Employees injured while sleeping on the job may or may not receive compensation depending on the circumstances. Sleeping on the job, unlike other personal activities, is a more substantial abandonment of work duties—it is unlikely to have a defined beginning and end as does a lunch break and is unlikely to be known about or allowed by the employer. On the other hand, if the employee sleeps during an unavoidable lull in the work, and certainly if the employee's fatigue follows long hours of work, courts are likely to deem the sleep incidental to the employment and thus compensable.

The outcome of any case that turns on the issue of personal activities depends heavily on the facts of the case. In almost all of these cases, the employee is injured on the employer's premises while not performing work duties. Claim representatives who investigate claims for such injuries should carefully determine how reasonable and customary the employee's activity was, whether the employer knew of or permitted the activity, and whether the employee limited the activity to a reasonable time or extended it into a deliberate departure from work. The principles underlying compensation awarded for injuries sustained during personal activities are illustrated by the following actual cases.

- A claimant was a member of a grounds maintenance crew that regularly took swimming breaks between jobs. On one such break, the claimant dove into a river and broke his neck. The court ruled the swimming to be an insubstantial deviation that was made necessary by the work conditions and awarded compensation.[41]

- A claimant was attacked by a fellow employee who believed the claimant had cut in front of him at the water fountain. Compensation was awarded.[42]

- A claimant was severely injured while using a large industrial oven to warm a frozen pot pie. The court denied compensation because the claimant had voluntarily chosen an unreasonable and unnecessary risk in pursuit of his own benefit, and the employer had no knowledge of the action.[43]

- During an unpaid lunch break, a claimant's hair caught on fire when she lit a match for a cigarette. The court ruled that the injury occurred in the course of employment, but did not arise out of it. The cause of the injury was deemed to be purely personal, and compensation was denied.[44]

- The claimant, a salesperson at a department store, was shopping on the store premises during her lunch break. During this time, she tripped on a hanger on the floor and was injured. She tried to pursue a liability claim, but the court ruled that the injury occurred in the course of employment and workers compensation was the only remedy.[45]

- The court found that a claimant was injured following an upsetting personal phone call when he accidentally thrust his hand through a window in a gesture of anger. The injury occurred during a paid lunch break on the employer's premises and was ruled compensable.[46]

Social and Recreational Activities. Employees have been injured at dinners, dances, cocktail parties, barbecues, Christmas parties, or while playing softball, basketball, volleyball, and other sports. Whether such injuries are compensable depends on the nature and extent of the employer's involvement in the activity and the benefit of the activity to the employer. These injuries have become so increasingly common that numerous state legislatures have enacted specific statutes concerning their compensability. See Exhibit 3-1.

Compensation is very likely to be awarded when the activity occurs on the employer's premises and with the employer's knowledge. This is true even if the employer has not explicitly sanctioned the activity. An activity that is regular, such as a touch football game during lunch break, is deemed incidental to the employment and is thus compensable. Courts might deny compensation for an injury resulting from a one-time or first-time activity, especially if the employer's knowledge of the activity cannot be demonstrated. The principles of compensation for recreational activities are illustrated by the following actual cases.

- A claimant suffered a ruptured kidney playing touch football on company property during an afternoon break. The employer knew of and acquiesced in the football games for over three months. The court ruled that the games had become incidental to the employment and awarded compensation.[47]

Exhibit 3-1
Compensability of Social and Recreational Activities

California:

Liability for...compensation...shall exist...where the injury does not arise out of voluntary participation in any off-duty recreational, social, or athletic activity not constituting part of the employee's work-related duties, except where these activities are a reasonable expectancy of, or are expressly or implicitly required by, the employment.

Cal. Labor Code § 3600(a)(9)

Colorado:

"Employee" excludes any person...while participating in recreational activity, who at such time is relieved of and is not performing any duties, regardless of whether he is utilizing, by discount or otherwise, a pass, ticket, license, permit, or other device as an emolument of his employment.

Col. Rev. Stat. § 8-41-106(2)

Illinois:

Accidental injuries incurred while participating in voluntary recreational programs including but not limited to athletic events, parties and picnics do not arise out of and in the course of the employment even though the employer pays some or all of the cost thereof. This exclusion shall not apply in the event that the injured employee was ordered or assigned by his employer to participate in the program.

Chap. 48 Ill. Rev. Stat. § 138.11

Massachusetts:

"Personal injury" shall not include any injury resulting from an employee's purely voluntary participation in any recreational activity, including but not limited to athletic events, parties, and picnics, even though the employer pays some or all of the cost thereof.

152 Mass. Gen. Law § 1(7A)

Michigan:

An injury incurred in the pursuit of an activity the major purpose of which is social or recreational is not covered under this act.

Mich. Stat. § 17.237(301)(3)

Nevada:

Any injury sustained by an employee while engaging in an athletic or social event sponsored by the employer shall be deemed not to have arisen out of or in the course of employment unless the employee received remuneration for participation in such event.

Nev. Rev. Stat. 616.110

New Jersey:

Compensation...shall be made by the employer...except...when recreational or social activities, unless such recreational or social activities are a regular incident of employment and produce a benefit to the employer beyond improvement in employee health and morale, are the natural and proximate cause of the injury or death.

N.J. Stat. 34:15-7

New York:
> Every employer...shall...provide compensation...except...where the injury was sustained in or caused by voluntary participation in an off-duty athletic activity not constituting part of the employee's work related duties unless the employer (a) requires the employee to participate in such activity, (b) compensates the employee for participating in such activity or (c) otherwise sponsors the activity.
>
> 64 Con. Laws of N.Y. § 10.(1.)

Oregon:
> Compensable injury does not include: Injury incurred while engaging in or performing, or as the result of engaging in or performing, any recreational or social activities solely for the worker's personal pleasure.
>
> Ore. Rev. Stat. 656.005(7)(a)(B)

Wisconsin:
> An employee is not performing service growing out of and incidental to employment while engaging in a program designed to improve the physical well-being of the employee, whether or not the program is located on the employer's premises, if participation in the program is voluntary and the employee receives no compensation for participation.
>
> Wisc. Stat. § 102.03(1)(c)3.

- A claimant was injured in a volleyball game at the employer's fire station. The court found that the volleyball games were a recognized activity at the station and that the supervisors and superior officers acquiesced. Because the recreational activity was considered to be a regular incident of the employment, compensation was awarded.[48]

Injuries related to recreational activities away from the employer's premises may be compensable if the employer requires or expects employee participation in, or derives benefit from, the activity.[49] Compensation will certainly be granted to an injured employee who is explicitly required to participate. In such a case, the social or recreational activity becomes a job duty. However, the requirement to participate need not be explicit. Many sales personnel and similar employees are implicitly expected to entertain customers. Other employees may participate in company-sponsored social events only because the alternative is to report to work.

Employers may derive benefit from social or recreational activities at which customers or suppliers are entertained or when the event is part of an advertising or marketing effort. Injuries to employees who participate in such events, even on a voluntary basis, are compensable. However, when the employer does not derive any real benefit, other than improved employee morale, and does not even tacitly require participation, the fact that the employer might help organize or finance the activity does not create a work relationship that is substantial enough to form the basis for compensating resulting injuries. Most courts would deny compensation when the employer merely encourages the activity. The principles underlying compensation for injuries sustained off-premises are illustrated by the following actual cases.

- A claimant was an employee of a law firm that directed him to maintain and participate in a softball league. An injury suffered while participating in the softball league was ruled compensable.[50]

- The court awarded compensation to a claimant for injury occurring during a company softball game because the employer organized and maintained the league, pressured the claimant to play, paid for the equipment, publicized and encouraged the games, and made company time available to create schedules and league bylaws.[51]

- A claimant drowned at a company picnic. The employer paid for the food, announced the picnic, and encouraged, but did not require, attendance. The court ruled that the claimant was in the course of employment and entitled to compensation.[52]

- An injury to an employee occurring at a company picnic was ruled not compensable when the only support for the event from the employer was allowing notices of the picnic to be copied and posted and tickets to be sold during work hours.[53]

- A claimant broke his leg while playing softball for a team sponsored by his employer. The employer paid for the equipment and jerseys, but games occurred off the employer's premises and were played mainly for employee enjoyment. Compensation was denied.[54]

Acts Outside Regular Duties. On the basis of the two preceding sections, it should be clear that under certain circumstances, workers can be compensated for injuries occurring while the worker is not engaged in work duties. This principle is applied to a number of situations, usually by the rationale that the activity in question is incidental to the employment or that it benefits the employer.

An employee who abandons work duties to help a co-worker with other work duties, even if forbidden to do so, remains within the course of employment. An employee who does so is, in fact, advancing the employer's interests even if the employee's only intent is to help the co-worker.

In contrast, an employee who abandons work duties solely to satisfy curiosity is likely not to be compensated for resulting injuries. Many courts would rule that employees who both abandon their own work and involve themselves with machinery, tools, or places that are none of their business should not be compensated for resulting injuries. However, other courts might overlook curiosity when a worker's lapse is momentary and spontaneous, granting compensation for resulting injuries.

An employee ordered to perform personal errands for a superior would likely be compensated for resulting injuries. A few courts might disagree on the grounds that the errand is obviously neither work-related nor something a superior is allowed by the employer to order. However, the better rule is to allow compensation, since a denial would place the financial burden of the injury on the employee, not the superior. Furthermore, employees cannot be put in the position of having to decide which orders from their superiors are appropriate and which are not. Injuries suffered while running a personal errand for a co-worker, not a superior, would not be compensable.

Injuries occurring to an employee acting in an emergency are compensable if the employer benefits from the employee's actions or if the circumstances of the employment caused the employee to become involved in the emergency.[55] An employee injured while rescuing a fellow employee or the employer's property from danger would certainly be compensated. Rescuing a complete stranger has a much weaker relationship to the employment, but courts have been generous toward those who act out of human decency, tending to grant compensation even in these situations. More difficult yet are cases in which there is no real emergency but only a need for help, such as a stranger with a broken-down car. Courts would probably not grant compensation for injuries resulting from such a situation unless ordinary standards of human behavior required the employee to get involved, such as if the broken-down car were in a remote, uninhabited area.

Pranks, Horseplay, and Practical Jokes. Employees often leave their work duties to engage in pranks, horseplay, or practical jokes. Certain employees are notorious for such behavior. They play hide-and-go-seek; chase one another; engage in play fights with tools, supplies, or trash; perform athletic or acrobatic stunts; sabotage the work stations of others; or prey on stuffy or fearful workers around them.

Those who are unwilling victims of such behavior can certainly receive compensation for their injuries. However, claim representatives investigating this sort of case should be aware that after being injured, a willing participant may not admit to having participated in the activity and may try to pose as an innocent victim.

Compensation for instigators and willing participants is much more doubtful. Courts are most likely to grant compensation when the behavior is momentary and spontaneous, is induced by boring lulls in work, or has become an established and tolerated part of the work environment. Nevertheless, courts will readily deny compensation in the absence of evidence that the behavior is an expected or an established incident of the employment. The principles underlying compensation for injuries sustained as a result of horseplay are illustrated by the following actual cases.

- During a lull in pipelaying work, a co-worker threw a vine at the claimant and yelled, "Snake!" The claimant jumped up, ran in fright, and suffered a myocardial infarction. The court found that such horseplay was foreseeable and the claimant was a victim rather than an instigator. Compensation was awarded.[56]

- While closing a service station, a seventeen-year-old claimant and another seventeen-year-old co-worker engaged in a sponge fight. The claimant tripped and fell through a glass door. The court ruled that because horseplay frequently occurred at this workplace, it was almost inevitable under the circumstances. Compensation was awarded.[57]

- A claimant was injured while attempting to perform a handstand on the arms of a swivel chair. The court found that physical exercises and horseplay had become a known and tolerated part of this employment and awarded compensation.[58]

- A claimant was injured when he fell from a stool after posting an offensive picture of another employee. The court ruled the injury noncompensable.[59]

- A claimant was injured when he struck his face on a hand truck after throwing a piece of rubber tubing at a co-worker. The court ruled that such horseplay was not compensable unless it was part of a series of similar incidents so known to the employer as to have become part of the employment.[60]

- A claimant abandoned his work of piling lumber beside a river to push a dilapidated wagon into the river. He became entangled in the wagon and drowned. The court denied compensation because the injury did not arise out of and in the course of employment.[61]

Dual Purpose Trips. Employees are covered by workers compensation during a business trip. An employee is sometimes injured while traveling for both business and personal reasons. These trips are known in compensation law as *dual purpose trips*. For example, an employee heading home for the day is asked by the employer to pick up or drop off something. Is this trip work-related, even though the employee would have undertaken the trip for personal reasons?

Some courts have approached this problem by weighing the relative importance of the business purpose and the personal purpose for the travel, awarding compensation only when the business purpose is deemed to be the more substantial of the two. The problem with this approach is that it is completely subjective. One court might decide that the business purpose of a given case is more significant, while another court might decide the opposite.

The better rule for deciding such cases was announced by the New York Court of Appeals (New York's highest court—the similar court in most states is the Supreme Court) in *Marks' Dependents v. Gray*.[62] The Court in *Marks'* stated:

> The test in brief is this: If the work of the employee creates the necessity for travel, he is in the course of his employment, though he is serving at the same time some purpose of his own. . . . If however, the work has had no part in creating the necessity for travel, if the journey would have gone forward though the business errand had been dropped, and would have been canceled upon failure of the private purpose, though the business errand was undone, the travel is then personal. . . .

Thus, if a business purpose makes a trip necessary, the entire trip is deemed a business trip, no matter how substantial the personal motive for the travel. Alternatively, if the business trip would have been postponed but for the personal purpose, the trip is deemed a personal trip. The issue is whether someone would have to be sent on the business trip, not whether the business purpose is more substantial. This principle is illustrated by the following actual cases.

- A claimant's husband was the president of her employer. The claimant accompanied her husband on a business trip that included a vacation in Yellowstone and Grand Teton National Parks. Before she was hired as an employee, the claimant had accompanied her husband on six of eight previous similar trips. After the claimant was killed en route from the national parks to the business meeting, the court ruled the trip to be personal. No evidence had been presented that someone had to accompany the husband for business purposes.[63]

- A claimant removed lumber from a worksite, loaded it in his truck, and headed home. He was injured in a collision en route. The court applied the dual purpose doctrine, since the claimant's employer had to remove the lumber at some point. The court ruled this was a business trip and awarded compensation.[64]

- A claimant was killed en route from a jobsite to his home in Phoenix, 300 miles away, where he planned to spend the weekend with family. He was also to pick up some fuel pump parts in Phoenix on Saturday. Fellow workers admitted that delivery of the fuel pump parts would have been arranged during the work week were it not for the claimant's trip home. The court found the trip to be personal and denied compensation.[65]

Deviations for Personal Reasons. Sometimes an employee departs from a business trip to a personal trip, identifiable by a distinct deviation from the normal route for the business trip. Courts generally deny compensation for injuries suffered by an employee when there is such a distinct deviation before the claimant returns to the business route. Nevertheless, other courts soften this rule of compensability by allowing recovery if the deviation is not too substantial or if the employee has completed his personal matters and is heading back toward the business route.[66] Claim representatives faced with this sort of case should carefully investigate the locations of the business and personal destinations and all alternative routes for reaching them. A determination of whether a particular deviation is substantial or not depends on the distance, duration, and alternatives.

A distinct business deviation from a personal trip remains a business trip until the employee returns to the personal route. An employee is therefore covered by workers compensation throughout such a business deviation even if it is not substantial or if the employee has completed the work-related business and is heading back toward the route for the personal trip. The principles underlying compensation for injuries sustained on dual purpose trips are illustrated by the following actual cases.

- A claimant was killed while driving a truck off of the usual route between Buffalo, NY, and Sioux City, IA. The court ruled that even if the claimant had stopped for personal reasons, he was heading back toward his business destination, and compensation should be awarded.[67]

- A claimant traveled from New Jersey to New York on business, then to Connecticut for a personal visit. After leaving Connecticut and returning to the route from New York to New Jersey, the claimant was killed in an auto accident. Compensation was awarded.[68]

- A claimant had to travel from Pittsburgh (in western Pennsylvania) to Bethlehem (in eastern Pennsylvania) on business. He left several days early and visited New York City for personal vacation. While traveling from New York to Bethlehem, the claimant was killed in New Jersey. The court ruled that the claimant was outside the course of his employment and denied compensation.[69]

The preceding two cases are illustrated in Exhibit 3-2. As shown by the diagram, compensability in these kinds of cases depends on whether the claimant is on an identifiable deviation from the business route at the time of injury, or if he or she has returned to the business route.

Relationship of Time and Place of Accident to Employment

The time and place of an employee's injury are extremely important in determining whether the injury is work-related. As a generalization, injuries occurring at the workplace during work hours are compensable, and those occurring away from the workplace outside regular work hours are not. Although these generalizations have important exceptions (as discussed in a large portion of this chapter), they nevertheless accurately apply to the outcomes of the vast majority of compensation cases.

The time and place of the accident are especially important in cases involving employees commuting back and forth to work, traveling employees, injuries to employees before hiring and after leaving the employment, and resident employees.

Commuting.   One of the most objective rules of compensation law is that employees are not compensated for injuries sustained while commuting to and from work although the trip would not be made except for the employment. Generally, this rule holds true no matter how close to the employer's premises the employee is when injured. Determining the boundaries of the employer's premises is the key issue in applying this rule.

The employer's premises include all areas owned, occupied, leased, or controlled by the employer. Therefore, an injury occurring in a private parking lot owned by the employer would likely be compensated, while one occurring in the public lot of an office complex or shopping center in which the employer is located probably would not be compensated. Certain courts have granted compensation for injuries occurring in areas over which the employer has some nominal control, such as common areas in an office building or sidewalks in front of the employer's premises. Other courts apply the premises rule very conservatively and have not awarded compensation for injuries occurring in such areas.

Travel from one part of an employer's premises to another is covered, since it occurs completely within the premises. An employee need not be injured at his or her work station to receive compensation. Coverage begins as soon as the employee sets foot on any part of the premises. Employees who travel from one location of the employer to

Exhibit 3-2
Personal Deviations from Business Trips

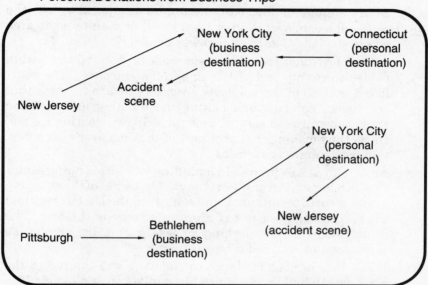

another are engaged in business travel and are thus not governed by the commuting rule. Injuries to such employees are compensable. Nor does the rule apply to workers who are injured on the way home if they are required by the employer to work upon returning home. However, as mentioned previously in this chapter, work taken home by the employee for his or her own convenience does not transform the commute home into a business trip. The principles of compensation for injuries sustained while on an employer's premises are illustrated by the following actual cases.

- An employee entering the employer's lot struck and killed the claimant as the claimant exited the lot on his motorcycle. The collision occurred four feet outside the employer's property. Compensation was denied.[70]

- A claimant slipped and fell on an icy public sidewalk while reaching for the door of his employer. The court ruled that the claimant could not be compensated for travel to and from the workplace and that the claimant had not been injured by any hazard of the employment. Compensation was denied.[71]

- A claimant was struck from behind while turning his car into his employer's property. The court found that no special risk of the employment was involved and denied compensation.[72]

- A claimant fell in the loading zone of a parking lot. Her employer was one of several stores in a shopping center, all of whose employees and customers used the parking lot. The claimant's employer did not own, lease, or maintain the area where she fell. Compensation was denied.[73]

- An employee fell on ice on a sidewalk in front of and within twelve to twenty feet of the employer's entrance. The court found that all of the employer's workers had to traverse that spot when entering and exiting the building and that the employer exercised control over the walk by clearing ice and snow, thus making that spot part of the employer's premises. Compensation was awarded.[74]

- An employee was injured in a parking lot at a shopping center in which her employer was a tenant. The owner of the shopping center owned, maintained, and controlled the lot, but required the tenant-employer to pay a pro rata share of the cost. The court ruled that the parking lot was part of the employer's premises and awarded compensation.[75]

- While heading out for lunch, a claimant was injured in the elevator of a building in which his employer was a tenant. The court ruled that the injury occurred on the employer's premises and awarded compensation.[76]

- An employer's premises were deemed to include an entire fenced-in 600-acre site at which the claimant's employer was working as a contractor. The employer's personnel had to traverse the site to get to the location of their work. The claimant was injured in a traffic accident on the site. Compensation was awarded.[77]

- A claimant was injured while walking from an office building in which her employer was a tenant to a parking spot leased by the employer. The court ruled that the employee was injured while traveling from one part of the employer's premises to another and awarded compensation.[78]

As an objective rule that is frequently the basis on which compensation is denied, it is not surprising that the commuting rule is subject to a number of exceptions. Transportation provided by the employer is an obvious exception. When the employer provides the means for commuting, the risks associated with employment begin as soon as the employee enters the employer's vehicle.[79] However, the usual commuting rule of noncompensability applies when employers reimburse the costs of commuting or if employees arrange their own car pools. Because control of the means of transportation does not rest with the employer in these cases, injuries occurring therein are not compensable.

Another exception to the commuting rule is for travel through dangerous spots, such as railroad crossings, that cannot be avoided when entering and leaving the employer's premises. The dangers of such places are considered a hazard of the employment.

Another exception to the commuting rule is for travel that in itself is a major part of the employee's duties. This exception is known as the *special errand rule.* For example, it is likely that an employee who must journey to the workplace just to open doors or lock up would receive compensation for injuries sustained during this time. In this case, the major part of the employee's effort is the trip back and forth at the required times. As a result, compensation for injuries sustained during the trip would reflect the fact that making the trip is considered a required, work-related activity. Likewise, employees temporarily assigned to a distant facility of the employer may be compensated for injuries occurring in transit. However, merely working overtime or different hours does not invoke the special errand rule. Applications of the special errand rule are illustrated by the following actual cases.

- A claimant was temporarily assigned by her employer to a location thirty miles from her usual workplace. She suffered injuries in an accident on the way back from this distant location. The court ruled that the claimant was on a special errand because the reassignment was temporary and unusual, because of the distance involved, and because the claimant was required to car pool with another worker. Compensation was awarded.[80]

- A nurse who gave lectures for her employer drove to another town, stayed overnight, gave her lecture the next day, and was injured on the return trip. The court ruled that her entire trip was a special errand for the employer and awarded compensation.[81]

- A claimant was injured while traveling home to change into a suit before going to a trade show that his employer required him to attend. Since the claimant normally wore work clothes at work and was required by his employer to change clothes and attend the show, the court ruled that the claimant was on a special errand and was entitled to compensation.[82]

- A claimant was required to return to a construction site at midnight and at 6:00 A.M. to light oil heaters. Travel time for each trip was about one hour, although the actual work required only fifteen to thirty minutes. The claimant was paid for three hours of extra time per day. The court found that the claimant was paid for his travel time and therefore awarded compensation for death occurring en route.[83]

- After a full day's work, a claimant was required to travel fifty miles to one of his employer's customers and work through the night. The claimant was injured while heading home the next morning on a significantly different route than his normal route home. The court found that claimant was on a special errand and awarded compensation.[84]

Traveling Employees. Certain employees are required by their jobs to travel. They include delivery personnel, solicitors, truck drivers, repairmen, construction personnel, and salespeople. While traveling from one place of business to another, these employees are covered by workers compensation. When it is clear that they are engaged in work-related duties, the absence of a fixed workplace should not jeopardize their compensation protection. Employees whose jobs require them to travel are covered by workers compensation as soon as they head for their first destination. This "door-to-door" coverage contrasts with the usual commuting rule for employees who work at fixed places.

Some employees are required by their jobs to travel overnight to distant cities. Most jurisdictions extend "twenty-four-hour" compensation protection to such employees. They are covered continuously until they return home for all expected activities, including eating at restaurants, sleeping in hotels, and engaging in reasonable relaxation. These principles are illustrated by the following actual cases.

- A claimant was killed in a fire in a room at the hotel where he was conducting meetings and conferences for his employer. Compensation was awarded.[85]
- A bus driver who was away overnight on a trip was accidentally shot at a bar where he had gone for drinks. The court ruled that the visit to the bar was a reasonable recreational activity, incidental to the employment, and awarded compensation.[86]

Courts that have denied compensation to overnight traveling employees have generally done so when the employee has deviated substantially from expected activities, such as becoming extremely drunk at a place far removed from the business destination.

Both employees who travel during the workday and those who travel overnight can make personal trips that take them outside the scope of workers compensation coverage. Whenever an injury occurs during an identifiable personal deviation from a business trip, compensation may be denied.

Before Hiring and After Discharge. Obviously, workers compensation does not apply before the employment relationship begins or after it ends. Nevertheless, claim representatives should be careful how they apply this rule.

The employment relationship begins when the parties agree to the employment and the worker is present at a place and time required by the employment. The employment agreement can be completely informal. The completion of personnel paperwork is not essential to confirm the employment relationship. The worker need not have begun any actual work duties to be in the course of the employment, as long as he or she is at a time and place required by the job.

After termination of employment, a worker is entitled to reasonable time to remove personal belongings from the workplace and to collect any pay that must be collected in person. Injuries occurring during any of these activities would be covered. However, the worker is not covered during subsequent and unnecessary visits to the workplace.

Resident Employees. Certain employees, including those at hotels, camps, and resorts, are required or allowed to live on the employer's premises. These employees have "twenty-four-hour" coverage if they are continuously on call. Injuries to resident employees who are not always on call are not necessarily covered by workers compensation. An injury occurring during off-hours and not caused by the premises would not be covered. The following case illustrates the principles that underlie compensation for injuries to resident employees.

- A fifteen-year-old laborer employed by a resort drowned in the resort lake while swimming during his lunch hour. Swimming was against the resort rules that required a lifeguard to be present and a swimming test to be taken. The court denied compensation because the cause of death did not arise out of his employment.[87]

SUMMARY

Although the vast majority of workers compensation claims seen by a claim representative arise out of and in the course of employment, some do not. Claim representatives must be alert to cases involving the following circumstances:

- Willful misconduct or violation of safety rules
- Intoxication
- Self-inflicted injury
- Street risk
- Acts of God
- Idiopathic injuries
- Assaults

- Lunch breaks and other personal activities
- Social affairs
- Recreational activities
- Acts outside regular duties
- Pranks, horseplay, and practical jokes
- Dual purpose trips
- Personal deviations from business trips
- Commuting
- Traveling employees
- Injuries occurring before hiring and after discharge
- Resident employees

Although a majority of the cases involving these circumstances are compensable, the circumstances create the greatest doubt about compensability. A claim representative who encounters a claim for injury involving these circumstances must investigate the facts very carefully, looking for indications of a relationship between the employment and the injury in terms of the following:

- Cause of injury
- What the employee was doing when injured
- Place of injury
- Time of injury

Compensation should not be denied unless the injury clearly does not arise out of and in the course of employment, and after the claim representative has consulted with local claims management, home office claims staff, or counsel.

Chapter Notes

1. Crites v. Baker, 276 N.E. 2d 582 (Ind. App. 1971).
2. R&T Investments Ltd. v. Johns, 321 S.E. 2d 287 (Va. 1984).
3. Orr v. Holiday Inns Inc., 627 P. 2d 1193 (Kan. App. 1981).
4. Craig v. Electrolux Corp., 510 P. 2d 138 (Kan. 1973).
5. Jordan v. St. Louis County Police Department, 699 S.W. 2d 124 (Mo. App. 1985).
6. Arthur Larson, *Workmen's Compensation* (Desk Edition), § 6.50.
7. Baker v. Orange County Board of County Commissioners, 399 So. 2d 400 (Fla. App. 1981).
8. Corken v. Corken Steel Products Inc., 385 S.W. 2d 949 (Ky. App. 1965).
9. Vanderbee v. Knape & Vogt Mfg. Co., 210 N.W. 2d 801 (Mich. App. 1973).
10. Globe Indemnity Co. v. Industrial Accident Commission, 171 P. 1088 (Cal. App. 1918).
11. Larson, § 29.10.
12. New York Consolidated Statutes, Workmen's Compensation, § 21.
13. Larson, § 32.00.
14. Larson, § 31.00.
15. Larson, § 34.31.
16. Larson, § 36.10.
17. Harlan-Wallis Coal Corp. v. Foster, 277 S.W. 2d 14 (Ky. 1955).
18. Wayne Adams Buick Inc. v. Ference, 421 N.E. 2d 733 (Ind. App. 1981).
19. Inglish v. Industrial Commission, 182 N.E. 31 (Ohio 1932).
20. Kristianson v. Lerman, 38 N.E. 2d 230 (N.Y. 1941).
21. Larson, § 8.00.
22. Reich v. A. Reich and Sons Gardens Inc., 485 S.W. 2d 133 (Mo. App. 1972).
23. Mobile and O.R.R. v. Industrial Commission 28, F. 2d 228 (E.D. Ill. 1928) (applying Illinois law).
24. Larson, § 12.10.
25. Collins v. Liberty Mutual Insurance Co., 561 S.W. 2d 456 (Tenn. 1978).
26. Ware v. State Workers Compensation Commissioner, 234 S.E. 2d 779 (W.Va. 1977).
27. Kennecott Corp. v. Industrial Commission, 675 P. 2d 1187 (Utah 1987).
28. Geeslin v. Workers Compensation Commissioner, 294 S.E. 2d 150 (W.Va. 1982).
29. Colvert v. Industrial Commission, 520 P. 2d 322 (Ariz. App. 1974).
30. Larson, § 11.11.
31. Schwartz v. Golden, 338 N.W. 2d 218 (Mich. App. 1983).
32. Person v. Safeco Insurance Co., 637 S.W. 2d 461 (Tenn. 1982).
33. Swanson v. Lockheed Aircraft Corp., 354 S.E. 2d 204 (Ga. App. 1987).
34. B&B Nursing Homes v. Blair, 496 P. 2d 795 (Okla. 1972).

35. Toler v. Industrial Commission, 527 P. 2d 767 (Ariz. App. 1974).

36. Slotnick v. Howard Stores Inc., 397 N.Y.S. 2d 179 (1979).

37. Cedar Rapids Community School v. Cady, 278 N.W. 2d 298 (Iowa 1979).

38. Transactron Inc. v. Workers Compensation Appeals Board, 137 Cal. Rptr. 142 (1977).

39. Devault v. General Motors Corp., 386 N.W. 2d 671 (Mich. App. 1986).

40. Rogers v. Workers Compensation Appeals Board, 218 Cal. Rptr. 662 (1985).

41. B&B Cash Grocery Stores v. Wortman, 431 So. 2d 171 (Fla. App. 1983).

42. Liberty Mutual Insurance Co. v. Hopkins, 422 S.W. 2d 203 (Tex. Civ. App. 1967).

43. Segler v. Industrial Commission, 406 N.E. 2d 542 (Ill. 1980).

44. Coleman v. Cycle Transformer Corp., 520 A. 2d 1341 (N.J. 1986).

45. Chen v. Federated Department Stores, 489 A. 2d 719 (N.J. Super. 1985).

46. Carling Brewing v. Belsner, 291 A. 2d 175 (Md. App. 1972).

47. Mack Trucks Inc. v. Miller, 326 A. 2d 186 (Md. App. 1974).

48. City of Oklahoma City v. Alvarado, 507 P. 2d 535 (Okla. 1973).

49. Larson, § 22.00.

50. Law Offices of William W. Schooley v. Industrial Commission, 503 N.E. 2d 1186 (Ill. App. 1987).

51. Illinois Bell Telephone Co. v. Industrial Commission, 334 N.E. 2d 136 (Ill. 1975).

52. Feaster v. S.K. Kelso & Sons, 347 A. 2d 521 (Pa. Commonw. 1975).

53. Dapp v. New York State Liquor Authority, 377 N.Y.S. 2d 677 (1975).

54. Chilcote v. Blass, Riddick, Chilcote & Continental Insurance Co., 620 S.W. 2d 953 (Ark. 1981).

55. Larson, § 28.00.

56. Ivy H. Smith Co. v. Kates, 395 So. 2d 263 (Fla. App. 1981).

57. Peet v. Garner Oil Co., 492 S.W. 2d 103 (Mo. App. 1973).

58. Aucompaugh v. General Electric, 490 N.Y.S. 2d 647 (1985).

59. Bemis Co. v. Industrial Commission, 423 N.E. 2d 896 (Ill. 1981).

60. Ognibene v. Rochester Mfg. Co., 80 N.E. 2d 749 (N.Y. 1948).

61. Gaurin v. Bagley & Sewall, 80 N.E. 2d 660 (N.Y. 1948).

62. 167 N.E. 181 (N.Y. 1929).

63. Storm v. Karl-Mil Inc., 460 A. 2d 519 (Del. 1983).

64. Downs v. Durbin Corp., 416 S.W. 2d 242 (Mo. App. 1967).

65. Kriese v. Industrial Commission, 554 P. 2d 914 (Ariz. Ct. App. 1976).

66. Larson, § 19.00.

67. Hilliker v. North American Van Lines, Inc., 207 N.Y.S. 2d 753 (1960).

68. Neumeister v. Eastern Brewing Co., 179 A. 2d 551 (N.J. Super. 1962).

69. Hess v. Catholic Knights of St. George, 27 A. 2d 542 (Pa. Super. 1942).

70. Heim v. Longview Fibre Co., 707 P. 2d 689 (Wash. App. 1985).

71. Simpson v. Cady & Lee, 293 N.W. 718 (Mich. 1940).
72. Templet v. Intracoastal Truck Line, Inc., 230 So. 2d 74 (La. 1969).
73. Barham v. Food World Inc., 266 S.E. 2d 676 (N.C. 1980).
74. Frost v. S.S. Kresge Co., 299 N.W. 2d 646 (Iowa 1980).
75. Merrill v. J.C. Penney, 256 N.W. 2d 518 (Minn. 1977).
76. Chicago Transit Authority v. Industrial Commission, 491 N.E. 2d 27 (Ill. App. 1986).
77. Pineda v. Oliver B. Cannon & Sons, Inc., 93 A. 2d 902 (Pa. Super. 1953).
78. P. B. Bell & Associates v. Industrial Commission, 690 P. 2d 802 (Ariz. Ct. App. 1984).
79. Larson, § 17.00.
80. Winn-Dixie Stores v. Smallwood, 516 So. 2d 716 (Ala. App. 1987).
81. Lundgaard v. State Department of Public Safety, 237 N.W. 2d 617 (Minn. 1975).
82. Green v. Workers Compensation Appeal Board, 232 Cal. Rptr. 465 (Cal. App. 1986).
83. O'Reilly v. Roberto Homes, Inc., 107 A. 2d 9 (N.J. Super. 1954).
84. Nemchick v. Thatcher Glass Manufacturing Co., 495 A. 2d 1372 (N.J. App. Div. 1985).
85. Burton v. Broadcast Music Inc., 250 N.E. 2d 243 (N.Y. 1968).
86. Voight v. Rettinger Transportation Inc., 306 N.W. 2d 133 (Minn. 1981).
87. Martin v. Bonclarken Assembly, 251 S.E. 2d 403 (N.C. 1979).

CHAPTER 4

Workers Compensation Benefits

The accurate and timely payment of benefits is vital in workers compensation claims. Disabled workers depend on a compensation benefit to replace income during periods of disability and may also depend on other compensation benefits due them. Therefore, the claim representative must know the benefits prescribed by the applicable statute, when the benefits are due, for how long the benefits are due, and exactly how much to pay.

The prompt payment of benefits sets the stage for a harmonious relationship between the injured employee and the claims representative. The accurate computation of benefits avoids underpayment or overpayment. Underpayment causes anxiety and anger for the recipient and may cause legal problems for the insurer. Penalties may be levied for unjustifiable delay in paying benefits. Late or inaccurate payments may prompt litigation if the employee feels aggrieved and retains counsel. On the other hand, if all payments have been made and there is no additional sum due on which to take a credit, overpayments are generally not recoverable by the insurer. In any case, an explanation to the employee of the benefit computation helps to avoid a misunderstanding.

Workers compensation statutes provide for several categories of benefits. They include payments for disability during the period the worker is medically unable to work and compensation for degrees of permanent residual disability or loss of earning capacity. Medical care is furnished, usually without limit, so long as it is reasonable, necessary, and related to the injury. Rehabilitation services assist injured workers in re-entering the labor force by helping limit the effects of disability. When a worker dies from a compensable injury or illness, certain benefits are paid to survivors.

The scope of workers compensation benefits has broadened, and the level has increased since the 1970s as state legislatures have endeavored to accommodate federal guidelines. Organized labor and members of the bar who represent claimants have been increasingly active in seeking broader and higher benefits. There has been a surge in the use of the workers compensation system as people become more aware of its availability through advertising by the legal community and publications distributed by state administrative agencies. On the downside, the costs to employers for workers compensation have risen to the point where legislatures are concerned about employers losing their businesses and the inability to attract new employers. Legislative decisions regarding the scope and cost of workers compensation will undoubtedly determine the direction of the system.

Among the reasons for cost increases are wage increases, which cause maximum and minimum caps to climb each year. The increased cost of medical benefits has far exceeded general inflation as more and more medical specialties develop and diagnostic testing becomes increasingly sophisticated. Rehabilitation efforts have grown from a rarity fifteen years ago to a service as common as an x-ray today. The various causes of cost increases in the workers compensation system are explored more completely in Chapter 6.

The purpose of this chapter is to identify and describe workers compensation benefits in general. Because benefits vary from jurisdiction to jurisdiction, the claims person is advised to consult the applicable law for precise provisions.

INDEMNITY PAYMENTS— TEMPORARY DISABILITY

In the vast majority of cases involving any lost time from work, the injured employee is away for a limited period of time and then returns to work. This is called *temporary total disability*. In some cases, the employee is able to work to only a limited extent, but eventually returns to full duties and hours. This condition is called *temporary partial disability*. This section discusses the indemnity payments for both kinds of temporary disability.

Temporary Total Disability Compensation

Compensation for temporary total disability is known as TTD. It is an income replacement benefit payable to a disabled worker during the time he or she is temporarily totally disabled because of a compensable injury or illness. It provides income in place of the disabled worker's regular paycheck. The TTD rate, commonly paid weekly, is based on a percentage of the worker's gross average weekly wage—the AWW. The percentage is typically 66²/₃ percent. A claim representative should refer to the U. S. Chamber of Commerce Analysis of Workers Compensation Laws or the applicable statute for the exact rate to use in a particular jurisdiction. The TTD compensation rate is subject to a maximum and usually to a minimum. In certain jurisdictions the TTD rate is increased by an additional amount for dependents. For example, Massachusetts allows an additional $6 weekly per dependent for workers whose compensation rate is $150 or lower, not to exceed the state maximum.

Maximums and Minimums. The maximum TTD compensation rate is normally computed as a percentage of the state average weekly wage—from 66²/₃ percent in Delaware in 1990 to 200 percent in Alaska for the same year. The state average weekly wage (SAWW) is determined by dividing total wages reported by employers by the average number of employees reported on a yearly basis. This yields an average annual wage for employees. This figure is divided by 52 to compute the state average weekly wage.

Minimum TTD rates vary widely, from $20 in Florida to $139.67 in Pennsylvania in 1990. If the employee's average weekly wage is below the minimum, the base for the compensation rate changes from the SAWW to actual wages. These bases can also vary. In some states the compensation rate is the employee's actual wage if that wage is lower than the minimum. In other states, 80 or 90 percent of actual earnings is used, and in yet others, spendable earnings is the basis. Because of these variations, the applicable law should be consulted. The caps also increase yearly as the state average weekly wage changes.

Average Weekly Wage. The average weekly wage (AWW) is the basis for computing the TTD rate and is, therefore, a significant figure. The AWW is calculated by averaging the worker's actual wages, including overtime, for a prescribed number of pre-injury weeks. Statutes are not uniform in the number of weeks required. In addition, because tips, overtime, meals, lodging, car or fuel allowance, and other benefits may need to be included in the wages, arriving at a proper AWW is sometimes difficult. Disagreements over the correct figure may have to be resolved by the applicable administrative body.

In certain jurisdictions (the District of Columbia, for example) wages from more than one job may be stacked to determine the AWW. Therefore, if the injured worker is employed full time as an accountant and part time as a salesperson, wages from both jobs would be totaled to determine the average weekly wage. In other states only wages from similar employment may be stacked. For example, in Virginia a worker employed as a full-time police officer and as a security person on weekends may include earnings from both jobs for consideration of his AWW. Certain jurisdictions consider wages solely from the job the worker was performing when injured.

In some jurisdictions spendable earnings may be used as a basis for the average weekly wage. For example, in the District of Columbia the compensation rate is based on 80 percent of spendable earnings (gross wages net of taxes) or 66²/₃ percent of gross wages, whichever is less.

The wage history is typically provided by the injured worker's employer on a published form that simplifies computation. (See Exhibit 4-1.) The worker's wage history may not extend to the prescribed number of weeks. Statutes outline alternate methods for determining the average weekly wage in such cases; for example, wages of a "similar worker" may be used. This may be accomplished by averaging wage history from three to five workers in the same employment capacity with the same hourly rate. Many jurisdictions will accept whatever wage history is available. The object is to arrive at a fair reflection of the disabled worker's pre-injury earnings.

Illustrations of Computations of Average Weekly Wage. Glenda is employed as a file clerk. She is salaried at $13,000 per year. Her weekly wage remains constant at $250 ($13,000 divided by 52 weeks).

George is a worker earning $6.50 per hour. He does not always work a full week. George is employed in a state where the average weekly wage is based on a thirteen-week pre-injury history. Over the past 13 weeks, George's total gross income was $2,782; his AWW is $214 ($2,782 divided by 13 weeks).

Jane is a waitress; she earns $3.09 per hour plus tips. Jane is employed in a jurisdiction prescribing a 52-week history as the basis for the average weekly wage. Her gross earnings for 52 weeks total $6,000; she is able to verify tips received for the same period in the amount of $8,500; she also receives a meal valued at $2.50 each workday totaling $650 for the 52-week period. Jane's average weekly wage is $291.35 ($6,000 wages + $8,500 tips + $650 meals = $15,150 ÷ 52 = $291.35).

Bill is a maintenance worker for an apartment management company. He receives an apartment in addition to his weekly salary of $400. The apartment is valued at $300 per month, or $75 per week. While Bill is disabled, he must pay rent for his apartment. In this instance, the value of the apartment is added to the gross income to arrive at Bill's average weekly wage: $400 + $75 = $475.

Earl is a construction superintendent. His weekly salary is $500. He also receives a car allowance of $125 per week that may be added to his salary to yield an average weekly wage of $625.

Waiting Period and Duration of the TTD Benefit. A worker is not eligible for TTD until after a statutory waiting period. This means the disabled worker must "wait" a prescribed number of days before the temporary total compensation disability benefit begins. The waiting

Exhibit 4-1
Wage History

STATE OF MARYLAND

Employer: _____

Please complete the weekly earnings schedule below for the employee you are reporting injured. Provide the weekly earnings for each of the 13 weeks, or all if less than 13 weeks, immediately preceding the date of accident.

Injured employee name			Social Security number	

Week No.	Week Ending Month Day Year	Days Worked	GROSS Amount Paid Including All Overtime
1			
2			
3			
4			
5			
6			
7			
8			
9			
10			
11			
12			
13			

Was this employee given free rent, lodging, board, tips or other allowances in addition to the above earnings? If yes, state weekly value thereof.
$ _____

Signed _____

period, depending upon the jurisdiction, ranges from three to seven days. If a worker returns to work before the end of the waiting period, no temporary disability benefits whatsoever are payable. If the employee is disabled beyond a certain period (the *retroactive period*), benefits become payable from the date of disability. TTD benefits for the previously uncompensated waiting period therefore become payable. The waiting period does not apply to medical benefits.

Compensation benefits are based on calendar days, rather than work days; that is, they are based on a seven-day week. Therefore, a worker who is disabled on days he normally does not work receives benefits for those days, but his compensation for each day is one-seventh of his weekly benefit. The reason for using calendar days is that this method equitably accommodates various work schedules and days of disability.

Temporary total compensation benefits continue until the worker is able to return to work. A few jurisdictions impose a time or dollar limit on temporary total disability payments. Virginia, for example, limits total disability benefits to 500 weeks; Florida, to 350 weeks; and Kansas, to $100,000.

Illustrations of Waiting Periods. Joe is injured on June 2; he is able to return to work on June 10. Joe works in a state imposing a three-day waiting period. He was paid for the day of injury, June 2. Joe must "wait" June 3, 4, and 5 before he is entitled to temporary total compensation. He receives benefits for June 6, 7, 8, and 9—four days, or $4/7$ of a week. TTD benefits are calculated on a seven-day week.

Suppose Joe, in the example above, did not return to work until June 29. The retroactive period in Joe's state is fourteen days. Joe is out twenty-six days, June 3 through June 28. Since he is disabled more than fourteen days, the waiting period does not apply, and Joe receives compensation from his first day of disability.

Eleanor is employed in a jurisdiction with a seven-day waiting period and a twenty-one-day retroactive period. Eleanor is injured on March 4. She returned to work on March 8. Eleanor receives no TTD benefits because her disability did not extend beyond the waiting period.

Ann is employed in the same state as Eleanor. Ann is injured on March 4 and is paid for that day. She is unable to return to work until March 15. She is eligible for TTD from March 12 through March 14 (for three days) since she must "wait" seven days (March 5 through March 11) for benefits to begin. If Ann had not been able to return to work until March 30, her disability would have extended past the twenty-one-day retroactive period and she would have received compensation from the first day of disability, March 5.

Tom is injured in a jurisdiction with a three-day waiting period and a fourteen-day retroactive period. His accident happens at 8:05 A.M. on April 1; he is not paid for the day of accident. Tom returns to work on April 9; his waiting days are April 1, 2, and 3; Tom receives TTD for April 4, 5, 6, 7, and 8—five days or $5/7$ of a week. Had he not returned to work until April 17, the waiting period would not have applied, and he would have received benefits from April 1 through April 16, sixteen days or $2^2/7$ weeks.

Computing the TTD Benefit—Case Studies. The following hypothetical cases illustrate the various factors affecting TTD.

Donald Jones. Donald is thirty-seven years old and has been employed as a painter by Acme Decorating for five years. Donald earns $12 per hour and works a forty-hour week with occasional overtime. On August 12 at 3:00 P.M. as Donald was descending a ladder on the job site, his left foot slipped off the bottom rung and he felt immediate pain in his left knee. By quitting time, the knee was swollen and he had trouble walking. Donald reported the injury to his foreman, who suggested that he visit a nearby medical center for care. The medical center doctor diagnosed the injury as a strain and told Donald he did not want him to work until reexamined in five days. On the second visit five days later, the doctor felt there was improvement but not enough to allow Donald to use ladders. The disability continued for another five days. When seen by the doctor for the last time on August 22, Donald was released for full duty on August 23. The following facts apply in calculating Donald's TTD benefit:

1. The AWW is $500 based on a 13-week pre-injury history (some overtime was worked).
2. The TTD compensation rate is $66^2/3$ percent of the AWW.
3. The maximum is $473.
4. The waiting period is 3 days, retroactive after 14 days.

Below is the calculation of the TTD benefit.

AWW = $500 x $66^2/3$% = $333.33 (TTD rate—state maximum is not applicable)

Disability period = August 13 through 22 = 10 days, minus the 3-day waiting period = TTD due from August 16 through 22 = 1 week = $333.33

Amy Brown. Amy is a secretary for Apple Construction. She struck her right knee on an open desk drawer on February 5 at noon. Her knee became swollen and stiff and by 4:00 P.M. she had difficulty walking. Amy saw her family doctor that evening. The doctor advised her to stay completely off her feet for a week and to return to his office for a release-to-work determination at that time. When Amy saw her doctor on February 12, the swelling was down, and she was released for work the next day, February 13. To compute Amy's TTD benefit, consider the following:

1. Amy is salaried at $350 per week; therefore, her AWW is $350.
2. The TTD compensation rate is 66²/3 percent of the AWW.
3. The maximum is $367.
4. The waiting period is 3 days, retroactive after 14 days.

Below is the calculation of TTD benefit.

AWW = $350 x 66²/3% = $233.33 (TTD rate—state maximum is not applicable)

Disability period = February 6 through February 12 = 7 days, minus the 3-day waiting period = TTD due from February 9 through February 12 = 4 days = 4/7 week x $233.33 = $133.33

Andrew Smith. Andrew Smith, a thirty-one-year-old electrician for Atlas Builders, was employed for six months, earning $16.50 per hour and working a forty-hour week at the time of his injury. On July 10 at 4:00 P.M., Andrew attempted to move a 150-pound spool of cable, slipped in mud, and twisted his back. He experienced pain and reported the injury to his boss, who instructed Andrew to see the company doctor at once. The doctor saw Andrew on July 11, diagnosed a back strain, advised him to stay out of work, and sent him to physical therapy for three weeks. At the end of three weeks, on July 31, Andrew returned to the doctor, reporting that he was better but still had pain on bending. The doctor prescribed three more weeks of therapy and sent Andrew back to work full duty on August 21. The following facts apply in calculating Andrew's TTD benefit:

1. Andrew's AWW is $710 based on the available work history (overtime was earned).
2. The TTD compensation rate is 66²/3 percent of the AWW.
3. The maximum is $344.
4. The waiting period is 7 days, retroactive after 21 days.

The calculation of TTD benefit is shown below.

AWW = $710 x 66²/3% = $473.33. This is over the maximum, so the TTD rate is the maximum, $344.

Disability period = July 11 through August 20 = 41 days

The waiting period does not apply since Andrew was disabled more than 21 days—TTD due July 11 through August 20 = 5⁶/7 weeks at $344 = $2,014.86

Temporary Partial Disability Compensation

Temporary partial disability compensation is known as TPD. It is a "bridge-the-gap" benefit compensating a disabled worker for the wage differential occurring when the employee returns to light work or lesser hours resulting in a post-injury wage that is less than the pre-injury wage.

A doctor will often not release a patient for full duty until he or she can be certain that the patient has recovered 100 percent, but the doctor will permit a return to part-time or light-duty employment. For an employee who sustains a hand injury, a doctor may approve one-handed work. For an employee with a back strain, a doctor may permit a return to work with restricted lifting for half days until the patient resumes full duty.

Employers increasingly provide light duty for injured workers whenever possible. They have discovered that it is good business to accommodate a return to less than full duty in order to keep the employee from falling into a "disability rut," to encourage job interest, and to boost morale.

The TPD compensation rate is a percentage of wage loss, that is, a percentage of the difference between the worker's pre-injury AWW and earnings upon return to work. The percentage varies: Maryland pays 50 percent of the difference; the District of Columbia's rate is $66^{2}/_{3}$ percent. The applicable statute must be checked for the proper percentage.

Maximums and Minimums. These constraints apply to temporary partial disability compensation as they do to temporary total compensation, having the same upper and lower boundaries.

Waiting Period and Duration of Benefits. Like TTD compensation, TPD benefits are payable for the duration of temporary partial disability after a waiting period. These benefits contemplate a return to regular duty when full healing occurs.

Computing the TPD Benefit—Case Studies. The following hypothetical cases illustrate the various factors affecting TPD.

Walter Black. Walter Black suffered a left knee strain on August 12 and could not return to regular work until August 23. Suppose Walter's boss asked him to return to work answering the phone (a sit-down job) until he could resume full duty, and suppose Walter's doctor approved this adjusted work effective August 16. In calculating Walter's TPD benefit, the following apply:

1. The AWW is $500.
2. The sit-down job pays $6 per hour, or $240 a week.
3. The waiting period is 3 days.
4. The TPD compensation rate is 66²/₃ percent of the wage loss.

The TPD benefit is calculated below.

AWW = $500 − $240 (adjusted work earnings) = $260 (wage loss)
x 66²/₃% = $173.33 (TPD rate)

Total disability period—August 13, 14, 15—represents waiting period (no benefits payable) —TPD disability period—August 16 through August 22 = 1 week payable at $173.33 per week = $173.33

Joyce Harris. Joyce Harris is a twenty-five-year-old hostess employed by the Blue Star Restaurant, earning $10 per hour for a forty-hour week. Joyce slipped on a wet floor on November 15, twisting her right ankle. Joyce's doctor, whom she consulted the same day, diagnosed the injury as a sprain, wrapped the ankle, and instructed Joyce to use crutches and avoid putting her full weight on the ankle until her return office visit in two weeks. When Joyce's manager was informed of her disability, he asked her to return to work as a cashier (a sitting job) during the dinner hour (four hours per day) until she could resume full duty. Joyce's doctor approved this arrangement. She was released for regular hostess work on November 29. In calculating Joyce's TPD benefit, the following apply:

1. Joyce's AWW is for $400 per week, based on a 13-week pre-injury wage history.
2. The cashier position pays $10 per hour at 20 hours, or $200 per week.
3. The waiting period is 3 days.
4. The TPD compensation rate is 50 percent of wage loss.

Below is the calculation of the TPD benefit.

AWW = $400 − $200 (adjusted work earnings) = $200 (wage loss)
x 50% = $100 (TPD rate)

Disability period = November 15 through November 28 = 2 weeks minus the 3-day waiting period = TPD due from November 18 through November 28 = 1⁴/₇ weeks x $100 = $157.14

Computing a Mixed Benefit—TTD and TPD—Case Study. Monroe Office Repair employs Greg Miller as a serviceman. Greg is thirty years old, has been with Monroe for four years, and earns $15 per hour for a forty-hour week. On March 5, while attempting to move a copier that was positioned on an uneven floor, Greg strained his back. He could not continue working, called his office to report the injury, and visited the nearest hospital emergency room. The emergency room doctor felt that Greg had a low back strain, advised no work, and referred him to an orthopedist. Upon receiving this information from Greg, the Monroe manager asked Greg if the doctor would permit light-duty shop work until he could return to full duty. The shop work pays $10 an hour. Greg saw the orthopedist on March 12; the doctor approved light duty beginning on March 24, cautioned Greg against heavy lifting, and scheduled a return visit for April 12. Greg was released for full duty effective April 13. The following facts apply to calculating Greg's compensation benefit:

1. The AWW is $600 based on a 13-week pre-injury wage history.
2. The light duty wage is $400 ($10 x 40 hours).
3. The TTD compensation rate is 66²/₃ percent of the AWW.
4. The TPD compensation rate is 66²/₃ percent of the wage loss.
5. The maximum is $420.
6. The waiting period is 3 days, retroactive after 14 days.

Below is the calculation of the mixed compensation benefit TTD due:

AWW = $600 x 66²/₃% = $400 (TTD rate) (maximum does not apply)

TTD disability period–March 6 through March 23–18 days = 2⁴/₇ weeks (waiting period does not apply since disability extended beyond 14 days) x $400 = $1,028.57

TPD due:

Wage loss = $600 (AWW) – $400 (adjusted work wage) = $200 per week x 66²/₃% = $133.33 (TPD rate)

TPD disability period–March 24 through April 12–20 days =2⁶/₇ weeks x $133.33 = $380.94

Total benefit = TTD $1,028.57 + TPD $380.94 = $1,409.51

INDEMNITY PAYMENTS— PERMANENT DISABILITY

Although cases of permanent disability are a small minority of all disability cases, they account for a tremendous number of dollars. Permanent disability can be total, in which case no work of any kind can be performed, or partial, in which case the worker is unable to perform certain tasks or jobs. This section discusses indemnity payments for both kinds of permanent disability.

Permanent Total Disability Compensation

Permanent total disability is known as PTD and is paid for a permanent disability. A disabled worker becomes eligible for PTD benefits when he or she is unable to return to gainful employment because of a work-related injury or disease. Some statutes narrow the disability criterion to *suitable* gainful employment. This type of rule contemplates a return to employment comparable with employment at the time of injury. For example, a disabled journeyman plumber who earned $20 per hour at injury may, under some statutes, be found to be permanently disabled if the only job available to him is a security position paying $3.50 per hour. A worker will often request permanent total disability status after rehabilitation efforts have been fruitless.

The permanent total disability compensation rate is computed in accordance with the applicable statute; it is usually paid at the same percentage of the average weekly wage as the temporary total compensation benefit. Maximums and minimums apply. The upper and lower limits are typically the same as for TTD with a few exceptions. Some states, as in TTD, provide for an additional amount for certain dependents.

Presumption. Certain injuries are so serious that permanent total disability is statutorily presumed; that is, the law states that a worker is permanently totally disabled if his or her injury falls within a described category. Examples of permanent total disability include loss of vision in both eyes; loss, or loss of use of, both legs or both arms; and mental incapacity. Certain statutes permit rebuttal of the presumption if employment is found, but others do not even though a worker presumed to be permanently totally disabled actually returns to some type of employment.

Duration. Permanent total disability benefits continue as long as the disability continues, usually for life, unless there is a change in condition that would permit the individual to resume employment. Some states limit PTD benefits to a specified number of weeks or to a dollar amount. For example, PTD in Virginia is limited to 500 weeks with exceptions for loss of both eyes, both arms, both legs, or imbecility. Texas limits PTD to 401 weeks with exceptions similar to Virginia. The Maryland PTD dollar cap is $45,000.

In many jurisdictions there is an offset for social security benefits, and in others, social security payments are reduced by workers compensation. Social security disability benefits are based on earnings over a working career. To qualify, the worker must have a specified number of social security credits. Under the social security and workers compensation systems, vocational rehabilitation services may be offered, and all disability cases are reviewed from time to time to ensure that the disability is continuing.

Escalation. Many jurisdictions provide for an annual cost of living increase for permanent total disability. In a few states, this provision also applies to temporary total disability. The percentage of increase is determined and promulgated by the state administrative body on a prescribed anniversary date and may be based on the original PTD rate each year, or it may be compounded. Compounding is more favorable to recipients since it requires a given percentage increase to be applied to the most recent level of benefits, not to the level of benefits in effect when the injury was first suffered, possibly many years earlier. Escalation may not apply in some instances when a combination of benefits reaches a certain level of the pre-injury wage. For example, no cost of living increase is available to a Virginia worker if the combined permanent total and social security disability benefit equal 80 percent of the pre-injury wage.

States providing for escalation of benefits typically impose the maximum in effect at the time of escalation each year. In other words, the PTD recipient is not restricted to the maximum in force at the time of the injury.

Computing the PTD Benefit—Case Studies. The following hypothetical cases illustrate the various factors affecting PTD.

Amos Taylor. Amos, a construction worker, sustained injury to both eyes when cement splashed on his face on the job site five years ago. After unsuccessful surgery on both eyes, Amos lost total vision and was awarded permanent total disability three years ago. The following facts apply to a computation of Amos' PTD benefit:

1. Amos' AWW is $360.
2. The PTD compensation rate is $66^2/3\%$ of the AWW.
3. The maximum is $400.
4. There is a cost of living percentage of increase that is not compounded.

The PTD benefit is calculated below.

AWW = $360 x $66^2/3\%$ = $240 = PTD benefit for the first year of disability

Second-year PTD rate, presuming a 3% cost of living increase = $240 x 3% = $7.20 + $240 = $247.20—second year PTD benefit

Third-year PTD rate, presuming a 2.5% cost of living increase = $240 x 2.5% = $6 + $7.20 (first year's increase) + $240 = $253.20

Each year's increase is based on $240 and is added to the previous years' increases.

Robert Akins. Robert Akins was a computer salesman involved in an automobile accident on his way to call on a customer four years ago. He sustained a spinal cord injury resulting in paralysis below the waist. Robert was declared permanently totally disabled three years ago. The following apply to computing Robert's PTD benefit:

1. Robert's AWW is $600.
2. The PTD compensation rate is $66^{2}/_{3}$ percent of the AWW.
3. The maximum at time of injury is $500.
4. The cost of living increase is compounded.

The PTD benefit is calculated below.

AWW = $600 x $66^{2}/_{3}$% = $400 = PTD benefit first year

Second-year PTD rate—cost of living adjustment is 1.5% = $400 x 1.5% = $6 + $400 = $406—second year PTD benefit

Third-year PTD rate—cost of living increase is 2% = $406 (last year's benefit) x 2% = $8.12 + $406 = $414.12

Fourth-year PTD rate—cost of living increase is 1.5% = $414.12 x 1.5% = $6.21 + $414.12 = $420.33

Each year's increase is based on the prior year's benefit.

Hubert Tallman. Hubert Tallman was employed as an electrician for Orange Electric for forty years prior to his injury. Two years ago he received an electric shock causing injury to both arms that prevented his return to work as an electrician. Hubert was sixty years old at the time of his injury. He underwent a program of vocational rehabilitation, but no employment could be found because of his lack of alternative work experience and his age. The administrative body in Hubert's state awarded permanent total disability. The following facts apply in the calculation of Hubert's PTD rate:

1. Hubert's AWW is $800.
2. The PTD rate is $66^{2}/_{3}$ percent of the AWW.
3. The maximum is $450.
4. There is no provision for escalation.

The PTD benefit is calculated below.

AWW = $800 x $66^{2}/_{3}$% = $533.33 (over maximum)

Maximum is $450 = Hubert's PTD rate during permanent disability

Permanent Partial Disability Compensation

Compensation for permanent partial disability is known as PPD. This benefit covers disability that is permanent in nature but partial in degree. It is designed to compensate injured workers for diminished earnings and/or residual disability to the injured part of the body. Permanent partial disability to certain scheduled members is based on loss or loss of use of certain injured body parts. In theory, PPD indemnifies for a possible decrease in future earnings because of a disability. Compensation for loss of earning capacity is based on the decrease in post-injury income attributable to the work injury.

The degree of permanent partial disability is not measurable until maximum medical improvement is reached; that is, when it is apparent that there will be no further recovery. Since this point may not be reached until sometime after a return to work, benefits awarded may be payable beginning at various times according to the applicable jurisdiction, e.g., at the end of TTD disability or TPD disability, when PPD disability is measured, or when maximum medical improvement is reached. Therefore, the first payment of PPD benefits often includes an accrued amount or the entire amount due, depending on the amount of the award and the date the award orders benefits to begin. Payments may be ordered by way of an award by the state, or they may be voluntary on the part of the employer/insurer. For example, a PPD benefit award of 36 weeks of benefits is made. Assuming the award was made in December for an injury that occurred the previous January, the entire award would be due and payable.

Statutes vary widely from state to state in specifying the methods of compensation for permanent partial disability. The majority of states compensate permanent partial disability for specified body members according to a schedule. Body members typically "scheduled" include the toe, foot, leg, thumb, finger, hand, arm, and eye. Loss of hearing is compensated under many statutes according to a schedule. For disabilities not scheduled, such as a back injury that prevents a worker from returning to work at his or her pre-injury wage level, compensation may be based on loss of earning capacity. An injured worker cannot usually collect compensation for both disability to a scheduled member and for loss of earnings from the same injury. Statutes also provide compensation subject to a maximum dollar amount for permanent disfigurement, generally at the discretion of an administrative examiner. The examiner bases his or her opinion on the appearance of the disfigurement, its location (exposed or unexposed area), and its effect on the worker's future employment. For instance, a significant facial scar could influence a salesperson's employability and would be worth more than a minor scar on the finger of a construction worker.

If an injured worker dies from a cause not related to the injury, any award outstanding at time of death may be payable to eligible dependents or to a personal representative. This kind of claim arises when payments for a permanent partial disability award for a scheduled member have not been completed at the time of the worker's death.

Benefits for Scheduled Injuries. A *schedule* is a list of specific body members with an accompanying number of weeks that total loss or total loss of use of the specific member is worth under the law of any given jurisdiction. The number of weeks the body member is worth varies from state to state; it is therefore necessary to consult the statutes of a given jurisdiction for the precise number of weeks.

Shoulders and hips sometimes present a problem. The shoulder may be considered part of an "arm" or a nonscheduled area of the body; the hip may be considered part of a "leg" or a nonscheduled injury. Determining exactly where the disability lies, which body part the doctor rates, and/or the dictates of the statute help to resolve such questions. The permanent, partial disability schedule for the District of Columbia is shown in Exhibit 4-2.

In some jurisdictions, temporary total compensation benefits paid are deducted from the scheduled injury allowance. In other states a specified "healing period" is allowed in addition to the schedule, and any TTD paid in excess of that period is deducted from the scheduled benefits. The majority of jurisdictions allow compensation for scheduled benefits in addition to temporary total disability compensation without set-off.

Computing Scheduled PPD Benefits—Case Studies. The following hypothetical cases illustrate the factors affecting scheduled PPD.

Mollie Burns. Mollie Burns is a forty-five-year-old salesperson for Famous Department Store. On December 12 she slipped on a wet tile floor and fell with her left foot in a twisted position, sustaining a fracture of the left ankle. She received TTD compensation until her return to work on February 28. Mollie's doctor felt she had reached maximum medical improvement on June 30. He rated her residual disability at 25 percent of the ankle because of loss of motion and remaining stiffness. In Mollie's state, as in most, disability to the ankle is rated as disability to the foot. Therefore, Mollie's permanent partial disability award is for 25 percent of the foot in agreement with her doctor's opinion. The following facts apply in calculating PPD benefit:

1. Mollie's AWW is $240.
2. PPD benefits begin at the end of TTD compensation payment.

Exhibit 4-2
District of Columbia Scheduled Benefits

In case of disability partial in character but permanent in quality, the compensation shall be 66²/₃ percent of the employee's average weekly wages which shall be in addition to compensation for temporary total disability or temporary partial disability and shall be paid to the employee as follows:

(A)   Arm lost, 312 weeks' compensation;

(B)   Leg lost, 288 weeks' compensation;

(C)   Hand lost, 244 weeks' compensation;

(D)   Foot lost, 205 weeks' compensation;

(E)   Eye lost, 160 weeks' compensation;

(F)   Thumb lost, 75 weeks' compensation;

(G)   First finger lost, 46 weeks' compensation;

(H)   Great toe lost, 38 weeks' compensation;

(I)   Second finger lost, 30 weeks' compensation;

(J)   Third finger lost, 25 weeks' compensation;

(K)   Toe other than great toe lost, 16 weeks' compensation;

(L)   Fourth finger lost, 15 weeks' compensation;

(M)   Compensation for loss of hearing in 1 ear, 52 weeks' compensation.

Compensation for loss of hearing in both ears, 200 weeks provided that the Mayor may establish a waiting period, not to exceed six months, during which an employee may not file a claim for loss of hearing resulting from nontraumatic causes in his occupational environment until the employee has been away from such environment for such period, and provided further, that nothing in this sub-paragraph shall limit an employee's right to file a claim for temporary partial disability pursuant to subsection (c) of this section;

(N)   Compensation for loss of more than 1 phalange of a digit shall be the same as for loss of the entire digit. Compensation for loss of the first phalange shall be one-half of the compensation for loss of the entire digit;

(O)   Compensation for an arm or a leg, if amputated at or above the elbow or the knee, shall be the same as for a loss of the arm or leg; but if amputated between the elbow and the wrist or the knee and the ankle, shall be the same as for loss of a hand or foot;

(P)   Compensation for loss of binocular vision or for 80 percent or more of the vision of an eye shall be the same as for loss of the eye;

(Q)   Compensation for loss of 2 or more digits, or 1 or more phalanges of 2 or more digits, of a hand or foot, may be proportioned to the loss of use of the hand or foot occasioned thereby, but shall not exceed the compensation for loss of a hand or foot;

(R)   Compensation for permanent total loss of use of a member shall be the same as for loss of the member;

(S)   Compensation for permanent partial loss or loss of use of a member may be for proportionate loss or loss of use of the member. Benefits for partial loss of vision in 1 or both eyes, or partial loss of hearing in 1 or both ears shall be for a period proportionate to the period benefits are payable for total bilateral loss of vision or total binaural loss of hearing as such partial loss bears to total loss;

(T)   The Mayor shall award proper and equitable compensation for serious disfigurement of the face, head, neck or other normally exposed bodily areas not to exceed $3,500.

---

3.   The PPD rate is 66²/₃ percent of the AWW.
4.   The maximum is $300.
5.   The foot is equal to 175 weeks.

The PPD benefit is calculated below.

Foot = 175 weeks x 25% = 43.75 weeks
Rate = $240 x 66²/₃% = $160
Benefit = 43.75 weeks x $160 = $7,000, payable at $160 per week
   beginning March 1

Julia Redd.   Julia is employed as an assembly-line worker for Bruno Industries, a tool manufacturer. She injured her right index finger on June 12 in an attempt to cut a piece of metal. Julia's injury was diagnosed as a laceration of a tendon. The tendon was repaired, and the finger was splinted. She was unable to work until August 1 and received TTD compensation through July 31. Julia continued to experience some soreness and restricted motion of the injured finger. Disability ratings were given by the treating doctor, Dr. Long, and by the employer's doctor, Dr. Petrie. Dr. Long rated the disability at 50 percent of the index finger, and Dr. Petrie felt Julia had sustained 40 percent permanent partial disability to the injured finger. The administrative officer in Julia's state split the ratings and awarded her 45 percent permanent partial disability of the index finger. Consider the following in computing Julia's PPD benefit:

1.   Julia's AWW is $140.
2.   PPD benefits begin at the end of TTD.
3.   The state AWW is $327.
4.   The PPD rate is ¹/₃ of the state AWW or $109.
5.   The index finger is scheduled at 40 weeks.

The PPD benefit calculation is shown below.

Index finger = 40 weeks x 45% = 18 weeks
Rate = $109

Benefit = 18 weeks x $109 = $1,962, payable at $109 per week beginning August 1

Frederick Matthews. Frederick Matthews is a mechanic for Best Auto Body. On May 15 he tripped over a piece of equipment in his bay, twisting his left leg. The knee became swollen and painful. Frederick's doctor treated him conservatively with rest and medication for four weeks, but because of persistent pain, a diagnostic arthroscopy was performed. A torn meniscus was found and repaired. Frederick was released for work on August 1.

Frederick's doctor instructed him in post-surgical care to rehabilitate the knee. He was discharged from treatment on November 15 with some remaining restriction of movement and discomfort that his doctor felt was equal to 10 percent permanent partial disability. The following facts apply in figuring Frederick's PPD benefit:

1. Frederick's AWW is $660.
2. PPD benefits begin on the day of rating.
3. The PPD rate is $66 \frac{2}{3}\%$ of the AWW.
4. The maximum is $490.
5. The leg is worth 300 weeks.

The PPD benefit would be computed in the following way:

Leg = 300 weeks x 10% = 30 weeks

Rate = $660 x $66 \frac{2}{3}\%$ = $440

Benefit = 30 weeks x $440 = $13,200, payable at $440 per week beginning November 15

Emily Lee. Emily is a cook for Homewood Nursing Home. On January 5 hot grease splashed from a cooking utensil onto Emily's right forearm, causing a burn. Emily received treatment for the injury, but did not lose any time from work because of it. The burned area healed but left some discoloration. Emily felt she was entitled to compensation for this disfigurement and asked for a hearing before her state workers compensation administrative body. The officer awarded Emily ten weeks' permanent partial disability for the scar. The following applies in computing Emily's PPD benefit:

1. Emily's AWW is $350.
2. The PPD rate is $66 \frac{2}{3}\%$ of the AWW.
3. The maximum is $300.
4. The statutory maximum dollar amount for disfigurement is $3,500.
5. PPD begins at the end of TTD.

The PPD benefit is computed below.

Rate = $350 x $66^2/_3\%$ = $233.33

Benefit = 10 weeks x $233.33 = $2,333.30 payable at $233.33 beginning January 6 (no TTD paid—no time lost)

Benefits for Nonscheduled Injuries. The ultimate determination of the percentage of loss or loss of use rests with the administrative body of the applicable jurisdiction. In arriving at the percentage of disability, consideration is given to several factors, including the opinion of the treating physician, the opinion of the evaluating physician or physicians (if any), the appearance of the injured member, and the injured worker's post-injury occupation and earnings.

Disability percentages are commonly given according to prescribed guidelines, such as the American Medical Association's tables for rating. In rating a disability, the doctor may consider degree of motion, strength, stability, loss (if a full or partial amputation), pain, and other criteria common to the particular injured member. These conclusions, when compared to an uninjured member, provide a basis for rating. For example, using the latest edition of the AMA Guidelines, a patient has a 10 percent impairment of the body as a whole resulting from surgery for a herniated lumbar disc at L5 on the left. With an unoperated herniated lumbar disc at L4 – L5, the patient has an additional disability of 7 percent of the body. Using the appropriate tables, the patient has a 7 percent impairment for loss of flexion and extension of the back and a 2 percent impairment for loss of lateral bending. The patient experiences stiffness, soreness, and loss of endurance; he faces the possibility of additional surgery; he cannot perform his pre-injury job. These factors combine for an additional 20 percent impairment giving this patient a total impairment of 46 percent of the body as a whole.

Rating is not a precise science even with the best of guidelines because it is difficult to base a measurement on an injured worker's description of symptoms, demonstration of movement, and like factors that may be understated or overstated by the worker. It is therefore understandable that the degree of disability often becomes a controversial issue. On the other hand, there is often agreement between the doctor and worker. As mentioned above, the administrative body makes the final decision or approves the agreed percentage.

The PPD rate changes periodically as does the TTD rate. It may be based on a percentage of the employee's average weekly wage or on a percentage of the state average weekly wage. The rate is not constant from jurisdiction to jurisdiction. In certain jurisdictions, the percentage changes with the degree of disability; that is, a higher percentage is granted for a major or serious disability. Disability to certain members may be payable at a different rate from that payable to other members. Maximums also differ from state to state and from maximums for other benefit categories. *Because of these variables, it is important to refer to the statute for the proper number of weeks, applicable percentage, and maximum.*

Benefits for Loss of Earning Capacity. In many jurisdictions, compensation for nonscheduled injuries is based on loss of earning capacity. *Loss of earning capacity* is a reduction in earning ability and, in the workers compensation context, addresses a return to post-injury employment at a lesser wage because of incapacity attributable to the injury. For example, a construction worker earning $15 per hour who cannot return to construction work because of a back injury may find post-injury employment as a security person earning $7.50 per hour and, thus, has a loss in earnings of $7.50 per hour because of his injury.

Basis. Although the concept of loss of earning capacity is similar in all jurisdictions offering this benefit, the basis for the amount differs. The basis for determining loss of earning capacity may be actual economic loss or medically determined degree of residual impairment. *Actual economic loss* is the difference between pre-injury and post-injury earnings. *Medically determined residual impairment* refers to disability of the body as a whole. Thus, if the degree of disability is 20%, the basis for loss of earning capacity is 20 percent of the worker's pre-injury AWW. In certain cases, this type of benefit may be payable in addition to an award for disability to a scheduled member.

Although it may be theoretically reasonable to provide benefits based on a percentage of earnings lost because of a compensable injury or illness, this rationale can in practice be problematic. In the attempt to establish an agreeable post-injury earning figure or degree of loss, problems are created by differences in medical opinion concerning work restrictions (for example, lifting limits), and this influences the kind of employment the impaired worker can assume post-injury and, therefore, his or her earnings. There may be controversy over placement efforts—personality conflicts with the counselor, arguments over the kinds of jobs found, and the necessity for retraining. The job market at time of post-injury placement is another factor that can affect the loss.

Duration. Loss of earnings benefits are normally payable until there is a change in actual earnings or earning ability.

Computing Loss of Earning Capacity Benefits—Case Studies. The following hypothetical cases illustrate loss of earnings claims.

Kent Green. Kent Green earned $18 per hour as a carpenter for Star Homes. Kent's state provides loss of earning benefits for nonscheduled injuries. Kent injured his back lifting a scaffold on August 12. The diagnosis was a herniated disc requiring surgery. Because the carpentry job was physically demanding, Kent's doctor felt he could not return to that employment after his back surgery. A rehabilitation counselor working with Kent found him a job, approved by his doctor, delivering building supplies. This was a driving job that required no lifting or repetitive bending. The post-injury job pays $10 per hour. He started the new job June 15 of the next year. In computing Kent's loss of earnings benefits, these conditions apply:

1. Pre-injury AWW is $720.
2. Post-injury AWW is $400.
3. The loss of earnings benefit is 66²/₃% of the difference.
4. The maximum is $327.

The LOE (loss of earnings) benefit is calculated below.

$720 pre-injury AWW − $400 post-injury AWW = $320 x 66²/₃% = $213.33 = weekly benefit beginning June 15

Jean Moore. Jean Moore earns $350 per week as a salaried housekeeping supervisor for Sunshine Motel. She injured her neck when she slipped and fell on a wet floor on May 10. She underwent a period of physical therapy to heal her neck, although there was no significant improvement. Her doctor felt she could not return to her pre-injury job because of its physical demands. Sunshine Motel offered Jean a job as a front desk clerk paying $250 per week. The position was approved by Jean's doctor, and she started on August 20. The following are facts to consider in Jean's case:

1. The pre-injury AWW is $350.
2. The post-injury AWW is $250.
3. The LOE rate is 66²/₃% of the difference.
4. The maximum is $315.

The LOE benefit is computed below.

$350 pre-injury AWW − $250 post-injury AWW = $100 x 66²/₃% = $66.67 weekly benefit beginning August 20

OTHER BENEFITS

Indemnity benefits for loss of earnings are the most important benefit of the workers compensation system. However, increases in the other benefits, especially medical benefits, have made them almost as significant in size as indemnity benefits. The most important other benefits are for medical expense, rehabilitation expense, and death.

Medical Benefits

Reasonable and necessary medical care is provided to injured employees under workers compensation laws. This is a valuable coverage that entitles the worker to quality medical care including sophisticated diagnostic testing, referral to the appropriate specialist, state of the art treatment, and surgical procedures. The scope of care is wide and may include the following:

1. Initial doctor or emergency room visit
2. Referral to a specialist
3. Surgery
4. Hospital care
5. Diagnostic testing; e.g., x-rays, CAT scans, myelograms, magnetic resonance imaging, nerve conduction studies
6. Nursing care
7. Medications
8. Physical therapy
9. Occupational therapy
10. Travel expense to and from place of care
11. Prosthetic devices including glasses, contact lenses, hearing aids, dentures, artificial limbs
12. Repair or replacement of prosthetic devices when damaged in a compensable accident

Workers compensation is primary medical coverage that should cover every aspect of the necessary medical care. No other health insurance plan or coverage is usually necessary.

Limitations on Medical Benefits. Although medical coverage is very broad, it is not unlimited. All medical care must meet the following conditions:

1. Related to the injury
2. Reasonable in amount given and amount charged
3. Necessary to cure or relieve the claimant

Determining whether or not these conditions apply to specific cases requires a great deal of knowledge of medicine and medical procedures by the claim representative.

Independent Exams. The employer typically has the right to have the injured worker examined by the physician of its choice if the care appears to be inappropriate or excessive. Requests for such examinations must be made at reasonable intervals and scheduled with physicians whose expertise extends to the type of injury involved. The location of the exam should be within a reasonable travel distance. The injured worker may object to, or fail to appear, for the examination. These issues can be controversial, and may need to be resolved by the administrative body.

Choice of Physician. The right to choose a physician varies from state to state. Most states allow the employee to choose his or her doctor; others permit the choice to be restricted to a list provided by the employer or from a "state list." If the employee frequently changes physicians without referral or without approval by the employer or administrative agency, the employer should request an opinion by a doctor of its choosing.

Duration. The employee becomes eligible for medical care immediately following a compensable injury; there is no waiting period. The worker need not be disabled to receive medical care under workers compensation. As long as the care is causally related to the injury or illness, medical benefits are provided as long as necessary.

Trends. The medical field continues to expand, and the injured worker can benefit from new technologies. Many jurisdictions now recognize practitioners whose cost of care may have been disputed in the past; for example, treatment by prayer or spiritual means alone is recognized in the District of Columbia when there is agreement between employer and employee, and Maryland approves acupuncture treatments.

With the expansion of medical technology and care comes a corresponding increase in costs. In an attempt to contain the cost of medical benefits, many states have adopted a medical fee schedule that establishes guidelines for charges for medical procedures. The medical provider is obligated to accept the allowed amount without recourse to the injured worker for any balance. A procedure for review of charges is commonly provided in "fee schedule" states. Chapter 6 elaborates on trends in medical costs.

Medical Benefits—Case Studies. The following hypothetical cases illustrate medical benefits.

Joan Wilson. Joan works for Printers, Inc. as a secretary. She twisted her knee while getting up from her chair on July 15 at 10:00 A.M. The knee became painful at once and began to swell within an hour.

When Joan reported the incident to her boss at 1:00 P.M., he suggested she visit an industrial clinic in the next block. The doctor took x-rays, read as negative, diagnosed a strain, prescribed medication, and suggested that Joan stay off her feet for three days and return if there was no improvement. Joan's knee remained painful, and she was referred to a specialist who performed diagnostic surgery and repaired a torn ligament. After a recuperative period, Joan was sent to therapy to strengthen her knee.

The medical benefit: All care is covered—the industrial clinic, specialist, surgery, hospital, physical therapy, x-rays, medication, and crutches.

Brian Bean. Brian cut his thumb on a utility knife while working for Printers, Inc. on August 1 at 10:00 A.M. He cleaned the wound, wrapped it in a towel, and was sent to the same industrial clinic Joan visited. The doctor diagnosed a superficial laceration, cleaned and bandaged it, and sent Brian back to work.

The medical benefit: All care is covered—industrial clinic charges.

Eugene Phillips. Eugene Phillips, employed as a salesman for Printers, Inc., was involved in an automobile accident on December 1. He was en route to visit a customer on a snowy day. His car skidded off the highway and struck a pole. Eugene was taken by ambulance to the nearest hospital and was admitted through the emergency room for head and neck injuries. A battery of tests was run. The diagnosis was a cervical dislocation. Eugene was hospitalized for a week and recuperated at home for a month, returning to the hospital outpatient clinic at two week intervals for monitoring. He was given a cervical collar and medication as part of his care.

The medical benefit: Eugene's care is covered in full under the workers compensation law in Eugene's state—ambulance, physician's care, hospitalization, medication, testing, cervical collar, outpatient clinic care.

Scott Ames. Scott is employed as a laborer for Acme Decorating. On August 10 at 11:00 A.M., his left eye became irritated. He was sent to a nearby clinic for care. The doctor removed a dirt particle from the left eye and referred Scott to an ophthalmologist for follow-up. The ophthalmologist performed a refraction and prescribed corrective glasses in addition to examining Scott's left eye for remaining irritation. The doctor acknowledged that the refraction had no relation to the injury.

The medical benefit: Clinic charges for initial care and ophthalmological care for the left eye irritation are covered under workers compensation. Charges for the unrelated refraction and for glasses are not covered.

Rehabilitation Services

Under the workers compensation system, rehabilitation services medically and vocationally assist the disabled worker. Medical rehabilitation includes supervising and coordinating care, counseling, emotional support, and assistance in adjusting the worker's lifestyle to accommodate his or her disability.

Vocational rehabilitation services assist an injured worker's return to the work force. This is an important part of the workers compensation benefit program. Returning to work gives an injured worker self-respect and earning power, and lends purpose and structure to his or her life. Employment provides a positive emotional outlook that often improves an injured worker's physical status. Employers encourage rehabilitation efforts to reduce the cost of paying open-ended TTD benefits.

Rehabilitation services are provided in all states either by order or voluntarily as extended by employers or insurance companies. The cost is borne by employers and insurers in most states. Some jurisdictions have established a fund to cover all or a part of the expense. Rehabilitation efforts are monitored by state administrative agencies.

Injured workers who are disabled from their pre-injury employment are candidates for the rehabilitation process. The worker may need one or more of the following services:

1. Physical rehabilitation—a program of physical and occupational therapy to heal and condition

2. Modification of the pre-injury job to accommodate the disability; for example, providing a stool, raising or lowering the work station, automating a machine, altering a foot pedal or button, furnishing a truck with automatic drive

3. Assistance in applying for and finding a new job compatible with the disability

4. Retraining in a new career

The Rehabilitation Process. The rehabilitation process is conducted by counselors with a medical or a vocational background or both. The counselor may be employed by the state or by a private company. The disabled worker is interviewed for background information including medical status, education, work history, skills, interests, and financial and family situation. Tests may be given to determine academic level and vocational aptitude. The counselor works with the treating physician to establish physical ability. A rehabilitation plan is formed. The worker is schooled in preparing resumes, in job-search techniques, and in interviewing. If it is decided that retraining is a viable option, assistance is given in choosing a career field and in exploring and applying to appropriate educational institutions for necessary training.

The professional help a rehabilitation counselor offers to a disabled worker is valuable and costly. The unjustified failure by the worker to cooperate with this effort will jeopardize the continuation of temporary total disability benefits in most jurisdictions.

Rehabilitation is not always successful. Workers can develop a negative attitude, refuse to cooperate, or cooperate half-heartedly. Sometimes no suitable employment can be found because of a poor job market, lack of marketable skills, age, and extent of disability. The earlier the process is begun, the better the result may be. If a worker is given a positive and structured program early on, it will keep him or her from falling into despair, or from becoming apathetic or comfortable with disability.

Benefits. Benefits may include the cost of the rehabilitation services, TTD compensation during rehabilitation, a specified maintenance allowance (board, lodging, travel if services are given away from home), tuition, and the cost of books and supplies. The law of the applicable jurisdiction must be consulted for the specific benefit provisions.

Duration. The duration of rehabilitation benefits varies from state to state. Many states set a time limit on rehabilitation benefits. Rehabilitation services that are voluntarily provided normally continue until the worker is placed or the effort fails.

Rehabilitation Services—Case Studies. The following hypothetical cases illustrate rehabilitation benefits.

Susan Sims. Susan, twenty-eight years old, was employed as a machine operator for Molded Plastics. She sprained her right ankle when she slipped at work. The sprain was severe. Susan could not return to work for Molded Plastics because she was unable to stand for the required eight hours. The employer had no modified employment available. Susan had some office experience but needed a refresher course in typing to market her clerical skills. During rehabilitation, a counselor helped Susan enroll in a refresher typing course. When Susan completed the course, the counselor helped Susan search for a job. A receptionist position in a law firm was found and approved by Susan's doctor. The rehabilitation benefit included the following:

- TTD compensation continues until the return to work.
- Tuition and books for the typing course are provided.
- Cost of the rehabilitation vendor's service is covered.

William Evans. Bill sustained a back injury working a construction job for Gene Brothers. After the necessary surgery, he could not return to construction work because of lifting and bending restrictions. Bill was forty-four years old at the time of injury and had worked in construction for twenty-six years. The rehabilitation counselor assigned to Bill's case worked with his doctor and employer in placing him in a supervisory capacity using his experience and accommodating his limitations. The rehabilitation benefit included the following:

- TTD compensation is paid during the placement process until return to work.
- The rehabilitation counselor's services are provided.

Thomas Worth. Tom is a thirty-five-year-old house painter who broke his heel when he fell from a ladder on the job site. He was left with residual pain and swelling in the injured foot. Tom's doctor advised against returning to a job involving work using a ladder. The painting company had no other work to offer Tom. A rehabilitation counselor helped Tom find employment as an estimator for another painting firm. The estimating job did not require climbing ladders and was approved by Tom's doctor. Tom was pleased with his new career that paid him more than his painting job and offered him a promising future. The rehabilitation benefit included the following:

- TTD compensation is continued until the return to work.
- Cost of the rehabilitation vendor's service is covered.

Death Benefits

Workers compensation statutes allow benefits for dependent survivors of workers who are killed in a compensable accident or who die from a compensable injury or disease. This is a weekly benefit designed to partially replace the support the deceased worker would have provided to those dependent upon him, had he lived. Certain jurisdictions grant a lump sum in addition to other benefits. Those eligible for death benefits include the surviving spouse and minor children. In many jurisdictions, others who are financially dependent on the deceased worker may be eligible for benefits. The applicable statute should be carefully reviewed in all death cases to determine criteria of eligibility for benefits.

Funeral expenses are covered by statute, subject to a maximum. Many jurisdictions provide for transportation of the body, sometimes subject to a maximum.

Duration. Benefits payable to a surviving spouse typically cease upon remarriage, with a lump sum (for example, two years of benefits) awarded at that time. Some states limit survivorship benefits to a specified number of weeks or dollar amount. Virginia, for example, limits benefits to 500 weeks. Benefits to children terminate at a certain age, usually eighteen, but may continue for an additional period while the child is enrolled in an approved school. Again, the law must be consulted because there may be special circumstances; for example, a mentally or physically incapacitated child or a disabled spouse may be treated specially.

Amount of the Benefit. The typical death benefit is $66^{2}/3$ percent of the deceased worker's AWW, subject to a maximum and a minimum. If there is a spouse only, or one child only, the percentage may be less, and it may change as the child reaches majority or other statutory limitation. Many states provide for escalation of benefits in the same manner as for permanently totally disabled workers. Others grant an additional benefit for a dependent child or children.

Computing the Death Benefit—Case Studies. The following hypothetical cases illustrate death benefits.

Horace Means. Horace Means, age forty-five, employed as an administrative manager for Peak Computers, died in an automobile accident when he skidded on ice and ran off the road on his way to a business meeting. At the time of his death, Horace was salaried at $650 per week. Horace and his wife Phyllis had no dependent children. Phyllis remarried four years after his death. The following facts are applicable to this case:

1. The benefit rate is $66^{2}/3\%$ of the AWW.
2. The maximum is $450.
3. There is no provision for escalation of benefits.
4. At time of remarriage, the spouse receives two years of benefits in a lump sum.

Below is the calculation of the death benefit.

AWW = $650 x $66^{2}/3\%$ = $433.33 = weekly benefit until remarriage

Remarriage benefit = 104 weeks (2 years) x $433.33 = $45,066.32, payable at time of remarriage

Edward Bush. Edward Bush died at age twenty-five because of massive internal injuries when he fell from a roof at a construction job. Edward was married to Helen and had two children, Edward, Jr., four years old, and Kelly, three years old. Edward's wage at the time of death was $12.50 per hour. These facts apply in calculating the benefit:

1. Bush's AWW was $570 (overtime was worked).
2. The death benefit is $66^{2}/3\%$ of the AWW.

3. The maximum is $400.
4. Escalation of benefits is provided.
5. The widow's benefit drops to 50% of the AWW when the last child reaches 18 or age 21 if in an accredited school.

The death benefit is computed below.

AWW = $570 x 66²/₃% = $380 = weekly benefit

This benefit rises each year by a stated cost of living percentage compounded on the previous year's benefit (refer to PTD escalated benefit calculation). The benefit to Helen falls to 50 percent of Bush's AWW (escalated for time) when the last child is no longer eligible for benefits.

SUMMARY

Workers compensation laws support disabled workers while they are unable to work by providing income replacement in the form of temporary total, temporary partial, or permanent total compensation benefits. A worker left with residual disability is entitled to permanent partial compensation for a scheduled member and/or loss of earning capacity benefits. Medical care and rehabilitation services are supplied. Death benefits are available to eligible dependent survivors of workers who die because of a compensable injury or illness.

The trend for the future is continued expansion of benefits, but at a pace slowed by sharply rising costs. Few systems are perfect. Workers compensation is sometimes cumbersome and slow, is sometimes abused, and sometimes invites controversy. On the whole, though, it works well in accomplishing its purpose of caring for the injured worker.

CHAPTER 5

The Administration of Workers Compensation Claims

This chapter discusses the procedures used by claim representatives in handling workers compensation claims. Many of these procedures are required by, or provided for in, the state compensation law. Many other important procedures are the responsibility of and are initiated by insurers and the claim representatives who handle claims for them.

REQUIREMENTS UNDER COMPENSATION LAW

To serve the purpose of being a quick and certain remedy for work-related injuries, compensation laws provide that certain procedures must be followed in the handling of a claim. The two most important of these procedures, discussed in this section, concern the requirement of notice of injury and the adjudicative methods for handling contested and uncontested cases, questions of evidence, and appeals. Also discussed are second injury funds, a common remedy for employers of workers who have suffered a previous injury.

Notice Requirements

Workers compensation systems were created to establish prompt and responsive methods to compensate workers for work-related inju-

137

ries and illnesses. These systems replace the common-law system, which was painfully slow largely because workers had to sue their employers in tort. The design of current compensation systems sought to remedy this problem. As a result, promptness in claim handling is emphasized, starting with the initial notice of the claim.

The administration of any given workers compensation claim is initiated with a notice of injury. There are four kinds of notices: (1) notice of accident from the employee to the employer, (2) notice of claims from the employee to the state compensation agency, (3) notice from the employer to the state workers compensation board, and (4) notice from the employer/insured to the insurer. These kinds of notices and requirements for each are explained below.

Notice From the Employee to the Employer. Since the intent of the current workers compensation system is promptness, every state specifies a time limit in which accidents must be reported. This emphasis on timeliness is reinforced by insurers that provide workers compensation insurance since they also stipulate in the policy a time limit for the reporting of claims. Under state law, thirty days is the most common period in which notice must be given, although some statutes require notice "immediately," "forthwith," or "as soon as practicable." Others allow as long as ninety days.

Notice need not be in writing. Verbal notice from the claimant or employee is sufficient. In some cases, constructive notice such as a witnessed slip and fall is sufficient. Virtually no compensation commission will deny benefits simply because the claimant's notice of accident was unwritten.

There is no legal requirement that a claimant's accident be witnessed. An absence of witnesses may be one sign among many that a claim should be closely investigated, but this fact alone, often touted by employers as a reason for denying a claim, is given little or no weight by industrial commissions. Further, even though the injured employee may have many personnel problems such as absenteeism, poor work performance, or write-ups for disciplinary reasons, employers must remember that "bad" employees can get hurt too. Other factors, however interesting, are extraneous to a worker's entitlement to benefits.

Excuses for Late Notice. Although there is statutory and procedural emphasis on timely notification, a claim representative must be aware that tardiness in injury notification is unlikely to be a sufficient reason to deny a workers compensation claim. Late notification is tolerated for several reasons. The first is that most compensation statutes concerning notice requirements contain the word "excusable" when discussing an employee's late notice of injury. In addition, compensation boards usually tolerate late notification, or even lack of notification, based on several arguments:

- The claimant was not *initially* aware of the severity, extent, or the prognosis of the injury.

- The employer had verbal or *constructive* notice of the accident. *Actual* notification occurs when an employee informs the supervisor, "I injured my back moving that pallet." Constructive notice of injury means that the supervisor observes the employee being injured. In this case, no formal report of claim need be filed. The fact that the supervisor observed the accident is interpreted by many courts as constructive notice. The employee's failure to give formal notice does not allow the employer to avoid paying a claim.

- The absence of prompt notice did not prejudice the employer or the employer's insurer's ability to properly investigate or defend against the claim. Prejudice means that the employer's or the insurer's ability to investigate or defend against the injury claim was hampered by the delay in notice. For instance, prejudice would exist when key witnesses are no longer available or cannot accurately recollect the circumstances leading to the injury, or when evidence has been destroyed. It is important to note that it is not necessarily the duration of the delay that is the important factor, but the effect that the delay, whether brief or prolonged, has on the employer's or insurer's investigation into the accident and subsequent ability to defend against the claim.

Notice From the Employee to the Compensation Commission. Many state laws also require the employee to notify the Workers Compensation Commission of the accidental injury, or the commission may receive such notice from the employer. Compensation commissions are usually flexible about the form such notice from the employee must take. A handwritten note may suffice.

Notice From the Employer to the Compensation Commission. Most states require the employer to file an Employer's First Report of Injury within a prescribed number of days after the accident. If the employer fails to do so, the employer may be subject to fines or penalties. It is important to counsel employers that completing the form neither means the employer accepts the claim, nor does it lend legitimacy to the claim. Claim representatives must convince the employer that regardless of their reservations concerning a particular compensation claim, they are legally obligated to file an Employer's First Report.

If the employer thinks a claim is unfounded, the wording in the report should carefully reflect that belief. The accident description may begin with the phrase, "It is alleged that...." In some jurisdictions, the Employer's First Report is considered an admission against interest, which makes it admissible in court as proof of its contents. Under these circumstances, an employer who writes the Employer's First Report stating that the accident happened may be later estopped from asserting that the accident never occurred.

Notice From the Insured to Insurer. Workers compensation policies require prompt, if not immediate, notice of injury from the insured/employer to the insurer. The NCCI standard workers compensation and employers liability insurance policy states: "Tell us at once if injury occurs that may be covered by this policy." Because promptness is not quantified, courts are free to determine what is a reasonable or an unreasonable delay. Usually, in order to deny coverage because of late notice, the insurer must prove that its ability to investigate or defend against the workers compensation claim was prejudiced. Claim representatives trying to deny coverage based on late notice must have an extremely strong position.

Coverage Questions. Although insurance policy coverage questions are not common in workers compensation cases, they can arise. Below are some examples of situations that could raise coverage questions:

- Insured's prejudicial delay in reporting a claim to the insurer
- Injury to an out-of-state employee
- Injury in the context of illegal employment of minors
- Material misrepresentation of the type of risk (Example: an insured who completed the insurance application as a toy company is found to be manufacturing fireworks)
- The named insured as a sole proprietor
- Failure to cooperate with the insurer in the investigation or defense of the claim
- Suspected collusion between the employer and the claimant to obtain workers compensation benefits when payment is unwarranted

Whenever a claim representative is faced with an insurance policy coverage question, the considerations for workers compensation claims are no different from those in handling a coverage problem on any other policy. To avoid waiver and estoppel of coverage defenses, the claim representative must immediately issue a reservation of rights letter to the employer or obtain a signed nonwaiver agreement from the insured. Beyond this, the claim representative may wish to retain an attorney as coverage counsel to review the facts as they apply to the law of that state, to render an opinion, and perhaps even to seek early judicial resolution of the issue. Judicial resolution can come in the form of a declaratory judgment, by which the insurer seeks the court's determination as to whether coverage exists.

Adjudicative Procedure

In addition to notice requirements, compensation laws require certain adjudicative procedures to be followed in claims handling. State procedures vary. At least fifty different workers compensation systems exist throughout the country. Few claim representatives could keep track of each procedural wrinkle or every change in each state. Claim representatives therefore need a frame of reference for categorizing workers compensation procedures. This may be even more critical for claim or risk professionals reviewing claims in several jurisdictions. Although each state workers compensation system differs, they do have certain common features. Each state must address the same types of questions: how are payments made and stopped? How are contested cases handled? What rules of evidence apply? How are appeals handled? The following discussion addresses these questions.

Uncontested Cases. Procedures in cases in which the insurer accepts the initial compensability of a case are straightforward. Individual states oversee the administration of workers compensation within their jurisdiction. Usually a single agency within the state government is dedicated to this purpose. In some states, the agency is a department within the state Department of Labor. Some common titles for such state boards are Industrial Commission, Workers Compensation Commission, and Industrial Accident Board. These agencies promulgate rules and regulations for applying the workers compensation statutes. State boards and agencies are responsible for administering the workers compensation law in a manner consistent with that state's legislative history and the law's humanitarian intent.

Claim representatives must be familiar with the procedural requirements of the states in which they adjust or supervise claims. At a minimum, this means obtaining a copy of the state compensation statute and administrative rules and becoming very familiar with them. Supplemental material may also be available to claim representatives, including circulars from the compensation commission, opinions of the commission, periodic updates, and newsletters from the legal community.

In an uncontested case the claim representative accepts the claim, and payments are made until (1) the claimant returns to work or (2) is judged fit to do so. When one of these two conditions exists, the claim representative must make the appropriate agreement with the claimant or file the suitable form with the compensation commission. The claim representative pays any final medical bills. Once the claim representative rules out permanent disability, the file may be closed. (Procedures become more involved in disputed claims. This is discussed in a subsequent section.) Some observers find it useful to categorize compensation programs as either filing systems or agreement systems.

Filing Systems. Under a filing system, the claim representative submits one form when compensation payments begin and another when they end. The claim representative does not need the claimant's signature. Filing systems are somewhat unilateral, and the claim representative has more leeway. The claimant's explicit consent to the terms or cessation of payment is unnecessary. The form signifying the start of payment and the form showing termination of payment have different names in various states. Claim representatives must familiarize themselves with the nomenclature of the forms used in their jurisdictions. Under the Longshore and Harbor Workers' Compensation Act, for example, the claim representative files a Form LS-206 when payments begin. When payments end, the claim representative files with the compensation commission a Form LS-208. A claim representative who contests a claim, either initially or during payment, must file a Form LS-207 or "Notice of Controversion."

Agreement Systems. Many states require the employee's signature on the forms officially signifying acceptance or termination of compensation payments. Getting the claimant's signature to begin payments is usually no problem. The injured claimant is usually eager to cooperate. Some states call the form signifying employer/insurer acceptance of a claim a "Memorandum of Agreement." The claim representative files the completed agreement with the state workers compensation commission, which then issues an *award*.

Awards normally set forth the terms and conditions governing payment of compensation, the employer's name and address, the employee's name and address, date of loss, the average weekly wage and weekly compensation rate, date first payments are due, and the commission's claim number. The employer/insurer must typically pay compensation until the commission terminates the award.

Obtaining the employee's signature on the form ending compensation can sometimes pose a problem. The claimant may not agree that payments should stop. If the claim representative cannot get the claimant to sign the form, then the claim representative must meet some very specific and rigorous requirements in order to stop payments. Often, the employer/insurer must file an application for a hearing. The employer/insurer may have to continue payments to the claimant while it awaits a hearing date and decision. Some states call the form ending payments an *agreed statement of fact.* It contains language stating that the claimant "returned to work/was able to return to work on (date)."

Time Limits for Payments. All state laws have time limits within which the employer/insurer must start payments. The limit is often fourteen days from the date compensation becomes due or fourteen days from the accident date. Whether the deadline is seven days or thirty, the act of payment is key. There are penalties to the employer/ insurer for late payments. Claim representatives handling workers compensation must be intimately familiar with their state requirements, or they will expose themselves, their employer, and their client to sanctions. Failure to start or continue payments on a timely basis as required by statute may also form the basis of a *bad faith claim* from the injured worker. In some states, it is permissible to issue a *pro forma denial* within the time limit for payment, pending a complete investigation. Upon completion of the investigation, a real decision to pay or deny must be made.

Methods of Contesting or Ending Payments. Most workers compensation cases are routinely investigated, adjusted, and paid. In some cases, however, the entitlement to compensation may be in question. Where the claim representative rejects a claim outright, most states require that the insurer send a letter to the claimant giving reason for the denial. This often results in an invitation by the compensation commission to the employee to file for a hearing. At that point, the next move is up to the employee.

In some cases, it may be wise for a claim representative to accept a questionable compensation claim rather than expose the employer to a third-party tort action. Because of the *exclusive remedy doctrine* operating in most states, compensation is the claimant's sole source of recovery vis-a-vis the employer. The law fixes compensation benefits at a set amount, but recovery in tort is theoretically unlimited. Pain and suffering are not compensable in workers compensation cases, but are legitimate general damages in tort claims.

Thus, in some instances the employer may actually be limiting its exposure by taking its chances with a compensation claim rather than exposing itself to a third-party action. Two scenarios illustrate this possibility:

- A laborer slips and falls on ice when walking into his employer's building. If the employer denies the claim, arguing that the claimant was outside the scope of employment at the time, it may expose itself to a premises liability claim.
- A hospital worker says he contracted AIDS from his repeated exposure to patient body fluids and substances. The hospital

accepts a questionable workers compensation claim rather than allowing a jury to decide its liability in a tort claim.

The claim representative initially views a case as compensable. Later, however, the claim representative finds grounds for contesting continued payments. Several scenarios can arise: the claimant's doctor may have cleared the claimant for work; an independent examining doctor may have cleared the claimant for work; the claim representative may find the claimant gainfully employed elsewhere while collecting workers compensation payments; or through surveillance or other means, the claim representative may discover that the claimant is engaged in physical activity that would prove his or her ability to work. When a dispute over termination of payment occurs, there are procedures to resolve the impasse, which are explained below.

Informal Conferences. In many jurisdictions, the first step in the adjudication process is an informal conference. Many states use this mechanism to encourage early resolution of disputes. At this stage, the claim representative represents the employer/insurer. Special claim representatives, often called *hearing examiners*, may specialize in taking files to these informal conferences. The employer can send an attorney, or both the claim representative and attorney can appear. The employee is usually present with an attorney. A representative of the commission supervises the conference, which aims to (1) identify items of agreement, (2) isolate areas of contention, and (3) encourage low level, informal dispute resolution.

As the name indicates, the setting for these conferences is informal. Each side informally presents its position. Commissions do not observe strict rules of evidence. The claim representative may have a chance to question the claimant. A commission representative may make a recommendation at the conference or may issue one within a certain number of days. Adverse recommendations are appealable to the next level, which is usually a formal hearing.

Formal Hearing. At this stage, the claim representative normally needs an attorney. Rules of evidence are more relaxed than they would be in a typical civil trial. However, the setting and procedure are not nearly as casual as in the informal conference. A compensation hearing resembles a mini-trial before a single commissioner. Results normally come weeks after the hearing. Adverse hearing rulings are often appealable.

Role of Courts. In a few states, the courts have the original jurisdiction to hear and decide workers compensation cases. This is different than the court's appellate role, which is discussed below. In these few states, the courts handle matters that are handled by a commissioner or hearing officer in most states.

Full Commission Appeal. In some jurisdictions, employers can appeal from the formal commission hearing to the entire assembled commission. This would involve filing briefs. One criticism of full commission review is that the full commission may be loath to overrule one of its members. There is often a presumption of correctness on the part of the single commissioner's opinion. In many states, the appeals board within the commission is a body separate from the hearing officers.

Appeals to State Courts. A claimant or employer, convinced that a bad decision was reached, may appeal to the state courts. These appeals usually go to appellate level courts within the state courts. The higher the appellate level, the more difficult it is to be heard. The case must involve fundamental interpretation of the workers compensation law or an issue of state constitutionality. The state supreme court only agrees to hear a case by granting a writ of certiorari, which is completely discretionary. In a majority of states, the courts in a appeal may only review issues of law, not the facts related to the case. In the remaining states, both issues of law and fact may be retried. Nevertheless, only a few of these states allow jury trials.

Grounds for Appeal. Losing parties can appeal compensation decisions for one of two reasons: an *alleged error of law* or an *alleged error of fact*. In about half the states, alleged errors of fact are not a basis for appeal. Only errors in law are grounds for appeal. Claim representatives contemplating appeal must understand the difference between the two before they proceed. In states in which only legal issues may be appealed, the appellate forum will not reconsider the circumstances of the accident or medical issues.

Alleged errors of fact arise over whether the commission correctly determined some element of verifiable truth. For example, a witness for the claimant testifies that she fell from a ladder and injured her back. A witness for the employer says that no such fall occurred. The two sets of testimony are mutually exclusive, and therefore raise a legitimate question as to the facts of the case. In states in which only alleged errors of law may be appealed, the commission's determination as to which witness to believe is not appealable.

Alleged errors of law include questions related to the interpretation of a legal issue. For example, do usual activities like walking up and down steps constitute an accidental injury within the meaning of the compensation law? Must a slip, twist, fall, or unusual exertion accompany lifting in order for such lifting to be compensable? These are questions of law, and alleged errors therein are appealable.

The stakes—and expenses—rise with each appeal level. The factors a claim representative should weigh in pondering an appeal include what legal costs will be incurred in pursuing an appeal? What, objectively, are the odds of success? How much money is at stake? Will the compensation award be precedent-setting if unchallenged? In many states the losing employer/insurer must pay the claimant pending an appeal.

Settlements. In some jurisdictions, a workers compensation claim can be settled by agreement of the insurer and claimant like any third-party tort claim. Unlike liability claim settlements, however, the settlement terms often must be approved by the state agency overseeing the compensation system, especially if the settlement is for less than the statutory amount of compensation. Commissions usually have the power to reject the terms of the proposed settlement.

Before approving settlements, commissions look at many factors. The settlement amount must appear reasonable given the severity of the injury. Commissions take a paternalistic view toward workers to ensure that they are not being exploited. Thus, some claim representatives believe that a settlement with a claimant represented by an attorney has a better chance of commission approval than settlement with an unrepresented employee. If the commission believes that settlement is not in the employee's best interests, it will likely reject the agreement. Settling compensation claims is tougher than settling third party liability claims, but it is possible, especially during litigation, as both sides ponder the protracted expense and delays inherent in the appeals process.

Rules of Evidence. Unlike civil trials, workers compensation hearings have fairly informal and relaxed rules of evidence. Commissioners may allow hearsay testimony and other evidence that would be inadmissible in court. Medical reports may be admissible evidence in lieu of having the physician physically present. Most jurisdictions allow any evidence to be admitted but require that the ultimate findings rest upon some evidence that would be admissible in civil courts. This is known as the *residuum rule*: the ultimate findings must rest on some "residuum" (literally, residue) of appropriate evidence.

Use of Statements and Reports. Hearsay that might be inadmissible in a civil trial may be allowed in a compensation hearing. This underscores the importance of the claim representative's signed statements. The claim representative may use a claimant's signed or recorded statement to impeach the claimant's testimony at a compensation hearing.

As mentioned, medical reports are often admitted as evidence in lieu of testimony from a physician. Nevertheless, the employer may have its physician testify in person. All other factors being equal, a compensation commission may weigh more heavily the opinion of a testifying practitioner than that expressed in a written report.

Unlike many civil trials, compensation procedure in most states does not usually require the parties to exchange witness lists and other evidence in advance. Thus, the element of surprise is often used in compensation hearings. Commissioners have denied benefits in many cases, having been persuaded by still photos or film of the "injured" claimant gainfully employed or working vigorously. Well-prepared claim representatives will have the investigator who did the work present to testify.

Burden of Proof. In most areas, the claimant has the minimal burden of proof to show that he or she sustained an accidental injury arising out of and in the course of employment. This is not a rigorous standard. A claimant's uncorroborated testimony may establish a prima facie case of compensability. Once the claimant meets this burden of proof, the burden shifts to the employer/insurer to show why the claimant's injury is not compensable.

Presumptions. In most jurisdictions, hearing commissioners act as though it is presumed that a claim falls under the workers compensation act and that the claimant sustained an accidental injury arising out of and in the course of employment. This effectively places the burden of disproving the claim on the employer/insurer even though the legal burden of proof remains on the claimant. This presumption is consistent with the liberal interpretation of workers compensation laws, as explained in Chapter 1. Legislative histories of state laws reflect a system aimed at a humane, compassionate system of payment for injured workers. In some jurisdictions, the law requires that the commissioners resolve any reasonable disputes in the employee's favor. This often makes claim denial and defense difficult for the employer/insurer/claim representative. To win a workers compensation case, the employer must have a stronger and more convincing case than the claimant. In New York, there are various presumptions explicitly created by statute. It is presumed that the claim is covered, that sufficient notice was given, and that the injury did not result from willful wrongdoing of the employee.

The Claim Representative's Role. The claim representative should attend compensation hearings regularly even if not required to be present. Every claim representative handling compensation cases should witness how commissions adjudicate disputed cases. The claim representative may also be able to assist the defense attorney by suggesting lines of questions or reminding counsel of key points. It may be helpful in the future for the claim representative to have seen how the defense attorney performs. A lawyer can make a very commanding impression on paper, but may be passive and ineffective at hearings.

At the hearing, the claim representative cannot ask questions or actively participate in any other way. However, the claim representative should seize any chance to discuss the claimant's testimony with the defense attorney during breaks in order to be sure the attorney is covering what is needed and to point out any discrepancies in the testimony.

Claim representatives usually do not testify. However, they occasionally receive a subpoena, which requires their presence. Statements taken by the claim representative may be admissible evidence, so the claim representative may be called to testify about a written statement from a witness. Claimant's counsel may try to discredit the claim representative's testimony. As a witness, the claim representative should remember to (1) tell the truth; (2) be thoroughly familiar with the file ahead of time; (3) give brief, to-the-point answers, but do not volunteer unrequested information; (4) say, "I don't know" if such is true; (5) confer in advance with defense counsel to anticipate where the other side will probe—consider a dress rehearsal of cross examination; (6) not get angry or defensive; (7) give the defense attorney time to object to questions before answering; (8) look and dress conservatively—like a professional.

Attorney Fees. The award of claimant attorney fees is generally subject to statutory limits and to the commission's approval. Upon any award of compensation following a hearing, the commission can be expected to approve an attorney fee. If the employee loses, there is usually no fee. The fee of the claimant's attorney is generally restricted to about 20 percent of the award. Attorney fees generally come *out of* the award to the claimant, but in some states they may be *in addition to* the sum awarded.

Reopening Old Awards. Often, employees will return to work for some time and later go back out of work. This may be the result of a *reoccurrence* of the original compensable injury, or the employee's job duties may become more rigorous. For whatever reason, injured workers may seek to reopen an award and resume disability benefits, for which each state has procedures the employee must follow. In many cases, the employee must give formal notice to the employer and compensation commission within a certain period of time.

Second Injury Funds

Most state workers compensation laws include second injury funds. These funds aim to minimize employer reluctance to hire handicapped or previously disabled workers. The rationale is that without such a safety net, employers would refuse to hire persons with handicaps or disabilities. A new injury combined with a preexisting disability may produce an overall disability much greater than would normally be the case. Holding employers responsible for the greater disability is unfair to employers and harsh on disabled individuals seeking work. Though provisions vary, these funds try to limit the employer's liability for indemnity payments when the employee sustains a subsequent injury or disability. The second injury fund is usually financed with premium taxes and special assessments in death cases involving no dependents.

Operation of Second Injury Funds. Second injury fund laws generally require employers to pay benefits related to the disability that would exist *from the second injury alone*. This is true even when the claimant receives benefits relating to the combined total disability. The second injury fund makes up the difference. This feature usually applies only to cases of permanent total disability. In about one-third of the states, the disability need not be total to invoke second injury fund relief. About half the states limit the operation of second injury funds to the loss of a member or an eye.

Some claim professionals refer to second injury fund laws as *apportionment*. Strictly speaking, apportionment is different. Under the few state statutes providing for apportionment, the employer is responsible only for the subsequent injury. No state fund pays the difference, as under second injury fund laws. For instance, assume that an employee has already lost sight in one eye, and then in a current accident loses the use of the other eye. In apportionment, the current employer is responsible for compensating only for the loss of one eye, and no one pays for the difference in compensation between the loss of sight in one eye and total blindness. A second injury fund would pay for the difference between the compensation for the loss of sight in one eye and in both eyes, or full permanent disability. Apportionment is harsh on *employees,* since the *employee* must bear the burden of the full disability. All states now have second injury funds. The few states with apportionment statutes apply such law only to cases not covered by the second injury fund.

The physician should allocate the percentage of permanent partial disability respectively attributable to the two injuries or conditions. For example, the treating physician may give the claimant a 40 percent permanent partial disability (PPD) rating, but from statements, medical history, and knowing that the claimant has had one prior knee operation and arthritis, the doctor may state that 20 percent PPD was preexisting and 20 percent was the result of the recent (i.e., second) injury.

Most statutes require the fund to pay the difference between compensation payable for the second injury alone and the total disability. However, some statutes limit the employer's liability to a finite number of weeks. For example, the statutes of Alaska, the District of Columbia, Georgia, Hawaii, Montana, New Hampshire, and New York

150—Principles of Workers Compensation Claims

limit the employer's responsibility to 104 weeks. Beyond this period, the special fund picks up payments to the claimant and may even reimburse the employer for any payments it has already made in excess of 104 weeks.

Establishing Second Injury Fund Claims. Second injury funds can be a powerful adjusting tool in managing workers compensation claims and limiting the insurer's exposure. This can save the employer or insurer many thousands of dollars—with no hardship to the claimant. Limiting the employer's responsibility to "only" 104 weeks of compensation may initially seem inconsequential. However, in some severe cases, it represents a considerable savings. The claim representative's time spent in documenting a case for second injury fund relief is an investment that can pay huge dividends. Second injury funds typically include the following requirements by employers wishing to invoke special fund benefits: (1) that the claimant has a prior disability; (2) that the employer has knowledge—actual or constructive— of the preexisting disability; and (3) that the combination of the preexisting disability and the current injury produce a greater disability overall.

Documenting a preexisting disability tests the claim representative's ability to research a claimant's medical history. For example, back pain is common for many. A thorough investigation into a claimant's medical history is important. The original injury or condition need not be work-related for the second injury to be covered by a second injury fund. In the claimant's statement, the claim representative should cover prior back injuries, treatments, accidents, and hospitalizations. The claim representative should obtain a signed medical authorization form. Family doctors should be identified and complete copies of charts requested. Union health records, personnel files, and group health files may contain information on preexisting problems or disabilities. Previous employers may be fruitful sources of information. Checking with the Index Bureau and local compensation commissions may produce evidence of prior claims and disabilities. Any of these avenues can lead the claim representative to evidence of a claimant's preexisting problem or disability.

Once the claim representative documents a preexisting disability, the next step is to prove that the employer knew of the condition. The claim representative can do this in a number of ways. Pre-employment physicals or medical questionnaires are useful sources. Testimony as to a claimant's limitations from co-workers or supervisors may suffice. Some jurisdictions hold that the employer has constructive knowledge of a preexisting condition so long as the information is "manifest" to the employer. In such cases, the claim representative need only show that medical evidence reflecting the prior disability existed in material available to the employer.

Demonstrating the third requirement, that a combination of the prior condition and the recent injury has produced a greater disability, is usually the easiest of the three steps. This is a medical question that the claim representative can pose to the treating doctor or to an independent medical examination (IME) physician. When using an IME, the claim representative must take care that all relevant prior medical records have been sent to the consulting physician. Further, the claim representative must clearly communicate to the IME physician precisely what medical issue must be addressed. The use of IMEs is discussed in detail later in this chapter.

Neophyte claim representatives are often uneasy about seeking second injury fund relief. They are so accustomed to trying to prove that a claimant has *no* disability that it seems strange to gather evidence showing the claimant has a greater disability or, as required in some states, that the claimant is permanently and totally disabled. Developing the evidence required to build a good second injury fund case may be tedious, but many claim representatives fail to pursue second injury funds because they simply have no grasp of the special injury fund requirements and possibilities.

RESPONSIBILITIES OF THE CLAIM REPRESENTATIVE

Many important procedures in the handling of compensation claims may not be explicitly required by compensation laws but are crucial to the insurer's ability to pay claims properly. These procedures are the responsibility of the claim representative. Insurers and "self-insurers" require a thorough investigation of the facts of a case to determine compensability, a complete medical determination, the investigation and pursuit of subrogation possibilities, and proper reserving of outstanding cases. This section reviews these topics.

Factual Investigation

The extent to which a case should be investigated depends on the severity of the workers compensation exposure. Claim representatives should strive to avoid over investigating minor claims or under investigating claims that represent potentially large losses. In a case involving lost time from work, an effective factual investigation should include: (1) claimant investigation; (2) insured investigation; (3) witness investigation; (4) medical investigation; and (5) postaccident activities investigation. Subrogation, discussed in a separate section, should also be considered as a possible course of action in a factual investigation.

The investigation of workers compensation claims involving automobile accidents, fatalities, and product liability are also discussed.

Claimant Investigation. The key to investigating any claim is a thorough statement—signed or recorded—from the claimant. This chapter will not attempt to exhaustively cover all the key points in all types of statements because some good guides already exist. Also, key questions depend on the type of case under consideration. The claim representative should remember that statement guides are starting points. They are the means, not the end, of an investigation. One sample statement outline, with annotations, is shown in Exhibit 5-1.

Companies have different policies regarding the necessity of statements. In fact, statements are not taken on all claims. For instance, rarely are statements obtained on "medical only" or no-lost-time cases. Some insurers may have guidelines that statements are required only on cases that involve particular disabilities or severity of injury (e.g., hernia, disc surgery, amputation). Others require statements whenever the facts surrounding an accident are questionable.

In addition to a complete statement, the claimant investigation should include a signed *medical authorization* and *wage authorization*. The medical authorization enables the claim representative to obtain more easily the medical reports and records needed to evaluate the claim. A medical authorization can become an invaluable tool in researching preexisting medical problems. A wage authorization is useful if the claimant has dual employment. It allows the claim representative to monitor postinjury earnings over time and to compile records regarding prior earnings in order to verify or contest a claim for loss of wage earning capacity.

Insured Investigation. Investigation at the insured's end includes (1) statements from co-workers who witnessed the accident; (2) a statement from the immediate supervisor regarding the injured employee's job duties, length of employment, and the supervisor's opinions about the claim; and (3) a copy of the claimant's personnel file with the initial employment application, the pre-employment physical report, the group health claim history, copies of prior workers compensation claims that were submitted, information regarding any disciplinary action taken against the employee, and the employee's employment history.

Witness Investigation. A witness investigation involves obtaining statements from co-workers or others who witnessed the injury. These statements can confirm or rule out the incident as being responsible for the compensation claim. The purpose of these statements is to determine if there was an injury, and if so, whether it was work-related. Statements from witnesses are very important in assessing the

Exhibit 5-1

Suggested Claimant Statement Outline for Workers Compensation Claims

1. What is your full name?
2. What is your current address and phone number?
3. How long have you lived there?
4. Are you married? Number and ages of children who are dependent upon you. (Comment: This could be critical information if the claim ever becomes a fatality.)
5. Where are you currently employed?
6. Are they your only employer? (Comment: Some states may require that, in cases of "dual employment," the claim representative use earnings from both jobs when computing the rate for temporary total disability.)
7. How long have you worked for them?
8. Before you worked for your current employer, for whom did you work? (Comment: This provides information for subsequent checks on claims history and medical history.)
9. What is your work address or location?
10. What is your job title?
11. Briefly describe your job duties.
12. Name of supervisor?
13. Are you a union member?
14. Are you salaried or paid by the hour? (Comment: Compare this information with the wage transcript furnished by the employer, the W-2 form or tax returns.)
15. If hourly, what is hourly pay rate? How many hours per week do you average? Any overtime? How much is the overtime rate? (Comment: Overtime wages may have to be included in the TTD rate.)
16. If salaried, what is your current weekly/monthly/annual salary?
17. Are you paid any noncash wages? If so, describe. (Comment: Some states require that the imputed value of noncash wages (housing, company car, uniforms) be included along with cash wages in computing the TTD rate.)
18. Were you recently injured on the job? (Comment: This sets the stage for the specific claim to be discussed.)
19. What was the date of that accident?
20. What time of day?
21. Where did it happen?
22. When did you start work that day?
23. Did you feel fine, physically, before you started work?
24. How long had you been working when the accident happened?

25. What were you doing at the time the accident occurred? Is this a regular part of your job? Who told you to do this?

26. Were you working alone or with anyone? Names of people who you were working with. If working alone, names of closest people in the vicinity. (Comment: This provides leads for the claim representative's witness investigation.)

27. What happened? Briefly describe the accident.

28. Did you feel pain immediately? Where?

29. Did you stop work immediately? If not, why not?

30. Did anyone see your accident? (Comment: Again, assists in identifying witnesses.)

31. Did you report the accident immediately to your employer? If not, why not? When did you first report the accident to your employer? What was the name of the first person to whom you reported the accident? (Comment: The greater the delay between the date of the alleged accident and the date reported to the employer, the more the claim representative should investigate the claim's legitimacy.)

32. Did you seek medical care on the day of the accident? If not, why not? What was the first date you sought medical treatment for the accident? (Comment: The longer the gap between the date of accident and the first date of medical treatment, the more tenuous the causal relationship is likely to be between the two.)

33. Names and addresses of first medical care providers. Did you tell them you were hurt on the job? (Comment: The first part of the query lays the foundation for the claim representative's medical investigation. The second may be surprisingly revealing. It is amazing the number of times the claimant does NOT give a history of on-the-job injury and then later files a compensation claim.)

34. What did they do for you?

35. When did you first see a private doctor for this? Name and address of doctor. Who referred you to this doctor? (Comment: Claim representatives may learn that a certain law firm or attorney referred the claimant to a hand-picked doctor.)

36. When did you start seeing this doctor? Are you still under the doctor's treatment? Date of last appointment? Date of next appointment? (Comment: Frequency of treatments can trigger claim representative concern about over-billing or redundant and superfluous physical therapy.)

37. Had you ever seen this doctor before? What other doctors have you seen for this injury? Who referred you to them?

38. Has the doctor released you for work? Has he or she given you any idea as to when you can return to work? (Comment: The claimant's reaction to this question may give the claim representative some indication as to the claimant's motivation to return to work.)

39. Have you worked at all since the accident date? (Comment: If there is evidence that the claimant has been working, the claim representative may be able to use the statement to impeach the claimant's credibility.)

40. Were you paid in full for the day on which you were injured? (Comment: In many states, if the claimant was paid for less than a half day on the date of injury, the employer must pay a full day of TTD.)

41. Have you ever had any problems with this same part of your body before? (Comment: The claim representative should say *problems*, not *accidents*. The claimant may have had chronic back pain for 12 years, but he doesn't consider that an accident. Asking if he has had any problems of any sort with that same part of the body prevents hedging. The claim representative can use this data in conducting subsequent medical investigation and/or testing claimant credibility. If the claimant denies prior injuries, and further investigation discovers that he or she has had some, the claim representative should suspect the possibility of fraud and concealment in the current case.)

42. Have you ever been injured on *any* job before? Get details.

43. Have you ever collected workers compensation before? Get details. (Comment: If the claimant denies any prior compensation claims, and prior or subsequent investigation reveals that he or she has had them, the claim representative should suspect the possibility of fraud and concealment in the current case.)

44. Have you ever been injured in an auto accident? Get details.

45. Have you ever filed an insurance claim before? Get details.

46. Have you ever been hospitalized?

47. Any prior surgeries?

48. What part(s) of your body did you hurt in this accident? Were there any other parts of your body that you hurt? (Comment: This second question is VERY IMPORTANT. It can limit the claim in cases of some claimants who will later try to add other aches, pains and injuries as causally related to the original accident. Although latent injuries do exist, the claim representative can help prevent these "floating disabilities" by having the claimant say, "I injured no part of my body in this accident other than my lower back.")

49. Other than workers compensation, have you filed for any other source(s) (e.g., health, disability, social security, unemployment compensation) of benefits as a result of this injury?

50. Is there anything about the accident I haven't asked you that you would like to add?

51. Have the answers you've given been true to the best of your knowledge?

52. While giving this statement, were you under the influence of any medication or alcohol? If so, what type? For what reason? (Comment: Without this, a clever attorney or claimant may try to explain away inconsistencies by claiming he was not in full possession of his faculties due to pain, medication or other substances.)

cause of the injury. However, it should be noted that no jurisdiction requires that the claimant's injury be witnessed.

Medical Investigation. A critical evaluation of a claimant's medical situation is subsequently discussed under the section entitled

"Medical Determination." This section addresses the factual medical investigation that must first be conducted.

Current Medical Providers. A first step in investigating a claim should be a request for medical reports and bills from each of the employee's current medical providers, typically hospitals and doctors. A signed medical authorization is not normally required on a workers compensation claim. However, it is prudent to obtain one in anticipation that it may be needed.

The prompt request for medical records and bills has many advantages: (1) It assists the claim representative in assessing compensability by comparing what the claimant reported to the doctor against what the claimant reported to the claim representative. (2) It helps establish the existence of disability. The medical report may confirm a history of on-the-job injury, but it may also indicate that the claimant could return to work immediately. (3) It expedites payment. The sooner the claim representative gets the bills, the sooner they can be processed for payment. This enhances good will and increases control over the claim. In some instances, it may decrease the claimant's perception that he or she needs to retain an attorney.

Medical History Investigation. The claimant's statement or personnel file may contain information regarding the claimant's medical history. This is important in helping the claim representative to decide whether an alleged job injury is really a preexisting condition.

It is possible that a job-related injury aggravated a preexisting condition. If the claim representative knows that this is true, it may be instrumental in obtaining second injury fund relief or apportionment. For example, does a back injury claimant have a history of backache, or a hernia claimant a history of preexisting hernia? Has the claimant submitted a group health or disability claim form, checking the box, "Unrelated to Employment?" Does the personnel application not indicate a history of shoulder problems when medical records reveal previous shoulder surgery? In more serious cases, a thorough medical history of the claimant may be needed to determine the employee's right to benefits or to limit the insurer's exposure.

Prior Claim Investigation. Identifying prior injuries, accidents, and claims can have many uses, including (1) undercutting the claimant's credibility (if he or she denies prior accidents); (2) finding other sources of exposure to occupational disease; and (3) establishing second injury fund relief. The following sources concerning prior accidents or claims are available to the claim representative:

- Index Bureau. Insurers and self-insureds can subscribe to an Index Bureau, which can give them a printout on any prior claims a claimant has filed.

- Compensation Commission. The local Workers Compensation Commission may be able to confirm whether there are any claims on file for a particular claimant.
- Motor vehicle records. This record may provide evidence of prior auto accidents and injury claims.

Postaccident Activity Investigations. The claim representative's investigative responsibilities do not end when compensation benefits are awarded. Although a claim is accepted as compensable, the claim representative may defeat the claim by demonstrating that the claimant is not disabled from working. Medical evidence is important for this. However, nonmedical evidence may be obtained to show that the claimant's true abilities are not what they seem to the physician providing treatment. If the claim representative can prove that the claimant is working, or is engaging in vigorous physical activities, then a disability claim may be defeated. Claim representatives can use a number of tactics to investigate a claimant's postaccident activity.

Activity Checks. In an activity check, the claim representative goes to the claimant's neighborhood and questions neighbors about the claimant's general level of physical activity. For example, does he mow the grass? Does he take out the garbage? Does he play with his children? Does he work around the house? If the answers are "yes," then a claim for disability may be defeated. Claim representatives should candidly identify their interests and never misrepresent their identity. They should plan on visiting the neighborhood when families are likely to be home. They should not make any remarks impugning the claimant's integrity. They should plan ahead, check a city directory, and try to get the names of the neighbors whom they will be approaching.

The pitfalls are clear. Neighbors may be friends of the claimant and may be suspicious of an insurance claim representative. The claimant himself may come over as the claim representative questions the neighbor. Some may "cover" for the claimant. The odds are long in finding any conclusive evidence against the claimant, but in more serious cases, the claim representative should consider the activity check.

Sub Rosa Investigation. A claim representative sometimes performs sub rosa (undercover) surveillance. For example, photographs of a claimant performing strenuous activity can be used to refute a claim of disability. However, in most cases calling for surveillance, the services of a professional investigator are used.

Professional Surveillance Services. In serious cases, claim representatives retain a professional private investigator to observe the claimant. The goal is to impeach the claimant's credibility or to counter pro-claimant medical reports stating that the claimant is disabled. Many firms have specially equipped vans for staking out the claimant's neighborhood. These surveillance firms attempt to obtain still photos or videotapes to document claimants lifting, bending, walking, and playing golf, for example, all while supposedly disabled. A claim representative should consider retaining an outside surveillance firm when "surveillance signals" such as the following indicate the need to do so:

1. Inconclusive medical opinions in which doctors can only provide subjective medical findings.
2. The claim representative or rehabilitation nurse has difficulty contacting a claimant who is supposed to be home most of the time.
3. The claimant frequently cancels appointments with doctors, physical therapists, rehabilitation nurses, and the claim representative.
4. The claimant appears to be having an extended recovery for the type of injury incurred as compared to recovery guidelines and the experience of others with similar injuries.
5. There is premature involvement by the claimant's attorney.
6. The employer relates information from co-workers or anonymous tips that the claimant is active and requests action.
7. The claimant comes by the claims office to pick up his check dressed in an expensive jogging or warm-up suit.
8. The claimant comes by the claims office to pick up his compensation check and is observed walking effortlessly across the parking lot to the building's entrance, but then limping into the claims office.

Upon deciding to engage a surveillance firm, the selection process should include the following:

1. A reference check, which will help determine if the firm's specialty is insurance work. An insurance specialist is generally preferable to a firm that also handles divorce cases and criminal matters.
2. An analysis of the credentials of the firm's staff. Professionals with investigative expertise, such as with the police or the FBI, should be chosen.
3. An inspection of the firm's capital assets. The firm should have equipment like a van and video camcorders.
4. A review of the firm's professional demeanor. The staff should be experienced in testifying in court and being cross-examined.

Once a surveillance firm is selected, a budget should be established. Open-ended assignments invite problems. The investigator should be given a certain number of hours or a dollar threshold as a control point. The claim representative should also help to establish a plan and should divulge any suspicions, tips, or leads from the employer.

Specific Types of Investigations. Auto accidents, fatalities, and accidents caused by products present special investigative issues.

Investigating Automobile Accidents. For all auto accidents, the claim representative should cover the key points that would be required in any automobile loss investigation. They include statements from all drivers, statements from witnesses, the police accident report, photos and diagram of the accident scene, and statements from wrecker crews or paramedic services. This evidence may be useful not only for compensability purposes, but also in establishing (or defending) a subrogation claim.

The claim representative must confirm or rule out that the claimant was operating the car within the scope of employment. If the employee was within the scope of employment, the claim representative should search for subrogation possibilities. In investigating whether the employee was operating the car within the scope of employment, the claim representative should ask the following questions: Was it a company car? If not, did the employer own the car? How often did the employee drive the car? For what purpose? Did the employee's job description involve travel by car? Where was the last stop made by the employee? Where was the next destination? Was the employee reimbursed for mileage? Was he on a travel expense account? Did he have a company credit card or debit card for gas or other travel expenses? Does the claimant's supervisor confirm that the employee was operating the car within the scope of employment? Was there any evidence of drinking or intoxication? Was there any evidence that the car was used for a personal errand instead of for a job mission? Was the car marked by a sign or otherwise identified as belonging to the employer? Who paid title, taxes, tags, and insurance for the car—the claimant or the employer? In detecting a deviation from the scope of employment, it is often helpful for a claim representative to take a map of the area and mark or highlight the employer's location, the accident scene, and the employee's destination. This may display the likelihood that the employee deviated or did not deviate from the scope of employment. In a fatality, is there any evidence of suicide?

Fatality Investigations. In addition to the facts investigated in an auto accident, the following other investigative avenues should be pursued in investigating any fatality claim:

1. Death Certificate. This is normally a matter of public record. Death certificates usually indicate the cause of death, dependency information, whether the death was work-related, and whether an autopsy was performed.

2. Autopsy Report. This is also usually a document of public record. The pathologist performing the autopsy will dictate a detailed report, which may offer further clues to the cause of death and the claimant's general health.

3. Toxicology Report. This usually accompanies an autopsy. The pathologist runs a routine blood screen on the deceased to detect traces of alcohol and drugs. In states where intoxication or drug impairment are claim defenses, this report could be important in establishing or ruling out such a defense.

4. Marriage records or divorce decrees from the courthouse may give positive confirmation of dependency status.

5. A newspaper obituary may include dependency information. The claim representative should compare the newspaper report to the information the survivors have offered regarding dependency status.

6. Any newspaper articles about the accident may provide valuable investigative leads.

Product Liability Investigations. Without prejudging the manufacturer or retailer, the claim representative should investigate whether or not there was a defect in design, manufacturing, warning, or breach of warranty in all cases in which a product contributed to the claimant's accident. A compensation claim representative should seek any subrogation opportunities created when an employee is injured as a result of a product defect. The successful identification of product defects may permit the claim representative to offset the employer/insurer's financial loss from workers compensation. Product liability cases are legally and technically complex, and may involve different considerations for a retailer than for a manufacturer. Subrogation is discussed at greater length in a subsequent section of this chapter.

Medical Determination

The determination of a claimant's diagnosis and prognosis requires the assertive approach found in medical management. "Medical management" is a phrase that was first used in rehabilitation literature. It involves directing and coordinating the efforts of health care providers to meet the needs of the patient and insurer. The goal of medical management is to avoid undertreating or overtreating an injured worker. It can mean the difference between a medical-only claim or a lost-time case; between a worker who misses several days and a worker with a long-term disability. Medical management also ensures that health care providers do not treat insurers as "fair game" for high billing rates, continually making liberal "unfit for duty" prescriptions. Some of the essential tools of medical management in workers compensation cases are the choice of physician or panels of physicians and the independent medical examination.

Choice of Physician. The employer's right to choose the physician can be a key factor affecting the length of disability. Some doctors accept patient complaints as the truth and certify virtually anyone as being disabled. Others classify only the severely injured as unfit for duty. Within any locale, certain doctors are known for "playing the workers compensation game." This involves high fees, prolonged treatments, lengthening the claimant's time out of work, and high percentage ratings for permanency.

Many states give the employer the right to choose either the treating physician or a panel of physicians. Claim representatives should become familiar with the law in their state to learn about employers' rights. A failure to exercise these rights can impair the claim representative's ability to manage the claim. In California, for example, the employer can choose the treating physician for the first thirty days following an on-the-job injury. In Virginia, the employer can give the injured worker a choice of three doctors at the outset of a claim.

Physician Panels. Effective claims management involves providing employers/insureds with lists of recommended physicians and facilities that should include more than one physician within each specialty. For most injuries, the most frequently consulted specialists are orthopedists, neurologists, and neurosurgeons. Claim professionals should see that panel physicians are impartial, dispassionate, and board-certified. They should not be biased toward insurance companies; otherwise, every opinion from such doctors would be dismissed by the claimant's attorney and the Workers Compensation Commission as the view of the "company doctor." Panel physicians should be accessible to phone calls and inquiries. They should write prompt, thorough, clear, and unequivocal reports. They should be familiar with testifying and be comfortable on the witness stand.

Employers who are allowed to provide panels should hold regular meetings and educate employees about workers compensation procedure. Some states allow employers to limit the claimant's choice of doctors to practitioners on the panel. Claim representatives must educate employers as to the usefulness of this procedure. Too often the employer does not recommend a panel to the claimant until another physician has already been seen. The claim representative must then try to control matters by belatedly imposing a panel. Attempts to impose a panel retroactively are often futile.

Independent Medical Examinations. If wisely used, the independent medical examination (IME) remains one of the most effective strategies for managing workers compensation claims. Not every case is a candidate for an IME. The exam's cost must be weighed against the potential loss. It makes little sense to pay $500 for an IME if only a week's worth of temporary total disability is at stake. Claim representatives most frequently use IMEs in the specialties of orthopedics, neurosurgery, and neurology. With the increase in stress claims, psychiatric IMEs are becoming more common.

Claim representatives should ask the IME physician to address the following questions:

1. In all medical probability, are the claimant's ailments causally related to a specific on-the-job injury?
2. Is the frequency and type of medical treatment rendered reasonable and appropriate?
3. From an *objective* medical standpoint, can the claimant return to full duty?
4. Can the claimant perform light/limited/modified work, and what are the claimant's specific physical restrictions?
5. Does the claimant have any permanent disability, and if so, what is the percentage?
6. Has the claimant reached maximum medical improvement?
7. Did preexisting or unrelated medical problems contribute to the claimant's disability?
8. Is prospective medical treatment—surgery or hospitalization, for instance—medically necessary and appropriate?

The claim representative's cover letter to the IME physician should specify in detail what the claim representative needs. The letter should be accompanied by any medical records, including up-to-date copies of x-rays. A written job description from the employer may also be useful since the claimant's description of job requirements may not match the actual job duties.

The claim representative should give the claimant a reasonable amount of advance notice of an IME. Some jurisdictions allow termination of disability payments if the claimant refuses without good cause to attend an IME.

Many believe that the IME is an overrated tool. Compensation boards, mindful of the humanitarian aims behind compensation laws, tend to weigh more heavily the treating physician's opinion than the judgment of the IME physician. They reason that the treating physician is more familiar with the patient and is thus best qualified to speak about medical restrictions. The opposing argument is that the treating doctor may lack objectivity and may have become the claimant's advocate. Nevertheless, questions of fact—including medical fact—are frequently resolved in the claimant's favor.

Despite well-founded concerns, IMEs can be effective cost-cutting weapons in the claim representative's arsenal. However, IMEs are often misused. The following are some common pitfalls undermining the effectiveness of an IME:

- IME monotony. The insurer may adopt the routine of choosing the same doctor(s) all the time. Compensation boards give little credibility to doctors whose opinions are repeatedly paraded out by insurers. Ideally, doctors chosen for IMEs should derive only a fraction of their income from such consultations, having a substantial practice from ongoing treatment of their own patients.

- Choosing an "insurance company doctor" (physicians who do a great deal of work for insurers) may give claim representatives the opinion sought, but these practitioners generally have no more credibility in court than a known claimant-oriented physician.

- Using unqualified physicians. If the treating physician or the claimant's expert is board-certified, it is imperative that the IME doctor have comparable credentials. Some doctors have subspecialties. One should not send a back injury claimant to an eminent hand specialist just because that doctor is an orthopedist.

- Failure to provide adequate background information to the IME physician. Copies of all medical records should be sent to the IME doctor well in advance of the appointment. This will lend more credence to the doctor's opinion. Few tactics undermine the IME faster than opposing counsel revealing that the consulting doctor did not have the benefit of the complete medical history and picture. If credibility or causation issues exist in a claim, the background material need not be limited to medical records, but may include items such as statements from the claimant, supervisor, and witnesses.

- Poor communication with the IME physician. Form letters have the virtue of efficiency. Although the cover letter to the consulting doctor is very important, it must be adapted to the needs of a particular case. What is the purpose of the IME? What is the claim representative's prime concern? What major issues does the claim representative want the doctor to address in the medical report? Does the claim representative want to speak with the doctor before the latter commits his impressions to paper? The claim representative must spell this out clearly to the IME physician in the cover letter.

Chances of success from IMEs are directly proportional to the amount of intelligent forethought and groundwork given by the claim representative in the pre-IME stage. Used selectively and with appropriate timing, the IME remains perhaps the claim representative's strongest tool in managing longer term workers compensation claims.

Getting What Is Needed From Doctors. Claim representatives need information from physicians. Reports may not arrive when promised. When they do arrive, they may need to be clarified for the claim representative. Claim representatives must find effective ways to extract the needed information from physicians. If the claim representative needs information or clarification from a doctor and cannot get a reply, he should phone the doctor's secretary. Physicians also have medical records clerks who can be helpful. If they cannot readily answer the claim representative's question, they can relay it to the doctor and get back to the claim representative. This saves time for both the doctor and the claim representative.

Physicians are more accessible at certain times than at others. Claim representatives usually get nowhere in trying to phone a doctor between 9:30 A.M. and 4:30 P.M. They will have a better chance of reaching a doctor earlier in the morning or later in the afternoon. A claim representative should find out from the doctor's secretary what time the doctor will be able to speak by phone and should tell the secretary to have the doctor expect a call at that time. Questions should be written in advance. Claim representatives are often timid about talking to doctors or about pushing to get reasonable inquiries answered. Claim representatives somehow overcome their initial fright of dealing with attorneys. Talking to physicians—as one professional to another—is another hurdle good claim representatives must overcome.

As is often the case with attorneys, sometimes the prospect of a face-to-face meeting will prompt a physician to relent and return a claim representative's calls. Nevertheless, in some cases, there will be little alternative to making an appointment to meet with the doctor.

Subrogation

Subrogation involves the substitution of one party for another in respect to the exercise of certain rights. In the context of workers compensation, to subrogate means to transfer the right of recovery from an injured employee to the employer or employer's insurer. When an employee is injured because of the negligence of a third party, the employer paying compensation benefits is entitled to "stand in the employee's shoes" and seek reimbursement from the tortfeasor (wrong-doer). Subrogation rights are created as a matter of law, usually by a specific provision in the compensation statute.

Subrogation is important in handling workers compensation claims. It is one time that the claim department can be a source of revenue. Subrogation reimburses the employer/insurer the money it has paid out in medical and lost-time benefits. In some jurisdictions, employers and insurers may also subrogate for sums paid out in rehabilitation expenses.

Enforcement of Subrogation. To subrogate successfully, the claim representative must analyze the accident to determine whether there are any potentially responsible parties. In some respects, the employer/insurer becomes the claimant. On-the-job accidents with a good potential for successful subrogation include vehicular accidents, any accident involving a product, and slip and fall losses on the property of a nonemployer.

Once subrogation opportunities are identified, the claim representative should send out a *subrogation notice letter*. This letter should include the following information: the full identity of the employer/insurer/claim representative; a brief description of loss; the fact that workers compensation benefits are being paid; the assertion of a compensation lien; the amount of the lien; whether this is a final lien or an ongoing amount; a request for a response, and the name of the responsible party's liability insurer. Examples of subrogation letters are shown in Exhibits 5-2 and 5-3.

Many liability claims originate as subrogation letters from employers or their workers compensation insurers. The claim representative sending out such a letter may need to follow up for a response. Sometimes these letters are ignored or not accorded the same weight as a lawyer's letter of representation. The claim representative must place the subrogation notice letter in a diary for follow-up to ensure that the potential tortfeasor has contacted its insurer. The initial goal when pursuing subrogation is to identify and involve the third party's insurer.

For serious cases, a subrogation investigation requires all the activities of a proper liability claim investigation—witness statements, photographs, police reports, expert testing. Subrogation investigations may also involve checking the assets of the tortfeasor as follows:

• Is the third party insured? If so, who is the insurer? What are the policy limits? How solvent is the insurer (check A.M. Best rating)? Does the tortfeasor have a deductible? Does the tortfeasor have any excess insurance? How much? With whom?

Exhibit 5-2
Sample Subrogation "Notice" Letter on a Vehicular Accident

May 14, 19XX

ACME Trucking Company   Certified Mail
1453 Spinout Place   Return Receipt Requested
Whowho, NJ 04532

Re: Insured/Employer:
           Claimant:
           Your Driver:
           Date/Loss:
           Policy #:
           Claim Number:

Dear   :

Our office represents (name of employer or compensation insurer) regarding the above workers compensation claim. Our investigation has revealed that our client's employee was injured arising out of an automobile accident with your (employee/insured).

This is to notify you of our client's lien under the workers compensation claim. To date, indemnity payments have been made in the amount of _____ and _____ have been paid in medical benefits. This is an interim, not a final lien figure. The amount of payments are increasing.

Please bring this letter and situation to the attention of your liability insurance carrier. Please call me if you need further information or wish to discuss this matter. Please acknowledge receipt of this letter.

Sincerely,

_____ , Claim Representative

cc: Workers Compensation Commission
    (injured employee)
    (employer/insurer client)
    (employee's lawyer)

- If the third party is self-insured: What is its financial condition? Its credit history? Consider running a Dun & Bradstreet credit report or making a Standard & Poors analysis of the company's financial condition. The claim representative should examine whether or not there are sufficient assets to cover the costs of a prolonged workers compensation.

Exhibit 5-3
Sample Subrogation "Notice" Letter on a Product-Related Accident

---

May 14, 19XX

Zinger Heating Inc.   Certified Mail
456 Fahrenheit Road   Return Receipt Requested
Lima, OH 43219

Re: Insured/Employer:
           Claimant:
           Your Driver:
           Date/Loss:
           Policy #:
           Claim Number:

Dear   :

Our office represents (name of employer or compensation insurer) regarding the above workers compensation claim. Our investigation has revealed that our client's employee was injured in an accident involving one of your "Hot Boy" space heaters, Serial Number 4233367.

This is to notify you of our client's lien under the workers compensation claim. To date, indemnity payments have been made in the amount of _____ and _____ have been paid in medical benefits. This is an interim, not a final lien figure. The amount of payments are increasing.

Please bring this letter and situation to the attention of your product liability insurance carrier. Please call me if you need further information or wish to discuss this matter. Please acknowledge receipt of this letter.

Sincerely,

_____, Claim Representative

cc: Workers Compensation Commission
    (injured employee)
    (employer/insurer client)
    (employee's lawyer)

Letters may not elicit a response from the third party, and stronger measures may be necessary to enforce subrogation rights. After numerous follow-ups by mail or by phone, the claim representative should consider retaining a subrogation attorney.

When the claimant already has an attorney for the compensation claim, the claim representative may wish to authorize that lawyer to pursue subrogation recovery on the insurer's behalf as well. It is also common, however, for the claim representative to retain separate counsel to enforce the compensation lien. This avoids any potential conflict of interest on the claimant attorney's part from representing both the employee and employer. In addition, separate counsel may be preferred because the claim representative may not have a prior working relationship with the claimant's attorney.

Upon retaining an attorney to enforce a compensation lien, the claim representative must clarify the fee arrangements with the subrogation lawyer. Will the subrogation lawyer be paid on a contingency basis, that is, a percentage of the amount recovered, or on a time and expense basis? If done on a time and expense basis, the claim representative must beware that the legal costs do not exceed the compensation recovery or offset it so much that pursuit of recovery is financially unattractive. Some law firms specialize in subrogation recovery. Claim representatives should seek out those firms, checking their references, success rates, and billing practices. Well-managed compensation departments do this in advance and maintain and periodically update their list of approved subrogation attorneys.

Claim representatives handling compensation files with subrogation potential must be mindful of the statute of limitations. The claim representative must be sure that the compensation insurer's rights are legally enforced by filing suit before the statute of limitations expires. Failure to do so will nullify the employer's right to recover the sums it has paid in workers compensation. If an independent claim representative misses the statute of limitations, the insurer/employer can make an errors and omissions claim against the claim representative and adjusting company. Claim offices prevent such oversights in a number of ways, for example, by marking the word "SUBRO" in red letters on the front of the file jacket, along with the date the statute of limitations expires.

If the claimant settles a tort claim without the insurer's knowledge or consent, the employer may be relieved of any obligation to pay further workers compensation benefits. Thus, the compensation claim representative must periodically follow up with the claimant or his attorney to check the status of the third-party case. More important, the claim representative must keep both parties clear on the fact that the compensation insurer should be consulted before settling any third-party claim. As compensation payments continue over time, the compensation lien will grow. The claim representative must periodically update the notice of lien—and its amount—to the claimant, claimant's attorney, and the third party.

Workers Compensation Claim Reserving

Every insurance company sets *reserves* on claims. Reserves are liabilities on an insurer's financial records representing the amount expected to be paid on all existing but not yet settled claims. A reserve on an individual case is a sum of money the insurer sets aside, which the insurer believes should be sufficient to cover the cost of the claim. Reserves are set for reported claims and for incurred-but-not-reported (IBNR) losses. This section focuses on reserves for reported individual workers compensation losses.

Claim representatives handling workers compensation must be thoroughly familiar with proper reserve practices. Underreserving or overreserving can damage an insurer's financial health. Underreserving of losses is *the* leading cause of insurer insolvency. Insolvency is almost inevitable after losses have been understated for years. Overreserving causes an insurer's bottom line to look worse than it should, restricts the insurer's ability to write new business, and causes rates to be too high.

Reserves are very important to insureds as well as insurers. For example, many insureds have workers compensation coverage under a *paid loss retro* plan. These plans are among the most common ways to purchase workers compensation. The insured's premiums are tied, retrospectively, to losses incurred during a preceding policy period. Losses *incurred* include individual case reserves, not just amounts actually paid. Thus, overstated workers compensation reserves will cause a company to overpay premiums. The claim representative's individual case reserves can therefore have a direct financial impact on the insured's budget.

Factors Affecting Reserves. Whether handling medical-only claims or lost-time claims, the claim representative must have an analytical framework for setting reserves. Workers compensation reserves are typically separated into three components: (1) indemnity, (2) medical, and (3) expense. *Indemnity reserves* are for lost-time benefits. *Medical reserves* are for medical expenses. *Expense reserves* would likely include items such as rehabilitation expenses (in some jurisdictions), private surveillance firms, IME fees, medical record costs, legal fees for a defense attorney, and court reporter fees.

A common reserving method is to set a figure on a case-by-case basis. This requires the claim representative to set a reserve based on his or her experience applied to a composite of other factors. Generally, the worse the injury is, the larger the reserve. Beyond this axiom, the following factors are considered in setting a workers compensation reserve:

Nature and extent of injury. Generally, a soft tissue injury will be reserved lower than a fracture. A widespread burn may be reserved higher than a fracture. The diagnosis, from the medical reports, should give the claim representative some guidance as to the expected number of weeks of disability. Tables and guidebooks explaining the typical disability for various injuries are available to claim representatives.

Anticipated medical costs, including emergency room costs, ambulance fees, treating physician, specialist/consultants, x-rays, surgery, hospitalization, lab costs, medication, physical therapy, and nursing services.

Amount of average weekly wage. Since the weekly indemnity rate is a function of the average weekly wage, the higher the claimant's earnings, the higher the reserve.

Attorney involvement. The presence of an attorney usually calls for a higher reserve. This is true for two reasons: claimants are more likely to get an attorney for serious cases, and attorneys can cause a case to become more expensive. Claimants represented by counsel may remain out of work longer. With an attorney involved, communication with the claimant and scheduling of IMEs becomes more problematic. Retention of counsel may also signal an adversarial relationship between the employer and employee, a situation not conducive to a quick return to work.

Defense attorney. If issues are contested and a defense attorney must be retained, the claim representative must also factor in legal and defense fees. These are often identified as a separate expense reserve.

Claims history of this claimant. Is the employee a veteran of five prior worker compensation claims, or has the employee never been hurt on the job? Other things being equal, the reserve on a repeat claimant should be higher.

The realistic odds of winning contested claims. No matter how serious the injury, if the employer/insurer has an airtight defense and the claimant's claim is implausible, this should be factored into the reserve. However, such cases are extremely rare. Compensation commissions deny very few claims outright. In addition, some insurers have a reserve philosophy that dictates reserving on the basis of "injury exposure" alone, without regard for any perceived odds of successfully denying compensability.

Venue or jurisdiction. Some states have generous work compensation maximums. Others are somewhat meager. Some compensation boards have a reputation for being liberal toward the employee, denying virtually no claims. Other jurisdictions are perceived as more pro-business.

Claimant's age. Generally, the younger the employee, the better the chance for medical recovery. Younger bodies heal faster and are more resilient. A fracture of a weight-bearing bone may heal well in a young person. In a sixty-two-year old retail clerk, however, such an injury can be calamitous. Disc surgery on an older employee eighteen months from retirement may yield a longer TTD period than the same injury in a twenty-five-year-old salesperson.

Occupation. An orthopedic injury for a manual laborer should receive a higher reserve than the same injury for a desk worker. Some claim representatives believe that management-level employees, identifying more with company objectives, are more motivated to return to work. However, it may be that employers are more accommodating to management employees, allowing for light duty and job restructuring.

Availability of light or limited duty. When the employer is willing to offer modified duty, the injured worker is likely to return to work soon. This is a moderating factor in establishing reserves. Some employers take the position, "The worker must be '100 percent' to come back." Other employers state, "We will virtually invent a job, if need be, to get someone back to work." This depends on company philosophy toward accommodating job restrictions. The claim representative's reserve should reflect the likelihood that the claimant can return to some function other than regular work.

How employable, re-employable, or trainable is the claimant? Because of age, attitude, education, or other factors, some people are more trainable than others. Younger people may have less invested in a career interrupted by an occupational injury, and may thus be more amenable to vocational rehabilitation. A fifty-two-year-old man who has been a bus driver all his working life may be uninterested (or unmarketable) in many other vocations. This must be factored into reserves.

Union status. Many claim representatives feel it is easier to get nonunionized workers back to work. Union rules may forbid "light duty." Unions may also refer injured workers to certain law firms as a matter of course. Unions may reinforce the perception of workers compensation as an adversarial relationship between employer and employee.

Another consideration (that is admittedly subjective) factored into the reserve is the claim representative's judgment as to how motivated the claimant is to return to work. Many claim representatives develop a "sixth sense" about claimants; which are the ones who want to work, and which are the ones seeking to exploit the compensation system.

Reserving Fatalities. For death cases, only some of the preceding factors are relevant. The claim representative handling a fatality must also consider the following additional factors in order to reserve a death case:

Marital status. Most compensation statutes offer specific indemnity benefits to survivors of a deceased. The state's regulations about death benefit payments should be considered in the reserve. The reserve for a single person with no dependents will be lower than for a married person with three children. Whether married or single, the deceased may have had one or more financial dependents. Compensation statutes consider dependency in determining survivor's entitlement to death benefit payments. The claim representative should check birth and death certificates, court records, or get a statement from survivors to clarify the dependency status. The more dependents, the higher the reserve.

Surviving spouse's life expectancy. Some states pay death benefits to a surviving spouse for life or for a set time limit, say 500 weeks. In such cases, the surviving spouse's life expectancy and state of health affect the insurer's predicted liability. The death benefit reserve on a thirty-three-year-old widow in good health will normally be higher than on a sixty-eight-year-old man with chronic obstructive pulmonary disease. Then again, in some states, death benefits terminate upon remarriage of the widow or widower. In this respect, the thirty-three-year-old may have a better chance of remarriage than an elderly person.

Reserving Techniques. Reserving techniques include the individual case method, formula method, and the round-table approach. The *individual case method* is the most common technique. Each claim representative sets the reserve based on the factors described above and his or her experience in similar cases. The amount is produced by an essentially subjective process. Individual case reserving is more art than science. The strength of this approach lies in consideration of the many factors that affect each case's value. Each reserve is therefore tailored to a unique claim. The disadvantages of this approach are that it is so subjective that reserves can vary widely from claim representative to claim representative, new claim representatives may have insufficient experience to estimate well, and it may be time-consuming.

In the *formula method*, a type of mathematical formula is sometimes used. A formula may, for instance, say that a back surgery case would be reserved at the weekly compensation rate multiplied by "X" number of weeks. An arm fracture would be reserved at the TTD rate multiplied by a predesignated number of weeks. Another formula approach would be based on the assumption that a certain ratio exists between the medical cost and indemnity on a case. For instance, a formula could state that indemnity reserves should be 60 percent of the medical reserve. The weakness of the formula approach is that it fails to account for the differences that exist from case to case. Formula approaches appear to be precise and mathematically certain, but they can be arbitrary and not based on empirical data. The strengths of the formula approach are that it is quicker to learn, to teach, and to apply than the individual case method.

The *round-table technique* involves having the claim file evaluated by two or more claims people, each suggesting a reserve. Ideally, none should initially know the figures the others have selected. After the evaluation and a discussion, a consensus reserve figure may be reached, or an average of all the figures may be computed. Because this technique is so time-consuming, it should be used only for the most serious and prolonged workers compensation claims. Its virtue lies in the team approach to case-by-case reserve analysis.

As a practical matter, claim departments have review systems in place for reserves. Among other things, claim supervisors review the case reserves set by claim representatives. On an aggregate basis, claim managers monitor reserve trends within their office or department. Corporate management assesses reserve trends on a company-wide basis. Thus, there are checks and balances within insurance company organizational structures to monitor reserve adequacy.

Reserves are typically dynamic numbers. Many facts can change throughout the life of a case, and these should produce reserve revisions as well. Reserves should respond to the developments of each claim file. Claim departments need management controls to ensure that reserves are not only initially set in a proper way, but are regularly reviewed until a claim file is closed. Periodic review of reserves is critical in order to avoid the common pitfalls that inhibit a company's financial health.

An excellent work sheet that may be used to calculate workers compensation reserves is illustrated in Exhibit 5-4. Different insurers may have different forms, but some sort of reserve work sheet is a useful device for the claim representative to complete periodically as lost-time cases are reviewed.

Reserving Pitfalls. Three common reserving pitfalls are underreserving, stepladdering, and overreserving.

Underreserving may be caused by claim representative inexperience or inattention, or unforeseeable case developments, which produce an unrealistically low reserve figure. Excessive optimism about return to duty, wishful thinking about winning a contested claim, or simple lack of time to analyze case reserves sufficiently can all produce an unrealistically low reserve figure. Correction of understated reserves can have a devastating effect on an insurer's profitability and financial health.

In *stepladdering*, a claim representative may initially set a modest reserve. Payments quickly approach the reserve. The claim representative then raises the reserve a few thousand dollars more. Two weeks later, more bills arrive and the claim representative must again raise the reserve. Thus, the claim representative raises the reserves incrementally. The process of making too frequent reserve changes, prompted by poor planning rather than by unforeseeable factors, is called stepladdering. It is a symptom of the claim representative's weakness in reserving technique and planning.

Overreserving is caused by claim representatives setting an unrealistically high reserve. One way to avoid underreserving and stepladdering is to set a huge reserve. The claim representative may think it is better to err on the side of caution. However, overreserving can also be a problem. It distorts a company's financial picture. Otherwise productive funds sit idly in inflated reserves. This exacts an opportunity cost for the insurer or self-insured.

OUTSIDE PROVIDERS OF WORKERS COMPENSATION CLAIM SERVICES

Both employers and insurers regularly use the services of outside providers to handle workers compensation claims. The most important outside providers are independent claims services and defense attorneys.

Selecting and Managing an Independent Claim Service

The important issues to be considered when using a claim service provider are how it should be selected and managed. Selection and management considerations include how its costs and fees are determined; whether a large provider or a small one would be preferable; what ancillary services and computerization the provider offers; and the nature of the provider's relationship with the compensation commission.

Selection of a Claim Service. Insurers and self-insureds often use independent third-party administrators (TPAs) to handle their workers compensation claims. The following are sources for finding competent adjusting services and TPAs.

Best's Director of Recommended Insurance Adjusters is published annually by the A. M. Best Company, Oldwick, NJ, 08858.

National Association of Independent Insurance Adjusters is located at 300 West Washington Street, Chicago, IL, 60606.

Trade magazines contain advertisements from loss adjusting companies, which send free literature and in many cases, a free directory. Advertisements for adjusting services can be found in the magazines *Claims, Business Insurance, National Underwriter*, and *Risk Management,* to name a few.

Trade shows also feature the services of claim adjustment firms. The annual Risk and Insurance Management Society (RIMS) convention has an exhibition hall where claim service providers frequently appear. Prospective independent claim representatives and TPAs should be asked for client references in the workers compensation area. Some adjusting firms are property oriented. Others focus on casualty work. A minimum of three references in the workers compensation area should be obtained. A prospective client should not hesitate to ask the adjusting company representative, "How many cases like mine have you handled?"

The insurer or self-insured should see that the TPA has enough staff to competently handle the expected volume of workers compensation claims. Cost-cutting pressures often give unrealistically high caseloads to claim representatives. The most experienced or competent claim representative will do a client little good if required to handle 300 lost-time files. Insurance buyers and risk managers should be concerned with the extent of individual attention each of their claims will receive. The following are some questions the TPA should be prepared to answer:

- May we have the resumes of the claim representatives who will be handling our claims?
- What was the average number of years of *workers compensation* experience for your staff?
- How many files or claims do your claim representatives handle?
- Will the claim representatives who handle our account be dedicated exclusively to our account, or will other clients/ accounts compete for their attention?
- Will the claim representatives who handle our account be monoline workers compensation specialists or multi-line claim representatives?
- What was the turnover rate in your office/organization over the past twenty-four months?
- What is the manner and the frequency with which claim files are reviewed by a supervisor? Will the results of those periodic reviews be available to the client?

Geographic spread is also a vital consideration. Are losses expected within a certain geographic radius, or might there be claims over a large territory, or even countrywide? A local community hospital, for example, may reasonably expect all its losses will be within one locale and would not need a claim service company that can adjust in all fifty states. A multi-state hospital chain, however, needs more than a one-office adjusting firm to provide fast response on widely dispersed claims.

Exhibit 5-4

Workers Compensation Reserve Worksheet

Br. & File # _____

INJURY CLAIM OF _____ ☐ Initial   ☐ Revised _____ (Date)

GENERAL FACTORS: Date of Injury _____ Statute Tolls _____ Jurisdiction _____

☐ Medical Only   ☐ Lost Time   ☐ Death, Permanent Total Disability

Cause of Injury: _____ Subrogation: ☐ Yes   ☐ No

Nature of Injury: _____

Attorney Representation: ☐ Yes   ☐ No

ANTICIPATED MEDICAL TREATMENT:

Principal Treating Physician: _____   ☐ Approved   ☐ Not Approved

TYPE OF MEDICAL:

Emergency Room Costs	$ _____
Ambulance	$ _____
Treating Physician	$ _____
Specialist, Consultant	$ _____
X-Rays, Radiologist	$ _____
Surgery	$ _____
Hospitalization (____ days @ $ ____)	$ _____
Other Hospital Fees	$ _____
Laboratory Costs	$ _____
Drugs, Medical Supplies	$ _____
Physical Therapy	$ _____
Other Medical Cost (____)	$ _____
Subtotal	_____

FUNERAL BENEFITS: $ _____

TOTAL MEDICAL RESERVE WITHOUT CONSIDERATION OF SUBROGATION OR CONTRIBUTION $ _____

Less Anticipated Subrogation Recovery or Contribution   – $ _____

TOTAL ESTIMATED MEDICAL RESERVE $ _____

DISABILITY:

Required Compensation Rate: $ _____ Week   □ Applicable   □ Not Applicable

Anticipated Disability Period: _____ Weeks. Total Disability

Anticipated Disability Period: _____ Weeks. Partial Disability

$ _____

Waiting Period: □ Applicable   □ Not Applicable

Anticipated Disability Benefits Due:

PERMANENCY:

Nature of Disability:

Award Basis: Part of Body: _____ Percent of Body: _____ %

Anticipated Scheduled Award: Cash $ _____ No. Weeks _____ X _____ $ _____

Rehabilitation Costs $ _____ Attorney Fee: _____ $ _____

SUBTOTAL $ _____

DEATH BENEFITS:

No. Dependents _____ Age(s) of Dependent Children _____ Age of Widow _____ Widow's Life Expectancy _____

Maximum Award/Cost $ _____

TOTAL INDEMNITY RESERVE WITHOUT CONSIDERATION OF SUBROGATION OR CONTRIBUTION $ _____

Less Anticipated Subrogation Recovery or Contribution   – $ _____

TOTAL ESTIMATED INDEMNITY RESERVE $ _____

OTHER COSTS:

Defense $ _____ Other $ _____ Explain: _____

TOTAL ESTIMATED EXPENSE RESERVE $ _____

Completed By _____ _____ (Date)   Approved By _____ _____ (Date)

THIS WORKSHEET IS INTENDED TO BE USED ONLY AS A TOOL FOR PROJECTING MAXIMUM RESERVE EXPOSURE AND SHOULD NOT BE USED AS THE FINAL CLAIM EVALUATION OR AUTHORIZATION FOR SETTLEMENT PURPOSES.

Some adjusting companies resemble a department store. Others decide that they cannot compete on a multi-line basis and carve out a niche in a particular claim area. A prospective client should determine whether it wants (or needs) a full-service adjusting company, or whether it has only "spot" needs that adjusting firms with a narrower focus can handle. For example, choosing an adjusting company depends on whether the client wants investigations only or settlement negotiations as well.

Costs. A prospective client should inquire about the fees that will be charged. Some adjusting companies have the same hourly rate for virtually every claim representative. For others, field claim representatives, reflecting their greater skill levels and expertise, typically bill at higher rates than an inside/telephone claim representative. Are billing rates graduated by the claim representative's years of experience? Determine whether accounts are handled by an executive claim representative. There is often an initial flat charge simply for setting up a file. In many claim offices, clients are charged one hour to cover the adjusting company's costs for physically setting up a file, assigning a claim number, and logging the loss into the computer or tracking system. Ancillary expenses in adjusting claims may also be charged, such as mileage for claim representatives with automobiles, photographs, photocopy, long distance phone charges, and cassette tapes for recorded statements.

The adjusting company's policy concerning billing for travel time should be determined. Most firms bill "from portal to portal," that is, from the time the claim representative leaves his or her office until he or she returns. Travel expenses should be prorated among all the files that the claim representative worked on during that trip, but there is usually no way for a client to check whether the claim representative had other work to perform during a trip, or whether that client's case was the only one worked on.

Whether the adjusting company is open to discussing billing arrangements other than straight time and expense should be determined. Many adjusting firms are willing to quote on a flat-fee-per-case basis, both for medical only and lost-time cases. For budgeting and expense control purposes, this may be preferable to a time-and-expense billing.

Large Versus Small Adjusting Companies. Prospective clients can choose between huge countrywide adjusting companies, medium-sized regional firms, and small local firms. Each has advantages and disadvantages. Whether an entire catastrophe team of claim representatives may be needed to go to a construction site right away, or whether claims merely dribble in one at a time, are issues that frame a client's preference for a small or large adjusting service.

A large adjusting company offers many benefits. The sheer number of employees may increase the odds that they have enough personnel to service an account. Since they have more claim representatives from which to choose, they may be able to transfer personnel from one branch office to another if additional staffing needs are created. For example, an insured may have a boiler explosion, injuring fifteen employees, and may immediately need a team of experienced and qualified claim representatives. A large adjusting company is more likely to have this capability. There is also another advantage. If a client has a loss at 3 A.M. in a remote location, it is more likely that a larger adjusting company will have an office nearby that services that territory. A smaller company may be able to get a claim representative there eventually, but the client will pay in additional travel time and expenses, and even worse, the handling of the claim may be compromised.

Small adjusting firms also have important advantages. They do not have to maintain large offices or headquarters. They do not support a sizeable corporate staff or "bureaucracy," or investment in plant and equipment. Their leaner structure can translate into lower overhead and, therefore, lower costs in adjusting fees. With a smaller adjusting company, a client has a better chance of obtaining personalized service. Smaller firms may be less rigid and not bound to a manual of procedures that dictates how the typical claim should be handled. A client with atypical claims may want to explore the offerings of smaller adjustment services. It has also been observed that the typical claim representative at smaller adjusting companies has more experience than the typical claim representative at large companies. This may be because larger companies initially hire a volume of trainees, whereas smaller firms hire only experienced claim representatives. Smaller "boutique" firms can often carve out a niche and make a good profit with specialized claims such as aviation losses, structural collapses, or business interruption losses. Smaller firms may also be less bureaucratic in negotiating fees, granting fee concessions in exchange for a volume of business, or exploring creative alternatives to the time and expense approach. Finally, with a large adjusting company, a client may be just one of several thousand, whereas with a smaller firm that client may be the most important. A smaller firm may thus be eager to accommodate that client's needs in billing and performance.

Ancillary Services. A client for whom one-stop shopping is important should check on the availability of other claims-related services offered by insurers and adjusting companies. Vertical integration is common, and many adjusting and insurance companies offer services in addition to claim investigation and processing. The following are some ancillary services:

- Structured Settlements. Most claims are paid by way of a lump sum. In a structured settlement, payments are made over a period of time. Typically, the insurance company buys an annuity with the claimant as beneficiary. Structured settlements have tax advantages to the claimant. They usually save insurance companies money as well since the net cost is often lower than the cost of paying one lump sum. Selling annuities for structured settlements is a very competitive area. Some full-service adjusting companies provide structured services.

- In-House Defense Lawyers. Some insurers, worried about skyrocketing legal fees, have hired attorneys as employees. These lawyers, who may specialize in workers compensation defense, may work within the claim office or in a small firm associated with the insurer. This specialization and familiarity with insurer procedures is a plus. Since no outside legal fees are incurred, this is a big expense category that may not be factored into an insured's loss ratio.

- Rehabilitation Services. For employees with prolonged disabilities, a vocational rehabilitation specialist may be needed. This specialist works with the injured person in coordinating medical care, assessing physical and mental abilities, and aiding a full return to work. If successful, rehabilitation services can trim claim costs that would otherwise be spent on long-term workers compensation benefits.

- Risk Control Services. To many clients it is important that the adjusting company offer loss prevention services, safety seminars, audits, inspections, and underwriting recommendations. In the workers compensation area, this might include such specific recommendations as instruction on proper lifting techniques, the wearing of safety eyeglasses for certain work areas, or the creation of a fleet auto safety program to reduce employee accidents.

Computerization. Clients should look for the computer capability of an outside service. Computer-related services are key to handling workers compensation claims. They provide the following advantages:

- The ability to issue payment drafts quickly, regularly, and efficiently.

- The ability to generate periodic loss runs summarizing claims history, reserves, payments, and open and closed claims.

- Claim representative access to computerized claim information. When a client or an injured worker telephones, the claim representative should be able to access the case quickly on a computer rather than have to pull the file and call back. Can the claim representative make on-line changes and corrections on invalid reserves, misallocated claims, and inaccurate case status entries? Generally, the more interactive the computer system, the better it is for the client.

- State of the art claim offices use computers for other useful functions including (1) forecasting loss frequency/severity based on past trends; (2) structured settlement modeling with "what if" analyses; and (3) enabling the client to focus on particular categories of claims, such as producing a printout of all losses in California reserved over $50,000.

Relationship With the Compensation Commission. A prospective client should determine whether the TPA has a good working relationship with the local compensation commission, whether there have been consistent complaints to the compensation commission because of the handling of files, and whether the compensation commission has fined the TPA. Although such information is not easy to get, the purchaser of workers compensation claim services can ask candid questions of the TPA and the compensation commission. The relationship between the two entities should be harmonious. Some TPAs have the reputation—deserved or undeserved—among compensation commissions as being slow and uncooperative. Employers have a difficult enough task to defend claims without having to deal with this handicap.

Management of Litigation and Defense Attorneys

Claim representatives and risk managers need not be passive bystanders once a disputed compensation case enters litigation. There are litigation management techniques that claim representatives and risk professionals can use to monitor, manage, and improve the responsiveness of outside counsel. The most important steps are the selection of a qualified attorney to handle disputed workers compensation cases and the maintenance of service standards for those attorneys.

Selection of an Attorney. A claim representative or a company who self-administers workers compensation can use the following sources to find a qualified lawyer:

- *A. M. Best Directory of Recommended Insurance Attorneys.* This gives the specialties of each law firm. Workers compensation should be listed among them.
- *Martindale Hubbell.* Most law firm, law, or bar association libraries have a copy of this multi-volume tract. It gives extensive information on firms and individual lawyers. Fur-

ther, it often rates attorneys and firms by a confidential rating from peers and judges.

- Referral from other insurers or independent claim representatives. Word of mouth referrals are effective and are the good lawyer's best advertisement. The claim offices of insurers writing a great deal of workers compensation and local independent adjusting companies can make recommendations for workers compensation defense work. Some very candid and useful "off-the-record" evaluations not found in any bound directory are likely to come from such sources.

- Bar associations. Local bar associations often keep lists of lawyers and can provide lists of attorneys who specialize in workers compensation defense.

- Risk managers. Through professional associations or contacts within the industry, a claim representative or risk manager can approach other risk managers for their recommendations about high quality workers compensation defense lawyers.

There are several things to look for in a compensation attorney. Although an attorney may be a superb litigator in defending auto accidents or medical malpractice, this does not necessarily mean that the lawyer is adept at workers compensation defense. Someone whose caseload is predominantly or exclusively workers compensation defense is preferable. Prospective attorneys should be asked what percentage of their caseload is workers compensation defense and whether they handle any plaintiff cases. Insurers have different philosophies about attorneys who "work both sides of the fence." Some want their attorneys to be "ideologically pure" and to do no plaintiff work. Other companies feel it helps the effectiveness of their defense counsel to have experience on the plaintiff side as well. Obviously, no one wants as a defense attorney someone who also represents an employee against that same employer. This would be a conflict of interest for the attorney.

A prospective attorney should be asked about his or her win/loss ratio and how the attorney defines a win. In the context of workers compensation, a "win" can be anything from a defeated compensation claim to getting 40 percent PPD instead of permanent total. "Win" is a relative term, and attorneys can usually define any result they get as a "win" when compared to an alternative worst case scenario.

A claim representative should obtain the names, addresses, and phone numbers of at least three current client references in the workers compensation area, and should check out those references. The adjuster should ask such questions as what are the attorney's strengths and weaknesses? Why does this reference use a particular firm or attorney? The claim representative should also ask the lawyer for the names of *former* clients, then call them and ask them why they no longer use a particular firm or attorney. If the adjuster does not do this, a firm might handpick three current clients who are likely to give biased reviews.

For claim representatives or examiners handling claims for more than one state or jurisdiction, an attorney's flexibility is essential. Compensation attorneys are not interchangeable goods. Ideally, they should be familiar with the procedures and the findings of a given state's compensation procedures. A defense attorney may be superbly schooled in California compensation law, but not in claims involving the Longshore and Harbor Workers' Compensation Act. A claim representative should determine whether the firm has offices in all the states where claims are likely to occur, and whether there are compensation specialists in those other offices.

How close the lawyer is to the courthouse or commission office where the hearings are held is important. If the attorney has to travel far, the insurer may pay dearly in costs. Attorneys near the courthouse can also keep their fingers on the pulse of the compensation system. Which arguments succeed and which fail? The personalities and idiosyncrasies of the hearing commissioners are useful inside information in defending claims.

A claim representative should determine the firm's hourly rates for partners, associates, paralegals, and law clerks. Is the firm tied to time-and-expense-fee billing, or will it entertain alternatives such as flat-rate billing for certain functions? Buyers of workers compensation services can do some comparison price-shopping. However, price should not be the primary factor in choosing a defense lawyer. Getting the least expensive lawyer may cost more in the long run if low cost also means incompetent or inefficient service.

Claim representatives must decide if they want one or more than one firm handling their disputed workers compensation claims. The advantages of using one firm are simplicity and centralization. It is easier for that firm to notice the client and to become familiar with its procedures. It also opens the possibility of exploring fee discounts in exchange for exclusive representation or a specified volume of referrals. The primary drawback to using one firm is one that is inherent in any noncompetitive situation—possible complacency on the part of a firm because it begins to feel it has a "lock" on a client's business. Using more than one firm makes all firms aware that cases will be assigned based on good results. To the extent that all the lawyers stay motivated to obtain referrals, the client should enjoy superior service and responsiveness.

Aside from professional competence, compatibility should be another criterion for picking a workers compensation defense attorney. Do the claim representative and attorney get along? Does the attorney listen as well as talk? Does the attorney ask about the claim representative's needs? Is the attorney accessible by phone? Is the attorney likely to come across well and make a good appearance in front of a hearing examiner? As subjective as these factors are, they are legitimate considerations in choosing a good workers compensation defense attorney. The need for compatibility also underscores the importance of meeting face to face with counsel before making the selection.

Closely related to compatibility is claim philosophy. Does the insurer prefer to settle claims to avoid protracted litigation? If so, a bulldog litigator may not be a good fit. If the insurer prefers to take a stand and fight "gray area" cases, an attorney who is settlement oriented may be the wrong choice. Many lawyers tell an insurer that they will adopt its settlement philosophy, but their own philosophy is not easily put aside.

Service Standards. Accountability and control must be established. Most observers, consultants, and even a few attorneys agree that clients should "choose a lawyer, not a law firm." Law firms do not try cases. Lawyers try cases. If a case is assigned to an attorney because of his or her compensation expertise, it should not be relegated to a junior associate unless the case is so minor that it can be competently handled by a junior associate. In such a case, however, the claim representative should be consulted about the reassignment.

Many law firms are enamored with the "team concept" of handling cases. A partner assisted by one or more associates will handle a case. Paralegals may also become involved. Although some insurers and claim representatives may tolerate this, others are wary. The team concept may invite high bills because multiple attorneys have to review the same materials to bring themselves up to date on a claim. Conferences among different attorneys in the same firm may be billed to the client. The team concept also dilutes the concept of accountability. If claim representatives choose a specific lawyer, they should expect that lawyer to handle and be accountable for their claim.

Claim representatives should take care to ensure that they are not paying defense attorneys to do adjusting work. Claim representatives, not lawyers, should investigate claims, take statements, track down witnesses, set up IMEs, obtain medical records, or even, in some cases, attend informal conferences. Many attorneys are delighted to perform these tasks at their usual hourly rate. One need not be a lawyer to perform this work, however. It is much more cost-effective for the claim representative to do the investigative legwork, freeing the lawyer to file pleadings and motions, help evaluate the case, and try the case in court. As claim representative caseloads climb higher and higher, a great temptation exists to parcel out, under the guise of legal work, many tasks that rightly belong to claim representatives. Well-managed claim departments seek to avoid this cost-escalator, making sure that lawyers are *not* performing adjusting work and that claim representative case loads are realistic.

The client should communicate specific reporting standards to the defense attorney concerning how often update reports must be made, who should receive copies of reports, whether a standard report format must be observed, and whether copies of all enclosures are needed. Without accurate status reports, the claim representative cannot manage a litigated claim.

Claim representatives or self-insureds should also communicate billing guidelines, including how frequently they want invoices—monthly, quarterly, or at some other interval. Bills should be itemized in tenth-of-an-hour increments showing who did what work, when, and for how long. The client's policy on legal research, multiple attorneys at hearings and depositions, and out-of-town travel should be made clear. Expenses and costs advanced should be itemized with receipts attached.

For reserving, budgeting, and case evaluation, the claim representative or risk manager should ask the attorney to prepare a defense budget. This is the lawyer's estimate of the time it will take to defend the workers compensation claim. Although lawyers have not historically done this, more clients are requiring litigation plans and budgets. The budget is not a binding contract, and its accuracy depends on many variables. However, the budget helps to set an expense reserve, to make a decision to defend or settle, and to send a message to defense counsel that the client is concerned about costs. The mere act of setting a budget may have a salutary effect on attorney cost-consciousness.

Closely related to billing guidelines is the need for guidelines on expenses. Does the claim representative expect the law firm to advance certain costs? Is there a policy on travel, use of facsimile (fax), or overnight delivery? Is the client unwilling to pay for secretarial overtime or word processing expenses? Is there an expectation of prorated expenses? These issues should be clarified by the claim representative when the case is assigned, if not before.

Too often the case is loosely assigned to defense counsel: "Here is our file. Please handle." In a well-managed claim operation, a written set of guidelines is drafted for the defense counsel. These guidelines constitute the protocol to use in litigated workers compensation cases and prevent the need to repeat procedural reminders with each new assignment. Such guidelines might include an overall statement of principles or claims philosophy, where assignments will originate, reporting procedures, settlement policy, billing procedures, and policy on retaining experts and independent medical consultants.

Claim representatives periodically need to audit the performance of their workers compensation defense counsel. Are defense attorneys adhering to the guidelines? Are the results satisfactory? How do the prices and costs of one firm compare to another? It is a good claim management practice to periodically evaluate the firms used for workers compensation defense to see if costs can be reduced or service improved. The claim representative should develop some type of formal criteria for the audit and share the results with the law firm(s) in question in order to improve service and efficiency.

SUMMARY

This chapter covered the important procedures used in the administration of workers compensation claims. Every claim must be properly reported to the employer, compensation commission, and insurer. Investigation into the factual and medical aspects of every claim involves numerous procedures. When compensability is agreed on, procedures to begin and end payments are simple. Contested cases may move through various levels of the administrative agency and the courts. The rules of evidence and the nature of appeals are special in compensation cases. In all cases, the claim representative must understand and implement procedures for second injury fund relief, subrogation, and proper reserving. The selection and management of outside claim services are an important part of a compensation claim representative's work.

CHAPTER 6

Cost Problems in Workers Compensation

The workers compensation insurance business continues to face escalating costs for compensation of illness and injury "arising out of and in the course of employment." Although these increases are caused in part by new and broader interpretations of the scope of coverage (for example, stress-related disability), they also arise from the increasing costs of treating ordinary traumatic injuries.

The cost problems in the workers compensation system have two distinct but related aspects. First, and more important, is the social and economic crisis experienced by employers relating to the cost of providing benefits to workers injured on the job. As medical costs and indemnity benefits increase, the direct costs of providing injury compensation escalate. Second, there is a cost crisis related to the inability of insurers to realize an acceptable rate of return on their investment in the workers compensation line. Employers cannot absorb endless cost increases without suffering loss of competitiveness, both domestically and internationally, and without facing eventual economic destruction. Insurers that cannot realize a return on workers compensation business will eventually abandon the line, thus diminishing competition and leaving employers to a residual market mechanism.

The future of any role for private insurers in the workers compensation system may depend on controlling or resolving the cost crisis. The public has little tolerance for escalating costs, periodic unavailability of insurance, or premium hikes that are perceived as arbitrary. Regardless of the underlying causes of such problems, the public naturally blames the immediate source, insurers. Continuing public distress over workers compensation costs could lead to increased regulation or to additional state-run funds. The private property-casualty insurance industry cannot take for granted its future role in the workers compensation system. Indeed, solving the industry's problems with the system will likely worsen the public's problems with the system. Although higher workers compensation rates and premiums would certainly ease the industry's distress, they would also increase public outcry.

This chapter analyzes the various causes of the cost problem. Many of the causes arise from legislative and regulatory decisions, over which claim representatives have no more influence than any member of the public. In addition, economic, demographic, and technological factors play a part in the cost of workers compensation. However, many other causes arise directly out of claim settlements and practices. These causes include the use rate of the system by claimants, the prevalence of fraud and abuse, attacks on the exclusive remedy doctrine, and the increase of stress claims. None of these complex phenomena can be immediately eliminated by diligent claim work, but claim representatives should, at least, understand that the individual matters they handle have an effect on a broad social problem.

Apart from its effect on workers compensation, the rapid escalation of medical costs is a social crisis by itself. It may also be the leading cause of the workers compensation cost crisis. Beyond the scope of this chapter, the subject is treated in AIC 34 *Medical Aspects of Claims*, Chapter 7. This chapter focuses on all other causes of the workers compensation cost crisis.

LEGISLATIVE AND REGULATORY CAUSES

Legislators and regulators have simultaneously expanded workers compensation benefits and restricted the ability of insurers to charge an adequate premium. The expansion of benefits serves an important humanistic goal, but has undeniably had a role in creating the financial difficulties of insurers. The inability to charge an adequate premium would cause financial difficulties no matter how stable costs were. The financial hardship to workers compensation insurers affects society and businesses in general in two important ways: the residual market expands and "self-insurance" becomes more important.

This section describes how benefits have expanded, the specific issues that have affected rate adequacy, and the consequences of simultaneously expanding benefits and restraining rates.

Exhibit 6-1
Average Dollar Amounts Paid per Benefit Case

Year	Total	Medical	Indemnity	Benefits as a % of Covered Payroll
1978	$ 9,796	$2,980	$ 6,816	.94
1979	12,027	3,520	8,507	1.01
1980	13,618	3,947	9,671	1.07
1981	15,054	4,431	10,623	1.08
1982	16,407	5,058	11,349	1.16
1983	17,575	5,681	11,894	1.17
1984	19,685	6,424	13,261	1.21
1985	22,471	7,381	15,090	1.31
1986	24,647	8,654	15,993	1.37
1987	27,390	9,940	17,450	1.43

Benefit Levels Versus Rate Levels

As mentioned, the problem in workers compensation is really two separate problems—one associated with the cost to society of providing the legislated benefits, and the other with the inadequacy of revenues available to insurers to pay those costs.

The cost of providing benefits for the ten years from 1978 to 1987 is shown in Exhibit 6-1. This Social Security Administration data represent the most comprehensive available estimate of benefits; it includes payments made by private insurers, self-insurers, and state and federal governments. Based on this data, it is evident that the costs of medical and indemnity benefits have been growing rapidly: direct costs have nearly tripled, while benefits as a percent of payroll have increased at an annual rate of almost 5 percent. Stated differently, this means that growth in the benefits of the compensation program have substantially exceeded the rate of wage inflation.

Thus, the growth in costs has exceeded the growth in insurer premiums available to pay those costs. Workers compensation premiums are based on payroll. If premiums had been keeping pace with losses and expenses, and the line were providing an adequate rate of return, recent trends in medical and indemnity costs might have been viewed as somewhat less of a problem, at least from the outlook of insurers. However, this has not been the case. Workers compensation is the only line of property-casualty insurance that has failed to emerge from the bottom of the sharp underwriting cycle of the mid-1980s. From 1984 through 1989, workers compensation insurers failed to realize a profit from this line, even after including investment income generated by the cash flow from underwriting activities.

The Effect of Changing Workers Compensation Benefit Levels

One of the most significant research findings over the past decade has been the identification of the importance of workers compensation benefits as a determinant of both the frequency and severity of claims. As benefit levels increase and the replacement rate (i.e., the percentage of the injured workers after-tax wages that are replaced by benefits) grows, both the frequency and severity of injuries also increase. This is caused by several factors: with higher benefits available, workers may choose to incur more risk on the job; they may file claims that previously would have gone unreported; and they may choose to extend the duration of disability once they have been injured.

The increases in costs caused by the higher utilization of benefits are collectively termed *benefit utilization*. This phenomenon can be of substantial importance in the growth of costs over time. A recent review and study concluded that the impact of benefit utilization can be as much as 50 percent of the estimated direct cost of a benefit increase.[1] In essence, if benefits levels increase 10 percent, the direct costs of claims will increase 10 percent, assuming there is no change in injury frequency and severity. However, in addition, it is estimated that costs will increase another 5 percent as a result of the increases in frequency and severity induced by the benefit change.

These costs are not insignificant. As an indication of the potential size of the effect of benefits utilization, consider that several states have recently legislated large increases in benefits for temporary and permanent disability. For example, California increased the maximum weekly benefit for temporary total disability by 50 percent (from $224 to $336) effective in two steps taking place in 1990 and 1991. This should directly cause an approximate 7 percent direct increase in costs. The induced increase in costs attributable to the utilization phenomenon could amount to as much as 3.5 percent of premium, or more than a quarter of a billion dollars. Insurers must consider these changes when estimating the growth in benefit costs over time.

Regulatory Rate Delay and Denial

The crisis in insurer profitability in the workers compensation line of business is evidenced by a combined ratio (the percentage of premiums used to pay for losses and expenses) that has consistently exceeded 100 for many years. To some extent, this has been the result of the regulatory process, which can both delay and deny insurer rate requests.

It has been common for industry rate requests to be scaled back considerably by regulators. For example, rate increases in 1989 averaged approximately 65 percent of the actuarially indicated amounts. Moreover, the restriction of rate increases has most often occurred in states where rate inadequacy is most severe. As might be expected, the approval of large rate increases in states where costs are already high is politically tenuous. Although the approval of large rates is a notable aspect of the cost crisis, it may be a phenomenon of limited duration. As with other cycles in the insurance industry, the workers compensation cycle may at some point turn, and rate inadequacy will presumably be remedied. At that time, however, the more fundamental problem of providing for the medical and indemnity costs associated with workplace injury will remain. This is the real crisis in workers compensation since it affects employers and society generally.

The major issues of contention in the rate approval process are trend, loss development, expenses, and profit.

Trend. If costs are escalating faster than the exposure base, there will be a trend of the loss ratio increasing over time. In workers compensation, this trend exists because benefit costs are increasing more quickly than payroll, the basis for calculating premiums. This condition occurs because inflation in medical costs exceeds wage inflation, and because indemnity benefits in relation to payroll are increasing over time. The countrywide annual trends at the end of the 1980s, as estimated by the NCCI, were increases of approximately 8 percent for medical costs and 6 percent for indemnity costs.[2]

In rate proceedings, the NCCI must project future trends in wage and medical cost increases. In such proceedings, it is typically the size of the estimated trend, rather than the concept of trending itself, that is contentious. Arguments at rate hearings often focus on statistical methodology and the data used by the insurer in the estimation process. Although these subjects frequently create honest intellectual differences, the political process is such that uncertainty is usually resolved against the insurer.

Loss Development. To estimate future rate requirements, historical data must be used. However, because workers compensation claims are paid over a long period of time, historical data is not completely mature. In other words, data for years gone by are still developing and will continue to do so. The process by which the ratemaker estimates the ultimate costs attributable to such historical data is known as loss development.

There are a number of methods for calculating ultimate loss development, and with a given set of data these methods may produce substantially different estimates of ultimate claim costs. The choice of methodology and the resulting cost estimates can create major disputes in rate hearings and reviews.

Expenses. If the ratemaker establishes final rates that are fully loaded to account for expenses, the expense component attributable to the line must be estimated. This is typically done by using a "budgetary" expense loading, which represents the expense cost to a stock insurer of writing a small ($5,000) policy. This expense figure is a fair standard for the cost of developing business. However, in contrast, there are premium discount plans that reflect the reduction in costs attributable to writing business of large premium size. Arguments at rate hearings related to the expense loading usually center on the contention that the budgetary allowance exceeds the insurers' actual average reported expense ratios.

Profit. In addition to expenses, a profit loading must be estimated if the ratemaker is to establish final rates. This has traditionally been accomplished using a judgmental 2.5 percent underwriting profit factor. The choice of the profit factor, however, has become one of the most difficult areas in the rate approval process.

The dispute on profit typically relates to the argument that the profit factor does not explicitly consider investment income. Since losses in workers compensation may be paid with a lag of several years, a substantial amount of income is earned by holding premiums until payment is made. Critics claim that the profit factor should fully reflect the investment income attributable to the line, but insurers claim that actual pricing in the competitive market acts to fully reflect investment income. Supporters of allowing the profit factor point to the historic trends in the profitability of the line to demonstrate the lack of excessive profits.

Implications of Benefit Growth and Rate Delay

The simultaneous growth in benefits and restraint of rates has substantially affected the workers compensation market: the residual market has grown, self-insurance has increased, and legislative reforms have been attempted.

Residual Market Growth. As a result of delays in and denials of rate increases, insurers have not been able to realize a reasonable profit from the workers compensation line of business. As mentioned, this problem has often been most severe in states where the rate inadequacy has been most persistent. When rates are inadequate and expectations of profit are absent, insurers become unwilling to make a market for the line; as a consequence, the size of the residual market (the assigned risk pools) grows.

After a brief period of reduction in the early 1980s, the workers compensation assigned risk pools grew dramatically in the mid and late 1980s. From a low of 5.5 percent in 1984, the residual market share as a proportion of total premium grew to over 21 percent by 1989. In addition, the net operating loss of the assigned risk pools grew from $300 million in 1984 to more than $1.5 billion in 1989.[3] These developments indicate a substantial tightening of the market caused by the continuing absence of profitability for the line.

Growth of the residual market affects insureds in the residual market and in the voluntary market. Insureds in the residual market have no choice as to which insurer will handle their business. This choice is important to many insureds because of the different quality of loss control and claims service provided by different insurers. Participation in the residual market can have undesirable effects on insureds. Rates in the residual market are fixed, thus providing no incentive for the insured to prevent losses. This feature of the residual market is perverse from society's point of view: genuinely bad risks should pay higher rates; insureds who successfully prevent losses should receive some discount or other incentive. Insureds in the voluntary market subsidize the residual market. All losses in the residual market (in excess of premiums) are allocated among the insurers in the voluntary market. By the end of the 1980s, an average of over 12 cents of every premium dollar collected in the voluntary markets went to supporting the residual market.[4] This subsidy of one group of insureds by another is a political problem that could threaten the future of private insurers in the workers compensation market.

Growth of Self-Insurance. The increasing benefits and increasing costs of workers compensation have increased the use of self-insurance by many insureds. By the late 1980s, over 15 percent of workers compensation "premiums" were devoted to self-insurance.[5] Over half the states allow self-insurance upon proof of adequate security. Nevertheless, the financial security of self-insurance mechanisms is generally less than that afforded by private insurers. The surplus of private insurers is generally far greater than the security posted by self insurers. In addition, the obligations of private insurers are generally backed by state guaranty funds. It remains to be seen whether, or on what conditions, society will allow self-insurance should a recession or other problem cause widespread bankruptcy of self-insured employers.

Self-insurance mechanisms affect the rest of the insurance industry more than they affect claims personnel. Self-insureds must employ outside claim adjusting firms or develop in-house expertise. In either case, claims personnel will still be handling claims. However, the environment is likely to be quite different from that of working for an insurer. Self-insureds are likely to be acutely conscious of claims service and competence, yet they may not understand workers compensation laws or claims procedures.

Legislative Responses. Legislative efforts to provide relief from the cost problems of workers compensation have involved compromise of the various competing interests. This pattern of compromise is likely to characterize all future legislative efforts in the area of workers compensation because of the politically powerful, but competing, interests at stake. Employers, labor unions, insurers, attorneys, and doctors all have a substantial interest in the workers compensation system.

For example, in 1989, California passed a law with five significant requirements:

1. Employees must notify employers of an injury before that employee can hire an attorney.
2. Employers and their insurers must pay claims promptly.
3. Submission of medical disputes to a newly created Industrial Medical Council.
4. Higher standards of causation for stress claims.
5. An increase in weekly maximum, permanent partial, and death benefits.

Similarly, Texas modified its workers compensation laws in 1989 to eliminate the near automatic use of courts for hearing cases; to regulate attorney's fees and doctor "shopping"; to require use of an impairment schedule rather than loss-of-earning-capacity in disability cases; to raise the weekly disability benefit; and to require rate rollbacks when actuarially indicated. In contrast, in 1990, Florida attacked the problem of growing costs by simply cutting wage loss benefits and rolling back rates 25 percent.

ECONOMIC AND OTHER FACTORS

Numerous economic and other factors affect the cost of workers compensation. This section reviews both the economic and other factors. The problems of certain industries are set forth at the end of this section.

Economic Changes in Workers Compensation Costs

There has been a substantial amount of research in recent years regarding the impact of economic and demographic factors on workers compensation claims. This is an area of considerable significance since it affects insurers' ability to understand the history of cost increases and to forecast the future. However, before discussing these factors, it is important to note that workers compensation costs can increase over time as a result of two phenomena: (1) a real increase in injury frequency or severity and (2) an induced increase in the reporting of injuries or in the duration and costs of disability. These events are quite different, each calling for different public policy responses.

A real increase in costs as a result of an increase in injury frequency or severity could occur for a number of reasons. For example, jobs may become more hazardous, workers may have less job experience, the amount of overtime or the intensity of the work effort may be increasing, or the costs of medical and indemnity benefits may be escalating. Any of these conditions can lead to an increase in the real frequency or severity of workplace injury. Such an increase is termed "real" because it arises out of economic, social, or demographic changes that increase the actual number or severity of workplace injuries.

In contrast, increased "benefit utilization," as mentioned, is a phenomenon that is an induced increase in costs arising as a function of an increase in the relative value of disability benefits. For example, if indemnity benefits become more generous, some workers may file claims for injuries that previously would have gone unreported, or they may extend the duration of disability on a claim. Although such an increase in costs is no less real, it is the result of an induced change in injury frequency or average cost rather than a real change in either the number or physical severity of workplace injuries. This phenomenon has been termed "benefit utilization" to reflect the understanding that the cost increase has resulted from a greater utilization of benefits rather than from a real change in workplace injury. Following is a discussion of the economic and demographic factors relating to both types of cost increases.

Economic and Demographic Factors Affecting Workers Compensation

Recent research has confirmed much of the conjecture regarding the relationship between economic and demographic characteristics and workers compensation costs. The following are six of the variables that have been shown to have an impact on costs:

1. *Economic Activity.* As the level of economic activity increases, the frequency of job injury also increases. Quite simply, injuries are a by-product of the production process, and as the intensity of work increases, the expected costs of workplace injury will go up. Two reasons for this are an increase in the amount of overtime and the entry of newer, less experienced workers who tend to be more injury prone. However, during the 1990s, and in contrast to the 1970s and 1980s, most economic growth is expected to result from higher productivity

rather than increases in the labor force. This could have beneficial effects on affordability of workers compensation. Real wages (and thus premiums) should increase faster than indemnity costs as many worker's earnings exceed the weekly maximum.

2. *Industry Mix.* Certain types of employment, notably in the manufacturing and construction sectors, tend to be more hazardous, thus producing a higher level of injuries. As the economy shifts away from these types of jobs toward service-sector jobs, injury costs should fall. However, most of this reduction in costs will not be enjoyed by insurers since insurers charge much lower premiums for service-sector jobs. In addition, insurers may see both higher vocational rehabilitation costs needed to retrain workers displaced from manufacturing jobs and a higher incidence of stress claims.

3. *Interest Rates.* High interest rates lead to an increased employment of labor and a decreased investment in safety. As the cost of using capital becomes more expensive, employers tend to use labor rather than capital *when such a choice is possible.* Therefore, as more labor is used, the level of injuries tends to rise. In addition, to the extent that interest rates affect the cost of investing in workplace safety, higher interest rates may cause a fall in such investments and a resulting increase in injuries and compensation costs. Following the growth of the federal deficit during the 1980s, interest rates were well above historic norms. Even if the federal deficit is eliminated and there are thus no additions to the accumulated debt, the federal government will still have to borrow extensively to service its existing accumulated debt. In addition, worldwide demand for capital for economic growth and the internationalization of capital markets will likely keep interest rates above historic norms.

4. *Age of the Workforce.* Older workers tend to have lower injury rates, presumably as a result of greater on-the-job expertise. At the same time, they tend to have higher severity for a given injury, presumably because as age increases, the recovery period for any given injury is longer. On balance, however, an older workforce results in lower compensation costs. Since the late 1970s, the average age of the workforce has been increasing and will continue to increase through the end of the century. This is expected to be a favorable trend for restraining workers compensation costs.

5. *Gender and Marital Status.* Gender alone is not a significant determinant of workers compensation costs. Thus, the fact

that women will account for most labor force growth in the 1990s will not affect compensation experience. Women tend to be employed in less hazardous occupations and are therefore injured less frequently. However, the costs of disability for identical injuries do not seem to vary by sex. As for marital status, to the extent that there is a working spouse in the household, the loss of real income subsequent to injury is somewhat tempered, and the resulting duration of disability may be higher.

6. *Unemployment Rates.* As the unemployment rate increases, the probability that an injured worker can return to previous employment or find a new job decreases. Thus, the duration of disability tends to increase. In addition, as workers become unemployed, remaining workers may tend to file workers compensation claims as a form of supplemental unemployment insurance.

Other Factors

Factors other than economic ones affect compensation costs. This section briefly introduces a variety of such factors.

Geographical Locations. The location of a plant or other work site can affect the numbers of claims filed and the length of time benefits are paid out. Many workers with mild disabilities are willing to return to work or to continue to work, especially if workers compensation benefits are much lower than the working wage. Thus, the extent of disability is strongly affected by compensation rates that vary considerably from state to state. It is wise for claim representatives to know about employment trends in a given location. Those trends can provide clues as to which claims should be investigated more thoroughly.

Strikes, Layoffs, and Plant Closings. Claims seem to abound when a strike, reduction in force, or plant closing occurs. In many states, strike benefits and unemployment insurance are quite low as compared to workers compensation benefits. Many pre-existing back injury cases or other claims involving some form of permanent disability seem to become suddenly more painful during strikes, layoffs, and closings. This phenomenon can be especially troublesome because employees with previous workers compensation claims will know what to say in order to begin collecting compensation benefits once again. There is not necessarily dishonest intent in these situations. As a result of psychological stress that can intensify physical pain, a person who is unemployed may be more likely to suffer from a given pain than someone with a job who has the same pain.

Employee Age. Older employees tend to have more ailments of a debilitating nature, such as arthritis, back problems, and other symptoms of advancing age. The claims from these employees are usually more severe because (1) a preexisting disability is more easily aggravated than that of a younger employee and (2) it is more difficult for older employees to find a new job. Older workers are more reluctant to seek new work, and despite laws making age discrimination illegal, employers often disqualify an older employee for a new job because "the work is too strenuous."

Underwriting Cycles. Until the 1970s, workers compensation was generally insulated from the peaks and valleys of the underwriting cycles experienced by other commercial lines of insurance. This stability in workers compensation results was caused by several factors. First, medical inflation was essentially equal to, or less than, wage inflation. Second, the wage replacement rates of workers compensation benefits was such that there was little incentive to stay off work any longer than necessary. Third, workers compensation results were fairly predictable, which made it easier to establish loss reserves.

However, by the mid to late 1970s, workers compensation had gone through dramatic changes. The most significant was that weekly benefits sharply increased. In many cases, the weekly workers compensation benefits equaled, or in some cases exceeded, the workers pre-injury after-tax wage, thereby reducing the incentive to return to work. The duration of benefits was also lengthened. These changes made it much more difficult to predict loss reserves accurately, which in turn made adequate pricing more difficult.

Occupational Disease. The incidence and costs of occupational disease (as opposed to occupational injury) remained relatively constant throughout the 1980s. Recent studies by the NCCI show that occupational disease (excluding black lung) accounts for 1 to 1.5 percent of all workers compensation claims and approximately 3 percent of costs. Although these costs have been stable, the increased prevalence of right-to-know laws (which require employers to inform workers about hazardous substances in the workplace) suggests that the costs of occupational disease could increase in the future.

Increasing Medical Complexity. Workers compensation medical costs are affected by numerous factors, not the least of which are the advances in medical technology. As technology increases, so does the extent, sophistication, and cost of health care. New tests and procedures are regularly introduced into the medical community, and a "market" is created for the new procedures and tests. The injured worker makes the initial decision to seek the care and services of a physician. However, beyond that, it is likely that the physician determines what additional services are needed. The tendency to provide more services and more complex services drives up the medical cost of compensation.

AIDS. The acquired immune deficiency syndrome (AIDS) is rapidly becoming one of the most devastating health emergencies in history. AIDS is caused by a virus known as human immunodeficiency virus (HIV). AIDS has reached epidemic proportions.

HIV transmission occurs primarily through sexual contact, exposure to infected blood or blood components, sharing a contaminated hypodermic needle, or perinatally from mother to fetus. Scientific evidence thus far indicates that transmission is not possible through casual personal contact and activities at the workplace (such as sharing bathrooms and phones, sneezing, coughing, and casual touching). From the standpoint of the workers compensation insurance industry, the greatest AIDS-related impact is expected to be felt from stress-related claims filed by fearful coworkers of AIDS victims or from people—such as emergency medical personnel and laboratory technicians—whose work can bring them into contact with infected blood. Despite public health officials' assurances that AIDS cannot be spread by casual contact, the public remains skeptical, and fear of associating with AIDS victims creates high levels of stress.

Cost Containment Programs. According to the NCCI, national health expenditures were only $75 billion, or 7.69 percent of the gross national product, in 1970. By 1987, the $500 billion spent on health care represented 11.1 percent of GNP, and that figure is expected to rise to 15 percent by the year 2000. Considered in this estimate are increasing benefits utilization and rising overall prices.

Containing these spiraling costs is a priority for the workers compensation industry. Many of the cost containment approaches now examined by experts in the workers compensation system have already been applied successfully to health insurance. Among those being studied are preferred provider organizations, fee schedules and copayments by insureds, utilization review, preadmission screening, alternative delivery systems, second opinions, and active claims management. It is unfortunate that legal restrictions prevent workers compensation insurers from implementing some of the cost containment strategies that have been very successful for health insurers, such as the use of deductibles and copayment provisions.

Problems in Certain Industries

Although the cost crisis in workers compensation affects all employers, it has created special problems for several industries. For example, in industries where wages are very high, many workers with fairly serious injuries can and do continue to work. However, if no work is available or foreseen, the injuries may become more painful and can lead either to a new claim or to the reopening of an old one. Probably the most significant of these industry-specific problems occur in high technology industries, white-collar employments, and in contracting enterprises.

High Technology Industries. In high technology industries, new discoveries are constantly forcing old products off the market. A typical example is the introduction of automation in the work environment. Robotics, antiseptically clean environments, and computers characterize the high technology workplaces. The workplace is certainly advanced, and the assumption might follow that it is also safe.

However, this may not necessarily be the case. Recent studies on video display terminals (VDTs), for example, have suggested that various ailments may be related to them. According to an NCCI study, more than 30 million American workers use VDTs every day, and that number is expected to double by the end of the century. As public awareness of VDT-related problems grows, so will the number of VDT-related workers compensation claims. The majority of complaints thus far seem to be for eye strain and musculoskeletal discomfort. Many of these problems disappear after a short while away from the computer terminal. Some of these problems can be remedied easily with the use of non-glare screens, which reduce eye strain, and adjustable chairs and detachable keyboards.

So far it does not appear that the public's concern over the use and safety of VDTs has resulted in a significant increase in claims. However, data are compiled according to the nature of the injuries, thus making it difficult to estimate the number of claims that arise out of the use of a specific piece of equipment.

White-Collar Employments. Stress-related disabilities, discussed in a subsequent section, seem to appear disproportionately in white-collar employments, which are classified in the "all other" industry group in workers compensation terminology. This is important in that claim cost trends in these classifications should be monitored closely in the future to ensure appropriate pricing for this set of insureds.

Contracting Enterprises. With very few exceptions, total payroll is the basis of premium in workers compensation. This is the best exposure base since it most closely correlates to the expected costs of future claims. However, in certain classifications (particularly among contractors) employees who perform the same work for different employers may have substantially different wages. This can give rise to potential inequities. If the workers are subject to a similar risk of injury and can expect similar benefit costs, then the employers paying a higher wage will be paying higher premiums for essentially the same coverage. The problem is particularly acute in the construction industry where union employees may have substantially higher wages than nonunion employees performing the same work.

Although some have argued that this problem should be addressed by changing the basis of premium to hours of work, this modification would introduce a number of problems, particularly in relation to monitoring the exposure of individual employers. An alternative, and perhaps preferred, solution is to address the issue through a revision in classifications. Such a revision would recognize the dual-wage structure of certain industries and could adjust rates accordingly.

CLAIMS-RELATED PROBLEMS

Although many of the problems in the workers compensation system arise outside of the claims process, some of the most important ones are specifically claims-related. The most noteworthy are fraud in claims and abuse of the system; attacks on the exclusive remedy doctrine; and the compensability of stress-related claims.

Fraud and Abuse

Fraud is intentional misrepresentation of the truth in order to induce someone to part with something of value or to surrender a legal right. There is a fine line between fraud and abuse of the workers compensation system. The circumstances of each condition must be carefully examined to determine if a situation is actually fraudulent. In most cases, the decisive issue is the claimant's intent. Fraud requires deliberate dishonesty on the claimant's part. Any misuse or overuse of the system not involving deliberate dishonesty is abuse of the system. According to informed speculation, the American public pays an estimated $15 billion a year in fraudulent claims, and fraud accounts for approximately 25 percent of policy premiums. Although 25 percent may be an unrealistically high figure, the U.S. Chamber of Commerce estimates that 10 percent of claims submitted to American insurers contain some fraud.[6]

It is difficult to establish what portion of the above figures involves workers compensation. However, the problems of fraud and abuse are gaining increased attention from American workers compensation insurers. Fraud can range from malingering employees to dishonest billing by doctors and attorneys to a multitude of other schemes. In some states, attorney involvement in workers compensation cases exceeds 90 percent. This statistic indicates that the no-fault workers compensation system, where lawyers should be superfluous, is somehow being abused; perhaps by employees filing fraudulent claims, or perhaps by employers failing to pay legitimate claims. Whatever the cause, the currently adversarial nature of the workers compensation process has induced participants to seek legal counsel.

Types of Fraud. Malingering is probably the most widespread type of fraud in the workers compensation system. The claimant usually alleges that there has been a soft tissue injury and reports that there is pain. X-rays and examinations cannot confirm such an injury or the presence of pain, and physicians are often reluctant to refute a patient's statements. Insurers must often resort to the use of surveillance to show the claimant participating in activities that would be impossible with the disabilities alleged.

Another example of fraud is the so-called "Monday morning syndrome." Many cases of back strains, knee strains, or other injuries that occur in the latter part of the last shift on Friday are perfectly legitimate, even if not reported until Monday morning. However, some cases are the result of weekend activities, and employees decide that it would be more profitable to report their injuries to their employers as workers compensation cases. Claims reported on Monday mornings involving injuries allegedly occurring during the previous work week require extra attention to ensure that they are legitimate.

Another type of fraud that is gaining increased attention from workers compensation insurers involves physicians. Fraudulent activities may include billing multiple insurance companies, treating parts of the body that were not injured, and authorizing unnecessary disability. There are very few statistics to determine just how much of the fraud in the workers compensation system comes from medical practitioners. Several states have taken strong criminal action against practitioners who engage in fraud. Oregon, for example, has filed criminal charges against several physicians that have resulted in fines, suspension, revocation of licenses, and even imprisonment.

Responding to Suspected Fraud. Whenever fraud or abuse is suspected, it is important to investigate the claim thoroughly. The sooner the investigation begins, the better. The claimant should be interviewed in person if possible, the employer should be interviewed, and the personnel file may need to be examined. Any witnesses to the accident should be interviewed for their account of what happened. It is helpful to have a detailed description of the exact job duties the claimant performs, including any physical requirements that must be met. In some cases, a video of someone similar to the claimant in size and build performing the same work is useful to show the treating physician the nature of the job duties. It may also occasionally be necessary to interview the claimant's neighbors and examine past medical history.

Some cases appear normal after a reading of the accident report and medical reports, but turn out to be exaggerated after the statements made in interviews by the claimant, the employer, and witnesses are considered. When this information is presented to the treating physician, he or she may decide that the claimant is not disabled from work and would then terminate the disability authorization.

Despite the suspected prevalence of fraud, claim representatives should guard against being overly cynical or acting in bad faith in response to suspected fraud. Claim representatives have a good faith duty to promptly settle and pay workers compensation claims. The vast majority of claims are completely legitimate. Cases that are suspicious, but that the claim representative knows cannot be proven fraudulent, should also be treated as legitimate. Cases in which the claim representative suspects fraud and may be able to prove it should be handled with the advice and guidance of legal counsel experienced in such matters.

One effective weapon used by the NCCI in combating corporate fraud is the Federal Racketeer Influenced and Corrupt Organizations Act (RICO). Under RICO, insurers can file civil actions against practitioners of fraud, recovering triple damages plus legal costs. The primary goal, of course, is to deter fraud.

Challenges to the Exclusive Remedy

The exclusiveness of the compensation remedy is a universally accepted principle of workers compensation law. The purpose of workers compensation is to provide an injured worker with a quick, dependable source of compensation whenever the worker is injured in the course and scope of employment. In return, the employee loses his or her right to sue the employer in tort, and the employer is prevented from asserting certain common-law defenses such as contributory negligence and assumption of risk. Thus, although workers compensation was intended primarily to benefit injured employees, it also benefits employers because the employer receives tort immunity except under certain exceptions.

Employers are vulnerable to tort claims from employees in several circumstances. In these circumstances, the exclusive remedy of the workers compensation system does not apply. In other circumstances, the exclusive remedy doctrine has been challenged, so far with minimal success. The extent to which the law has allowed exceptions to exclusive remedy varies considerably from state to state. Claim representatives must become familiar with the applicable rulings in the states from which they handle claims.

Exceptions to the Exclusive Remedy Doctrine. Two recognized exceptions to the exclusive remedy doctrine are for third-party-over liability and intentional injuries.

Third-Party-Over Liability. Third-party-over liability arises when an injured worker who is entitled to workers compensation benefits alleges that he was injured through the negligence of another party, called the "third party." The injured worker may sue the third party for tort damages. However, the third party may then contend that the negligence of the worker's employer was solely or jointly responsible for the injury. The third party brings the employer into the employee's suit, usually by a cross complaint alleging that the employer negligently caused the accident. The joinder of the employer by the third party in this instance is referred to as a *third-party-over suit.* Such suits often occur, for example, when the employee is injured by a machine manufactured by the third party, and the manufacturer then alleges that the injury occurred as a result of a modification of that machine by the employer, or in construction accidents where multiple parties have responsibility for a job site or a particular piece of work.

Courts have generally held that the employer *cannot* be jointly liable. However, should the third party have an *independent* right of indemnity against the employer, usually based on contractual obligations, the third party can claim against the employer. For example, a subcontractor whose employee is injured at a job site may be contractually obligated to indemnify the general contractor and the owner should the employee file suit against them.

Intentional Injury. Over the years, another exception to the exclusive remedy principle has developed with respect to intentional torts of the employer. The rationale for this exception is that an intentional tort does not qualify as an accident arising out of and in the course of employment because it is not a function of the employment relationship. Therefore, it does not come under the provisions of the workers compensation statutes.

In cases of this kind, the claimant/employee usually seeks damages for misconduct beyond ordinary negligence. One case that attracted considerable attention was *Blankenship v. Cincinnati Milacron Chemical Company.*[7] In this case, eight employees filed an action seeking compensatory and punitive damages for their exposure to fumes and chemicals. They alleged that they were made sick, were poisoned, and suffered chemical intoxication, pain, discomfort, and emotional distress. It was further claimed that the employer's actions, by failing to correct the dangerous conditions and by failing to warn employees of the conditions, were intentional, malicious, and constituted a willful and wanton disregard of the employer's duty to protect the health of its workers. The court held that the employees had a cause of action.

The Ohio legislature has since enacted amendments to the law restricting the effect of *Blankenship*. Nevertheless, not all states have ruled against the *Blankenship* concept of "intentional," and efforts to expand this concept into a greater number of jurisdictions continue. However, in the vast majority of states, the law follows the eventual result of Ohio's law: employers are liable in tort for only truly intentional wrongdoing. Liability will not be founded on gross recklessness or any other lesser standard of intent.

Unsuccessful Challenges to the Exclusive Remedy. There have been a number of unsuccessful challenges to the exclusive remedy doctrine that are noteworthy for how often they have appeared. They include claims for loss of consortium; claims against the employer in some capacity other than as employer; and claims for wrongful discharge, sexual harassment, and other personnel-related matters.

Loss of Consortium. In this kind of action, the spouse of the injured worker claims damages from the employer for loss of services because of an injury to the spouse. Workers compensation laws generally continue to bar such actions.

Employer in a Capacity Other Than Employer. Under the so-called "dual capacity" doctrine, the employee may allege that the employer, in a capacity other than as an employer, has a tort liability that is separate from liability imposed by the workers compensation laws. For example, the Ohio court in *Mercer v. Uniroyal, Inc.*[8] held that the employee's action was not barred by exclusive remedy. In that case, a truck driver was injured when a tire manufactured by his employer blew out. The injured worker sued his employer in its other capacity as the product manufacturer. Most cases of this kind that have been filed in various jurisdictions have been rejected either by the courts or, as in California, by legislative change. Even the Ohio courts now reject dual capacity liability except when the employer operates as a separate legal entity.

Wrongful Discharge, Sexual Harassment, and Other Personnel-Related Actions. Claims for wrongful discharge, sexual harassment, and other personnel-related grievances have been filed with increasing frequency in recent years. Claimants often cite emotional injury resulting from an employer's personnel or disciplinary practices.

The claimant might allege wrongful discharge, demotion, harassment, discrimination, and other related allegations. Claimants often seek either statutory workers compensation benefits or damages in tort for stress created by such actions. Whether or not the claimant can assert a tort action against the employer generally depends on whether the claimant is asserting a claim that is primarily for physical injuries (including emotional distress). Claims for nonphysical injuries, such as defamation or wrongful discharge, are permitted to proceed as tort actions. Claims for physical injury (including emotional injury) are generally kept within the compensation system.

Fellow Employee Exceptions to Exclusive Remedy. As stated, the workers compensation system was originally intended to be an employee's sole means of recovery against the employer for a work-related injury. Whether the exclusive remedy extends to a fellow employee is an entirely different question. One example of this kind of attack on the exclusive remedy doctrine can be found in *Sullivan v. Streeter and Melcher*.[9] In this case, the husband of the branch manager of a savings and loan who was killed during an armed robbery brought action against the president and chairman of the board and the senior vice president of the bank. The Florida court concluded in this case that sufficient facts had been pled and raised in the record to establish material questions of fact as to gross negligence.

Only ten jurisdictions (Alabama, Arkansas, Maryland, Minnesota, Missouri, New Hampshire, Rhode Island, South Dakota, and Vermont) and the Federal Employees Compensation Act permit an injured worker to maintain a suit against a fellow employee. About half of the remaining states have established exceptions under which suits against fellow employees are allowed. Those exceptions range from intentional torts and willful and wanton acts to gross negligence, or they may be limited to the negligent operation of a motor vehicle. The *Sullivan* case, cited above, concerned Florida's "gross negligence" exception.

Dismantling of Some Workers Compensation Insurer Immunity. A developing challenge to the exclusive remedy rule involves actions against the insurer as a third party. The issue is whether or not the employer and the insurer can be held liable in bad faith for improperly processing a workers compensation claim. There has been a flood of rulings related to this issue both for and against employers and insurers. There is a similar question as to whether an employee, whose benefits have been unjustly denied by the employer's insurer, can go outside the compensation system and bring an action for bad faith for failure to pay benefits against that insurance carrier.

In determining whether or not a bad faith claim should be an exception to the exclusive remedy protection of the compensation statute, it is useful to consider the definition of such a claim. The case of *Noble v. National American Life Insurance Co.* defined a bad faith claim as follows:

> To show a claim for bad faith, a plaintiff must show the absence of a reasonable basis for denying benefits of the policy and the defendant's knowledge or reckless disregard of the lack of a reasonable basis for denying the claim. It is apparent, then, that the tort of bad faith is an intentional tort.[10]

If bad faith is an intentional tort, the next question to be answered is whether the claimant is entitled to bring civil action against the insurer. State courts are divided on this question, and an examination of their decisions is helpful in understanding how to handle these claims.

Some courts that deny an action against the compensation insurer for bad faith do so on the grounds that the exclusive remedy provision of the statute is absolute. They reason that circumvention of the exclusive remedy provision would undermine the entire compensation system. Some of these courts have noted that the statute itself provides for appropriate penalties in cases where the carrier does not comply with statutory requirements.

Courts that have allowed an action against the insurer for bad faith have generally done so on the basis of the following:

1. That acts committed in claims processing do not arise out of an employment relationship, holding that the bad faith tort falls outside of the workers compensation system

2. Where the jurisdiction's compensation system contains a penalty provision for improper claim processing, that the allowed penalty is inadequate to compensate for the wrong committed

3. That there is no applicable penalty provision in the jurisdiction's compensation law

4. That such penalty provisions were not intended to compensate for bad faith or intentional misconduct

State workers compensation statutes must be carefully evaluated when assessing an insurer's exposure to bad faith actions. Many statutes already have penalty provisions if benefits are not properly paid. If such provisions are already in place, it is less likely that a court will allow a civil action for bad faith. In many states, a cause of action against the insurer is permitted only if it is alleged that there was an intentional tort. Finally, one must consider the nature of the insurer's action or inaction. If the conduct complained of is particularly outrageous or reprehensible, then the bad faith action is much more likely to be permitted.

Another example of actions against insurers involves claims alleging that the insurer has been negligent in its safety inspections. In a majority of states, insurers are immune from liability in this area as a result of explicit statutory exemption or by judicial decision.

Coverage Provided by the Standard Workers Compensation and Employers Liability Policy. The standard workers compensation and employers liability insurance policy is used nationwide (except in the six monopolistic state fund jurisdictions) by all insurers providing workers compensation insurance. Part One of the 1984 policy provides insurance for claims brought under a covered workers compensation law by a worker injured by accident during the policy period or injured by disease if the last day of the worker's last exposure to the conditions causing or aggravating the disease occurs during the policy period. Part Two of the 1984 policy is intended to protect the employer against legal (tort) liability because of injury to an employee, arising out of and in the course of employment, where that injury or disease is not covered by the workers compensation law. Coverage for care and loss of services, third-party-over actions, work-related dual capacity or consequential bodily injury to immediate family members is specifically provided. Only employers named on the information page (formerly the declarations page) are insured. Since employees are not named insureds, employee suits solely against coemployees (including corporate executive officers) are not covered by the policy.

Cases with respect to claims involving alleged intentional acts must be defended since the pleading often raises a question of whether there was an accident. If an event was unexpected or unforeseen by the employer, it is likely that the "accident" test will have been met. However, should it ultimately be determined that damages are awarded because of an intentional, willful, or deliberate injury by the employer, then the policy would not apply because the event was not an accident and because the policy specifically excludes such events.

Wrongful discharge, harassment, and other personnel-related claims are not covered by the standard policy because of an exclusion that provides, "This insurance does not cover damages arising out of the discharge of, coercion of, or discrimination against any employee in violation of law." The standard workers compensation and employers liability insurance policy was never intended to cover personnel-related acts or omissions such as coercion, discrimination, or sexual harassment. This is true even though such acts may arise out of the employment relationship.

Psychic Injury and Stress-Related Claims

Stress claims are an emerging concern in the workers compensation system. In addition to rising numbers of claims filed and found compensable, costs associated with stress claims are generally higher than the average claim. Although such claims have been filed in virtually every job classification, they appear to occur most frequently in nursing, executive secretarial, teaching and managerial jobs.

According to a recent article by the NCCI, change is a primary cause of on-the-job stress. "Stressful change can involve promotions, demotions, transfers, higher levels of job responsibility, job termination, harassment, sex discrimination, and a host of other factors."[11] Stress-related claims are often filed when an employment relationship deteriorates. In the past, little data were available to confirm suspicions that claims of mental stress and mental disability were increasing. This is partly a result of the fact that claims related to mental injuries were actually filed as a claim for a physical problem. Moreover, there is often a fine line between what is mental and what is physical. When a shocking event occurs at the workplace, for example, the death of a worker, the event is certainly a physical occurrence to the victim, but the despair or fear felt by coworkers is mental. Similarly, a heart attack is plainly a physical event, but it is difficult to say whether the stresses that may have weakened the heart are mental or physical events. As a result, it is common for physicians, attorneys, and courts to disagree about whether a worker's injury is physical or mental in nature.

The available statistics, however, indicate a continuing increase in the number of claims for a mental disability caused by a mental stress without an accompanying traumatic physical event.

Trends in Stress Claims. A statistical study of information reviewed in a detailed claims study by the NCCI confirmed that in recent years, claims involving cumulative mental disorders sufficiently severe to prevent the worker from performing the normal duties of employment are a significant percentage of all occupational disease claims. The NCCI study was based on data collected from a random sampling of claims from 1980 to 1982 in thirteen states selected to provide a geographic sample of the entire nation. The results were weighted to avoid any statistical bias toward the less populated states in the sample. The study, as analyzed by the Economic and Social Research Division of the NCCI, revealed that the gradual mental stress claims accounted for about 11 percent of all occupational disease claims. Moreover, the study showed that mental stress claimants are younger than other claimants. Thus, approximately 59 percent of the mental stress claimants were age thirty-nine or younger, whereas only about 40 percent of the other occupational disease claimants were younger than forty. The results for the year 1981 showed that women accounted for more than one-half of the gradual mental stress claims, as compared to approximately 20 to 25 percent for other occupational disease and traumatic injury claimants.[12]

Perhaps more significant, the NCCI study indicated that the cost in indemnity payments and medical benefits of gradual mental stress claims is also increasing relative to other occupational diseases. The mean indemnity cost for gradual mental stress claims, which was less than 60 percent of the mean cost of other occupational disease claims in 1980, actually surpassed the non-stress claims in 1982. Similarly, average incurred medical costs for the gradual mental stress claims passed the average incurred medical costs of other occupational diseases in 1981.[13]

Stress claims constitute a small proportion of workers compensation claims (less than 0.1 percent of all workers compensation claims, according to NCCI studies). In California, approximately 17 percent of the lost-time injuries reported in 1986 were stress claims. This was an increase of 430 percent over a six-year period. These high percentages are caused primarily by the fact that California includes as a mental stress claim physical-mental and mental-physical as well as mental-mental cases. About one-third of the claims in California are classified as mental-mental.[14] Courts and legislators are increasingly being asked to consider whether and under what circumstances stress claims, particularly mental-mental stress claims, may be compensable.

Compensability of Mental Injuries. As noted in Chapter 2, mental injuries are categorized as mental-physical, physical-mental, and mental-mental. Both mental-physical and physical-mental claims are widely accepted as compensable, assuming they are work-related. States can be divided into four categories in terms of how they view compensability regarding mental-mental claims.

1. Mental-mental claims are not compensable under any circumstances.
2. Mental-mental claims may be potentially compensable if the stress is a sudden, frightening, or shocking event, such as witnessing the death of a co-worker.
3. Mental-mental claims involving gradual stress may be compensable if the stress is unusual, as in supervisory harassment.
4. Mental-mental claims may be compensable even without unusual stress.

With few exceptions, the category to which a particular state belongs is determined by case law, not by explicit statutory definition or limitation. Few state statutes were written with any contemplation of purely mental injuries.

The trend to regard mental-mental claims as compensable is an obvious one. Most state decisions recognizing compensability for mental-mental claims have been decided since 1980. It can probably be said that a majority of states are in, or are moving towards, one of the two more liberal categories—allowing mental-mental claims so long as the stress is unusual or allowing mental-mental claims without regard to whether the stress is unusual—in effect, treating mental-mental claims no differently from any physical injury.

Despite this trend, the courts have still been sympathetic to the fact that neither the stress nor the disability in a mental-mental claim can be physically corroborated. Thus, even those states affording relatively liberal recognition of mental-mental claims seem to be looking for safeguards to ensure reliability. In states requiring unusual stress, the "unusual" requirement is no doubt based on a belief that unusual events are more likely to be easily proved. In Pennsylvania, the case law has clearly established that in a mental-mental claim, the event or working environment must be abnormal. States that do not require stress to be unusual seem to be seeking similar assurances. New Jersey case law has emphasized that there must be objective medical proof of mental disability. Perhaps the most widespread limitation on the scope of compensable mental-mental claims is the near-universal rejection of the purely subjective standard of stress. Under a subjective standard, if a claimant with an emotional imbalance perceives as a source of stress a workplace condition not typically construed as stressful and suffers disability as a result of this condition, the injury would be compensable. With the possible exception of California, this liberal standard has now been rejected by every state court that has considered it, and was abolished by legislation in Michigan.

Reasons suggested for the increase in stress claims include publicity, economic conditions, and the legal environment. Whatever the cause, the increase will probably continue. The services sector of our economy continues to grow, and service-sector jobs are generally more stressful than other types of employment. Furthermore, employees have become more aware of their rights to file claims for job-related stress. This has placed increasing pressure on courts and state legislatures to develop a clear definition of job-related, compensable stress.

SUMMARY

The cost crisis in the workers compensation system has two distinct aspects: unprofitability for insurers and the price of workers compensation insurance for employers. The unprofitability of workers compensation for insurers is caused by regulatory delays and denials and by the behavior of insurers during the underwriting cycle. It is unfortunate that any solution to the problem facing insurers would exacerbate the problem facing employers, which would create a more significant problem for society. The overall cost of workers compensation has grown because of expanding benefits, economic and demographic factors that have increased benefit utilization, and expanded concepts of compensability resulting from attacks on the exclusive remedy and acceptance of stress claims. Fraud and abuse of the system have also contributed to expanding costs. Claim representatives have more power to control fraud and abuse than any of the other causes of increased cost. The future of private insurers in workers compensation may depend upon control or resolution of the cost crisis.

Chapter Notes

1. Richard J. Butler and John D. Worrall, "Labor Market Theory and the Distribution of Workers' Compensation Losses," from *Workers' Compensation Insurance Pricing: Current Programs and Proposed Returns.* David Appel and Philip S. Borba, eds. (Boston: Kluwer Academic Publishers, 1988), p. 30.

2. NCCI, *Issues Report*, 1990, p. 9.

3. *Issues Report*, 1990, pp. 4, 5.

4. *Issues Report*, 1990, pp. 4, 5.

5. U.S. Bureau of the Census Statistical Abstract of the United States, 1990, table no. 599, p. 363.

6. *Issues Report*, 1989, p. 25.

7. 433 N.E. 2d 572 (Ohio 1982).

8. 361 N.E. 2d 492 (Ohio-App.1977).

9. 509 So. 2d 268 (Fla. 1987).

10. 624 P. 2d 866 (Ariz. 1981).

11. *Issues Report*, 1989, p. 31.

12. Michael Camilleri, Senior Vice President and General Counsel, NCCI; and *Issues Report*, 1989, p. 31.

13. Camilleri and *Issues Report*, 1989, p. 31.

14. Camilleri and *Issues Report*, 1989, p. 31.

Bibliography

Butler, Richard J. and Worrall, John D. "Labor Market Theory and the Distribution of Workers' Compensation Losses." From Appel, David and Borba, Phillip S., eds. *Workers' Compensation Insurance Pricing: Current Programs and Proposed Returns.* Boston, MA: Kluwer Academic Publishers, 1988.

"Accident Cost Control." Bureau of Labor Standards Bulletin, 1965.

Larson, Arthur. *Workmen's Compensation*, Desk Edition. Albany, NY: Matthew Bender.

Malecki, Donaldson, and Horn. *Commercial Liability Risk Management and Insurance.* Malvern, PA: American Institute for Property and Liability Underwriters, 1978.

1990 Property / Casualty Insurance Facts. New York, NY: Insurance Information Institute, 1990. Based on statistics from A.M. Best Company, Inc. Oldwick, NJ: *Best's Aggregates and Averages.*

National Council on Compensation Insurance. *Issues Report.* New York, NY: Public Affairs Office, 1989.

_____. *Issues Report.* New York, NY: Public Affairs Office, 1990.

U.S. Bureau of the Census Statistical Abstract of the United States, table no. 599.

U.S. Chamber of Commerce. 1990 Analysis of Workers Compensation Laws.

_____. *Statistical Abstract of the United States, 1989.*

Index

B

C

D

E

T